W9-CNN-718

"*Heart & Soul Resumes* offers a treasure chest of golden guideposts that can truly illuminate the path for all who want to make the most of their business, career, and personal life."

—TAYLOR HAY, AUTHOR OF *SYNERGETICS* AND *YOUR WHOLE LIFE FITNESS PLAN*

"*Heart & Soul Resumes* is wonderful. Resume writing doesn't happen very well until **you** know who you are."

—JUDITH GRUTTER, MS, NCC, LEADING TRAINER AND AUTHOR OF *MAKING IT IN TODAY'S ORGANIZATIONS*

"Simple and thought-provoking, **Heart & Soul Resumes** provides career-oriented people with the tools to attain the rewarding positions all of us so desperately want."

—STEPHEN L. MEREDITH, CHAIRMAN, KENTUCKY HOSPITAL ASSOCIATION, AND CHIEF EXECUTIVE OFFICER, TWIN LAKES REGIONAL MEDICAL CENTER

"*Heart & Soul Resumes* is long overdue. It is a win-win situation for both the employer who's looking for an employee and the candidate who's looking for a job. By reading this book, both will open doorways to their inner selves. **Heart & Soul Resumes** is in essence about the heart and soul, and about how this is an important factor in all career objectives . . . a book that will be great reading for years to come."

—PHILLIP I. LEVITAN, M.D., PRESIDENT, NEW YORK STATE SOCIETY OF SURGEONS, TELEVISION MOVIE PRODUCER

"*This book teaches you to visualize the career you really want and then to write the perfect resume to land the job that's right for you. More than just a how-to resume book, it's essential reading for discovering what you truly want to be and then making it happen.*"

—KEN LINGO, LINGO CAPITAL MANAGEMENT

"**Heart & Soul Resumes** is not just about writing a resume, but about creating a vision for and about yourself, and learning how to effectively and creatively communicate that vision to others. Using the Heart & Soul techniques has completely changed the way I look at resume writing."

—STACEY L. MILLER, ATTORNEY AT LAW

"**Heart & Soul Resumes** gave me a fresh perspective on how to recognize, market, and capitalize on my strengths in order to be successful in the business world. The book went beyond the 'cut and paste' approach to career development and resume writing. It helped me discover my inner strengths and realize what motivates me."

—YOLANDA BRADLEY, RECENT UNIVERSITY GRADUATE, BANKING AND FINANCE PROFESSIONAL

heart & soul
RESUMES

heart & soul

RESUMES

**7** NEVER-BEFORE-PUBLISHED SECRETS
TO CAPTURING HEART & SOUL
IN YOUR RESUME

CHUCK COCHRAN
DONNA PEERCE

CERTIFIED PROFESSIONAL
RESUME WRITERS AND PARTNERS,
HEART & SOUL CAREER CENTER

FOREWORD BY
BARBARA BARRON-TIEGER

DAVIES-BLACK PUBLISHING • PALO ALTO, CALIFORNIA

NOTICE

*All names have been changed to protect the privacy of the individuals highlighted
in this book. Any similarities to actual persons, living or dead, are purely coincidental.*

Published by Davies-Black Publishing, an imprint of Consulting Psychologists Press, Inc.,
3803 East Bayshore Road, Palo Alto, CA 94303; 800-624-1765.

Special discounts on bulk quantities of Davies-Black books are available to corporations, professional associations, and other organizations. For details, contact the
Director of Book Sales at Davies-Black Publishing, an imprint of Consulting Psychologists Press, Inc., 3803 East Bayshore Road, Palo Alto, CA 94303; 650-691-9123; Fax
650-988-0673.

Copyright © 1998 by Davies-Black Publishing, an imprint of Consulting Psychologists
Press, Inc. All rights reserved. No part of this book may be reproduced, stored in a
retrieval system, or transmitted in any form or by any means, electronic, mechanical,
photocopying, recording, or otherwise, without written permission of the publisher,
except in the case of brief quotations embodied in critical articles or reviews.

Davies-Black and colophon are registered trademarks of Consulting Psychologists
Press, Inc.

MBTI and *Myers-Briggs Type Indicator* are registered trademarks of Consulting
Psychologists Press, Inc.

Strong Interest Inventory is a trademark of Stanford University Press.

Cover and interior design by Seventeenth Street Studios

02 01 00 99 98   10 9 8 7 6 5 4 3 2 1
Printed in the United States of America

Library of Congress Cataloging-in-Publication Data
Cochran, Chuck
    Heart & soul resumes : 7 never-before-published secrets to capturing heart &
soul in your resume / Chuck Cochran, Donna Peerce.
      p. cm.
    Includes bibliographical references and index.
    ISBN 0-89106-113-4
    1. Résumés (Employment). I. Peerce, Donna. II. Title.
HF5383.P37   1998
808'.06665—dc21   97-46374
                                                         CIP

FIRST EDITION
First printing 1998

Contents

Foreword

It's a sad fact of life that so many people are doing work that does not suit them, that drains them, that feels pointless and frustrating. Most people don't think work can be anything but drudgery. This is especially unfortunate because it is so unnecessary. Doing work that suits you, that energizes and inspires you, about which you feel rewarded, is within the reach of each of us. But even after we think we know what that work might be, we must embark on the important path of finding it.

How we go about presenting ourselves to potential employers is an essential piece of the sometimes puzzling process of finding true career satisfaction. We must communicate who we really are and why we are just the person the interviewer has been looking for—in a way that is positive and original—and we must convey it all in a matter of a mere page or two, which may be read in just a few minutes! It is a daunting task to many job seekers. The good news is that *Heart & Soul Resumes: Seven Never-Before-Published Secrets to Capturing Heart & Soul in Your Resume* makes the process of resume creation clear and fun. It is the ultimate guide to personally tailoring a resume to tell others who you really are and what you have to offer. A Heart & Soul resume sets you apart and tells others the most important things about you that a traditional resume can't.

We spend years at work—hopefully doing something that energizes us and helps us grow. Not only is positioning yourself for the right career for you easier with *Heart & Soul Resumes,* but it makes the selection of YOU easier for the employer!

BARBARA BARRON-TIEGER, COAUTHOR OF
*DO WHAT YOU ARE: DISCOVER THE PERFECT CAREER FOR YOU
THROUGH THE SECRETS OF PERSONALITY TYPE* (LITTLE, BROWN, 1992, 1995)

Preface

Chuck Cochran and I have been writing resumes professionally for many years. Chuck started the business ResumePLUS, Inc., in Nashville in 1991, and I joined him as a partner in 1993. Previously I had been a freelance writer for 15 years. As certified professional resume writers and members of the Professional Association for Resume Writers (PARW), together Chuck and I have written more than 10,000 resumes for all types of job seekers, from truck drivers to physicians to CEOs of large corporations. As time passed, we began to notice that our resumes were different from other resumes we reviewed—they got people interviews and jobs! We got phone calls literally every day from clients raving about the success of their resumes! It's not that other resumes are that bad. It's just that our resumes contain something special—something that was hard to define at first, until we began to examine our approach to resume writing. It's different from the methods other resume companies use. We use a *Heart & Soul* approach to resume writing. In this book we'll explain each step to this approach, so you'll be able to incorporate these same ideas into your own resume writing.

DONNA PEERCE, VICE PRESIDENT OF WRITING SERVICES
THE HEART & SOUL CAREER CENTER, RESUMEPLUS, INC., NASHVILLE, TENN.

Without a doubt, being a professional resume writer is the most unique and challenging career I could ever have imagined. I have met and enjoyed the most diverse group of professionals throughout my career, and they have helped me grow professionally as much as I have helped them.

The decision for us to write about our resume-writing business was really an easy one. With the exception of a few special books, we noticed a significant lack of reference material in the marketplace that effectively communicated how a *winning* resume is developed. Of course, there are many resume books that we call "style galleries," which are simply compilations of examples. While copying one of these styles may yield adequate results, that simply isn't good enough. Too much emphasis has been put on the various *styles* of resumes and not enough on the *process* needed to develop the content.

Popular resume books that teach you how to write your resume usually suggest the following: (1) List your past jobs. (2) List the functions of each job. (3) Put the information into one of our formats. (4) You're finished! now, go get a job! Sure, these are important steps, but we believe they are very elementary and greatly oversimplified. What about the real issues, such as "What do I want to do with my life?" "How can I get from here to there?" and "How do I communicate my objectives on paper?" The mental process of setting appropriate career objectives as well as high but realistic standards for yourself, and mentally working through all the personal issues that are of concern, should be mastered well before you begin your resume-writing and job search process.

CHUCK COCHRAN, FOUNDER AND PRESIDENT
THE HEART & SOUL CAREER CENTER, RESUMEPLUS, INC., NASHVILLE, TENN.

PART ONE

SEVEN NEVER-BEFORE-

PUBLISHED SECRETS

TO CREATING

A SUCCESSFUL RESUME

The heart has its reasons which reason knows nothing of.

BLAISE PASCAL

*T*HIS IS NOT YOUR typical "how to write a resume" book. If you've visited your local bookstore or library, you've seen many such books, all looking very similar. Our book is different—and, what's better, it works!

Heart & Soul Resumes won't bore you to tears like many of those other books. It doesn't elaborate on the consequences of "functional" and "chronological" styles of resumes—terms that have been overused in the resume industry. It doesn't list one hundred samples of look-alike resumes and tell you to copy one of the styles when you write yours. It doesn't give you a standardized format and instruct you to fill in the blanks with overused lines and phrases. You can get lost in the technicalities of writing a resume, but whatever resume format you want to use is up to you. You can even create your own format.

Our book takes you to another level in resume writing. It is essential to high-caliber, intelligent professionals (as well as professionals to be) who take a more in-depth approach toward life and their careers, and who believe that harmony of spirit, mind, and body is essential to well-being and success. Our book focuses on a more holistic, synergistic approach to writing a resume. It discusses the psychology of why it's important to utilize certain ideas, thoughts, and attitudes in your writing—all part of the Heart & Soul approach to resume writing.

No matter who you are—business professional, philosopher, student, first-time resume writer—you will benefit from this book. It will take you on a journey, a journey into your inner self, and will explain how you can truly integrate your heart and soul into writing your resume.

We've taken this holistic approach to writing resumes and divided it into seven secrets. Amazingly, these seven secrets to creating a successful resume have never been published before! These secrets will lift you to a higher echelon, a superior level of knowing yourself and understanding your life, its meaning, and its purpose. They examine the psychological nuances that are present in everything you do—in everything you are and want to be. They will make your resume better and will leave a lasting impression on anyone who reads it.

We recognize that even bad resumes get people jobs. But we're not talking about just jobs. We're talking about "cream of the crop" jobs and careers. This book is *especially* for individuals who want more than just a job and who want more than just an ordinary, run-of-the-mill resume. This book is for people who want to get to the heart and soul of the meaning of their life, to understand and know themselves better than before. They won't settle for anything less than doing the work they love. And if they're not sure what they do love, then they want to find out!

Whether you want to improve or update your current resume or write one for the first time after reading our book, your resume will be better and will reflect the very essence of your being—your heart and soul. This really isn't that difficult once you learn the basic concepts, something anyone can do. We have outlined our secrets in seven chapters. The seven secrets work together to create a holistic synergy that results in a personalized, true-to-self, Heart & Soul resume. They describe the psychological steps a person must incorporate into the process of writing to make a difference in the end. You don't necessarily have to practice each of the seven steps sequentially as we've placed them in this book, though for some that may be necessary.

When you write a resume, you become a writer. What you write may not become a best-seller or next year's top-rated movie, but you're a writer nonetheless. Your whole thought process, belief system, and attitude toward yourself and life become important parts of your resume, for the resume reflects *you*. Its job is to sell *you*. A resume that is written from a higher viewpoint will have greater impact on anyone who reads it because it is written from and appeals to the heart and soul.

Employers reading your resume won't be consciously aware that you used (or did not use) the Heart & Soul approach. They won't be aware of all the psychological nuances that are at play; whether it's written from the heart or not, they won't care. All they'll know is that they either like the resume and the person it reflects or they don't.

Remember, you want to reach the reader on the "heart and soul" level! And you'll know the seven secrets to writing this kind of powerful resume, provided you read this book. That's why, if you're one of those professionals who truly believe in a higher, deeper, more psychological approach toward mastering life, then it's vitally important to put your heart and soul into writing, improving, and/or rewriting your resume. Doing this separates the good resumes from the great resumes! By integrating these seven never-before-published secrets to creating a successful resume into your entire writing process, you will have a greater chance of getting the interviews and jobs you desire. So read on, for you are about to take the first step of an incredible journey into the heart and soul of your inner self, and this step in turn will enable you to write a Heart & Soul resume!

Creative Visualization

*Imagination is the beginning of creation. You imagine
what you desire; you will what you imagine; and
at last you create what you will.*

GEORGE BERNARD SHAW

Creative visualization is the first of the seven never-before-published secrets to creating a successful resume and is the first step to integrating heart and soul into your writing. You might be asking yourself with some surprise, "How can something like creative visualization have anything to do with resume writing? Isn't that just something New Age enthusiasts dreamed up?" You might be conjuring up images of crystals, pyramids, psychic phenomena, ESP—stuff like that. In fact, *creative visualization* is a very ordinary term that has been used throughout the ages in one form or another. It has also been called daydreaming, imagination, and positive thinking—just to give a few of its names. *Creative visualization* is simply a fancy term describing a very *normal* process in our everyday life. And this process is one of the most important secrets to writing a Heart & Soul resume.

HEART & SOUL TIP

You don't have to follow these seven secrets step by step, but consider each one as part of a greater synergistic whole. Master the concepts in each chapter, and not only will your resume win interviews and job offers, but your career will literally take off!

HEART & SOUL TIP

To help yourself use creative visualization, try repeating affirmations each day. Scott Adams, the creator of the comic strip "Dilbert," did this while a middle manager for Pacific Bell, and now he has the top syndicated comic strip in the U.S.!

If you ask successful people how they got that way, most of them will say that they always visualized themselves being successful. Scott Adams, the creator of the popular "Dilbert," said he always visualized himself as the nation's top cartoonist. He figured out that to live big dreams you must first visualize them. While working as a middle manager at Pacific Bell, he would write fifteen times a day, "I will be a syndicated cartoonist." This positive "affirmation" worked. Syndicated in 1989, Adams decided he wanted to have the top comic strip, so he also visualized the retirement of cartoonists Gary Larson ("The Far Side") and Bill Watterson ("Calvin and Hobbes"). And it happened.

Other examples of people using creative visualization to succeed are Jack Canfield and Mark Victor Hanson. Coauthors of the best-selling *Chicken Soup for the Soul* series, they continually visualized *Chicken Soup for the Soul* being number one on the *New York Times* best-seller list. They clipped the list and wrote their book in as number one, and then framed it and hung it in their offices. The original book became number one and remained there for more than ninety weeks, and the follow-up books also soared on the best-seller charts.

No matter in what form, creative visualization is a paramount tool for attaining what we want in life, whether it's a better job, a better place to live, a better relationship with our friends or family, or even a better physical body. Creative visualization is simply using our imagination to create what we

HEART & SOUL TIP

To succeed in your field, you must be able to see yourself (really see and imagine yourself) in the highest position you can dream of. This is creative visualization, and the focus you gain from this "vision" is vital to your Heart & Soul resume.

want—mentally, physically, and emotionally—in life, and we unknowingly use it every day. But, because we grow up in a basically negative world, we are conditioned to expect difficulties and, in one way or another, our lives reflect our difficulties rather than our triumphs over them. How often have you heard people say, "I have the worst luck—I can't find a good job anywhere"? Or "Well, I may as well not enter that contest. I won't win it. I never win anything"? These people visualize themselves in a negative way and unknowingly recreate that image in their life.

You Are What You Think

We create our own successes and failures. The mind is always busy feeding us messages. And these messages can be positive or negative. It's up to each one of us to determine what the message is going to be. In Chapter 6 we will explain more fully the importance of the right attitude, the "attitude of gratitude," in preparing a resume.

HEART & SOUL TIP

Use your imagination to create the position you want!

Right now let's focus on using your imagination to create a positive image in your mind of the career position you want before you even start to write your resume. There are many different ways to use creative visualization: some people daydream, some write down objectives and goals on an actual list, some use meditation or contemplation. No matter what techniques are employed, all of them use the imagination, and this is all part of creative visualization. Before writing anything, it's important to center yourself, focus your attention on the job at hand, and imagine, or creatively visualize, the position you want. Some techniques to assist you in opening your creative energies are outlined for you later in this chapter.

Nancy Smith

When we write resumes for other people, we always imagine them in the position they're seeking, not in the position they're leaving. This is the first step in integrating heart and soul into our resume writing, and it is reflected in the way we visualize people's goals. We use this creative visualization to clearly "see" them in the position they want. And it works.

For example, a woman named Nancy Smith, who had a job as a secretary, came into our office. She was bored with being a secretary and wanted a position in sales. We spent time with Nancy and got to know her—part of the Heart & Soul approach we use with our clients. We listened to her dreams. When we wrote her resume, we acted as if she were already in sales. We visualized this woman as a sales representative. Using creative visualization, we zoned right into the heart and soul of Nancy's dreams. We didn't write about her terrific computer and telephone skills. Rather, we highlighted her experience in client relations, her ability to interact with all types of clients, and her time management skills, all of which are necessary in sales. Taking this Heart & Soul approach, focusing on her real dreams, changed the whole tone of the resume and was successful in getting her an interview with a large sales organization.

Figure 1.1 illustrates the way we would write Nancy's "Professional Objective & Profile" and "Summary of Qualifications" on her resume if she were applying for a *secretarial* position. Figure 1.2 shows how we would write those sections for a *sales* position. Keep in mind that this is only an initial step, designed to illustrate how we would focus the resume for two different jobs. All the information is accurate and true in both summaries; in the second example, however, we took the focus off her secretarial background. The difference is in the wording and focus, and it would not have been possible if we had not visualized her in the sales position. We were able to "see" Nancy as a sales representative because we used creative visualization.

HEART & SOUL TIP

By acting and thinking as if Nancy were already in sales, we visualized her in this position and were able to successfully target her resume toward sales.

Nancy Smith's Resume Targeted for a Secretarial Position

> **HEART & SOUL TIP**
>
> *This resume is accurate, attractive, and well written. But, for a career in sales, she doesn't have a chance! She needs to bring out her sales experience.*

NANCY SMITH
1234 Anywhere Street
City, State 10000
Phone Number

Professional Objective & Profile

A highly motivated, goal-oriented secretary is seeking a position in Office Administration that will fully utilize 6 years of experience. Skilled in computers, office administration and accounting. Desires a secretarial position that will provide a challenging opportunity to significantly contribute to the development, support, and expansion of an organization.

Summary of Qualifications

Track Record of Success

More than 6 years of experience building and leading integrated office operations as a Secretary for a worldwide sales organization. Consistently assumed higher levels of responsibility and authority as a Secretary during tenure.

Office Administration

Talented in setting up and directing office operations for companies. Solid organizational, management, interpersonal and communications skills with a proven track record of making sound decisions.

Business Correspondence

Draft, design, and proof a diversity of marketing and sales materials targeted to professional, corporate and community markets.

Meeting Planning

Skilled in arranging and coordinating special events and meetings for staff members. Assisted professional staff with national meeting planning, member communications, marketing campaign, design and execution.

Computer & Typing Skills

Skilled in WordPerfect, Microsoft Word and Windows 95. Accurate typing skills of 60 wpm. Ability to perform in stressful, fast-paced environments.

Telephone/Receptionist Expertise

Ability to manage a multiline switchboard and coordinate messages for multiple personnel. Strong background as a Receptionist with strong interpersonal skills.

Employee Relations

Ability to work independently or as a team member. Supportive of sales staff and office associates.

■ **FIGURE 1.2**
Nancy Smith's Resume Targeted for a Sales Position

HEART & SOUL TIP

This resume is formatted in a similar manner, but it clearly illustrates her skills and experience in sales and marketing as opposed to her office skills. While remaining truthful, we refocused (or visualized) her resume toward sales. (It worked for her, too!)

NANCY SMITH
1234 Anywhere Street
City, State 10000
Phone Number

Professional Objective & Profile

A highly motivated, goal-oriented business professional is seeking a position in sales that will fully utilize 6 years of experience in sales and marketing support positions. Strong background in providing support to sales staff through research, market analysis, and client relations.

Summary of Qualifications

Track Record of Success

More than 6 years of experience building and leading integrated office operations for a worldwide sales organization. Consistently assumed higher levels of responsibility and authority in sales and marketing operations during tenure.

Marketing & Sales

Coordinate market research activities, maintain database and competitor information, and assist with product/service development and pricing strategy. Use proven methods in assisting sales staff in developing new sales and marketing strategies that maximize growth and profitability.

Customer Service/Client Relations

Assist clients by responding to inquiries and/or concerns, and by providing information regarding accounts. Serve as public relations liaison to a large regional customer base. Establish and maintain an exemplary network of business associates as a result of extensive interaction and superior service.

Communications

Write, design, and produce diversified marketing and sales materials targeted to professional, corporate, and community markets. Assist sales staff by utilizing multimedia techniques to produce high-impact materials and presentations.

Meeting Planning

Arrange and coordinate special sales events, annual meetings, and conferences for staff members. Assist sales staff with national meeting planning, member communications, marketing campaign, design, and execution.

Employee Relations

Lead administrative team in providing sales and marketing support for a worldwide sales organization. Work includes preparing direct mail and advertising campaigns and all business correspondence. Effectively interface with several branch sales offices.

This is just an example of how you can write two different versions of a resume to target two different jobs. We have discovered throughout our resume-writing careers that it is extremely important to target your resume to a specific job by highlighting specific skills and accomplishments that relate to the position you want.

We listened to Nancy's dreams and visualized her in a sales position. We were able to express her talents and skills that were directly relevant to sales. This is a very effective Heart & Soul approach to resume writing, and you can try the same technique by utilizing creative visualization to imagine yourself in a new job.

Creative Visualization—Try It, You'll Like It!

HEART & SOUL TIP

Creative visualization is just as important for short-term goals as it is for long-term goals. Even if you don't yet have a long-term career path in place, you can still use this skill to advance to the position you want right now.

HEART & SOUL TIP

To contemplate, sit in a quiet place and close your eyes. Silently or out loud, repeat a special word or mantra. Imagine yourself in the position you're seeking. Keep your inner self open to any messages. Chanting your mantra will open the creative channel within you and can be useful in guiding you to what you need to do next.

They probably wouldn't admit it, but many people, no matter how educated or intelligent, do not know how to use creative visualization effectively in realizing their dreams. While all of us use it on a subconscious level every day, it's much more effective to use it consciously and actually work with it to accomplish our goals.

Contemplation is one way to use creative visualization. It is similar to meditation except that when you contemplate you become a more active participant in the exercise. You actually *imagine* yourself doing something. In this case, focus on the kind of job or career you want. First, find a quiet place, sit down, and close your eyes. You might have a song, prayer, or mantra to help you relax and focus on your inner self. By chanting a special word, you open up a creative channel that helps you attain whatever it is you want. If you can't think of a mantra, use the word HU (pronounced *hue*), an ancient word for God used by the Navajo during sacred ceremonies and celebrations. You can also focus on a spiritual guide or inner master, if you have one, which will help open the creative channel within you. When you close your eyes, relax and chant your mantra three times and think about the job for which you are sending your resume. *Imagine that you already have the job!* For fifteen or twenty minutes imagine yourself in this job. Can you see what you're wearing? Can you hear the wind blowing outside? Are there other co-workers around you? Can you smell anything in particular? This is an example of using the "as if" principle, which we will elaborate on later in this chapter.

Don't be discouraged if you don't think you're getting immediate results from this creative visualization technique. It may take some practice for the actual visualization to manifest itself in reality, but every time you practice this technique, you'll be one step closer to achieving your dream. Remember, it takes time to change old habits and patterns developed over a lifetime.

However, creative visualization is such a powerful process that doing it only five minutes a day, every day, can make drastic changes in your life. So just be patient. With perseverance and the right attitude, you will succeed!

It is important to incorporate *feelings* into creative visualization. *Feel* confident as you imagine yourself in this new job. *Feel* your confidence grow as you visualize how you can significantly contribute your skills to this job. What a wonderful feeling this is! *Feel* how friendly the people around you are. Hold these images in your mind while you are contemplating for fifteen or twenty minutes.

You are experiencing the *first secret* to writing a successful resume, which is a very important tool to use in your Heart & Soul approach to resume writing. And if you keep practicing this technique, you will soon find out how creative visualization can be a very powerful tool in all areas of your life.

Like . . . Ya' Know . . . As If!

As we mentioned earlier, affirmations are another key aspect of creative visualization. They can replace our old, habitually negative way of thinking, and they are simple to practice. An affirmation can be any positive statement; the more specific it is, the more likely it is to get you exactly what you want. Remember the old cliché "Be careful what you wish for"? Creative visualization works the same way. You're wishing for something to come true, and acting "as if" will make it more real.

Again, incorporate *feelings* into this exercise. Remember, the more frequently you consciously tell yourself something positive, the more real it becomes, and it is even more powerful when you put feelings into it.

Perhaps, like our resume client Nancy Smith, you would like a job in sales. You might repeat the following affirmations over and over throughout the day:

"I am a dynamic, effective sales representative for a major corporation."

"I am surpassing my sales quotas on a weekly basis."

"I am confident in my new job as a sales representative, and I contribute numerous skills and talents to the job."

Always repeat the affirmations in the present tense and practice the "as if" technique. While repeating the affirmations, imagine yourself this way. Thoughts consist of mental energy. Everything on this earth is energy and energy is a real thing, and this means that thoughts are real things. The more you think something, the more real it becomes.

If you have trouble focusing on the type of job you want, you might want to skip ahead and read the next chapter, which explains methods for defining your career goals. You may want to contact a career development center or career counselor to help you discover and streamline your goals. Career firms

HEART & SOUL TIP

Remember to practice positive affirmations daily and to act "as if" to attain the goals and jobs you're seeking. Put "feelings" into these affirmations. Repeating these affirmations and writing them down will make them become real.

offer several types of tests that will provide insight into the pros and cons of career choices. These tests are excellent evaluations that offer vital tools for learning more about your strengths and weaknesses and provide a straightforward and affirmative path to self-understanding.

Self-understanding is an important step in the Heart & Soul approach to writing a resume. Without focus or knowing what kind of job or career you want, you are like a ship at sea without a destination. Plus, if you don't have the focus to know your inner self and what you want, it is very difficult to put your whole heart and soul into writing your resume. After reading Chapter 2, you may want to come back to Chapter 1 and practice *creative visualization.*

Planning Career Strategies to Guide Your Job Search

People are always blaming their circumstances for what they are. . . . The people who get on in this world are the people who get up and look for the circumstances they want, and if they can't find them, make them.

GEORGE BERNARD SHAW

THE SECOND OF THE seven never-before-published secrets to creating a successful resume is to base your job search on your long-term career goals. What kind of job are you looking for? Are you confused about your career choices? Have you gotten into a job-search slump? Is your only job-seeking activity that of perusing the classifieds, then sending your resume to any job that sounds interesting, regardless of whether it's the right job for you, or whether you're even qualified for the job? Do you spend day after day moaning to your friends that no company in town has any good job openings or that you can't seem to get an interview, no matter how many resumes you distribute?

If your answer is yes to any of these questions, then most certainly you need to read this chapter. How can you put your whole heart and soul into resume writing if you don't have any career goals? Without career goals, you're being very *reactive* and not *proactive*. But don't worry. You're not alone.

I Know There Aren't Any Jobs—I Looked in the Paper!

Just as creative visualization is a key secret to integrating heart and soul into writing a successful resume, and an important step in defining and attaining your goals, so is taking a *proactive* approach. When clients come into our office moaning and groaning with complaints that no one is hiring and that they're not getting calls for interviews, we tell them it's time for them to take charge of their life and create their own opportunities. The same goes for you: don't sit around and wait for the "right" job to be advertised in the newspaper. Be proactive instead of reactive.

HEART & SOUL TIP

When you respond to job leads without any real career focus, your resume will reflect your ambivalence. If you take a proactive approach in your career and job search, your resume illustrates your commitment, confidence, and desire.

Rather than sending your resume randomly to any job that sounds interesting, take an active step in researching and deciding what type of job you want. This is taking a proactive approach toward developing and planning your career. A proactive approach will involve several steps in strategic planning and vision regarding what you want to accomplish on a long-term basis. These steps are important and necessary at any stage in your career if you want to be successful in Heart & Soul resume writing.

Being reactive is a trap that all of us have fallen into from time to time. Being reactive in your career means you have no long-term goal or vision about who you are or where you want to be. You react to circumstances around you rather than creating your own opportunities, based on your interests and skills. This trap keeps you from being able to creatively visualize your dreams or tune in to the heart and soul of your inner self. That's why we strongly stress being proactive as one of the seven secrets to creating a successful resume. You must take charge of your life; once you've done this, you'll be one step closer to putting your heart and soul into everything you do, including resume writing.

For example, one of our clients is a college graduate with a four-year degree in management. She had interviewed with a wide range of companies on campus in her senior year and landed a well-paying but extremely stressful job as a front-line manager for a unionized crew in a manufacturing plant. After two years she was totally burned out and, frustrated, came to us wondering where she had gone wrong. She was so distraught that the idea of focusing on her inner self and creatively visualizing her dreams seemed far-fetched and impractical.

Hers is an example of a *reactive* career plan. The lure of a good starting salary right out of college kept her from researching and identifying what she truly wanted in life. She hadn't taken the time to put her heart and soul into planning her life. What did she dream of doing? What made her the happiest? She didn't know. She had never stopped long enough to contemplate or listen to that inner voice that guides us throughout life. She had no real clue as to what her strengths and weaknesses were, and where she would be most productive. How could she possibly write a great resume?

HEART & SOUL TIP

Take the time to know your heart's dreams!

Remember, writing your resume when you have no proactive career plan will be less than effective. Without heart and soul, it simply won't be as successful. Naturally, we recognize that some resumes—even the worst of resumes and those without heart and soul—get people jobs. What we're talking about are the "cream of the crop" jobs and careers for high-caliber professionals who want more than just any old job.

Jeff Whitney

One of our clients, Jeff Whitney, came into our office very discouraged. He slumped down in a chair and sighed, "No one seems to be interested in me. I've sent out about fifty of these resumes and they just don't seem to be working." We took his resume and noticed that he had an extensive background with diversified experience in several areas. However, there was no real focus, no objective—just a listing of random jobs. When we questioned him about his career focus, we understood why he had been unsuccessful in getting interviews. "I don't know what I want to do," Jeff shrugged. "I just want a good job. It doesn't really matter what it is."

Alert! Red flag! We knew immediately where the real problem was with his job-seeking process and why his resume hadn't been successful. He had no career plan, no job focus. He was far too frustrated to even think about the "heart and soul" meaning of his life. His resume simply didn't stand a chance without focus. He had been sending out his resumes to any job that sounded good. He had sent his resume to manufacturing plants, retail stores, transportation companies, and restaurants—in other words, anything that was listed in the paper. We immediately informed him that he had to focus on the career or job he wanted before we could write a successful resume and that, after we determined his career goal, creative visualization would be very effective in helping him target that specific goal.

Figure 2.1 is Jeff's undeveloped, unfocused, "before" resume. We'll explain later how we determined his career needs and more clearly focused the resume that was successful in landing him several good job offers.

■ **FIGURE 2.1**
Jeff Whitney's "Before" Resume

HEART & SOUL TIP

From this resume, you would not think that Jeff is really a bright, motivated, and intelligent young man. Many readers would classify Jeff as a slow, unmotivated learner. Not a very strong or favorable first impression!

Jeff's unfocused, poorly written resume

JEFF WHITNEY
715 Anywhere Street
City, State 10000
Phone Number

WORK EXPERIENCE

October 1992 to Present

UNITED PARCEL SERVICE, Nashville, Tennessee
Work consists of sorting mail for shipment.

January 1994 to July 1995

WICKER INTERNATIONAL, Dayton, Ohio
Field Engineer: Work consisted of working on film
processor and CADI systems as well as all other brands.
Trouble-shot and did preventive maintenance on the
processors.

June 1991 to Present

Freelance Electronic Technician and Handyman.
Work consists of television and stereo repair, installing
home security systems, installing car stereos, washer
and dryer repair, and small appliance repair.

April 1993 to Present

SNS PHOTOGRAPHY
Self-owned business specializing in weddings and
self-portraits.

June 1992 to April 1993

GOODMAN'S RETAIL STORE
Sales Associate responsible for selling clothing to
retail customers.

1990 to 1991

WINE & DISTILLED SPIRITS COMPANY
Filled orders for distribution to various grocery stores.

1983 to 1990

MARTIN-THOMAS & OWENS PLASTIC DIVISION
Work consisted of operating and maintaining special
equipment. Set up lines and inspected for quality
control. Operated lift truck when necessary.

EDUCATION

R.E.T.S. Electronic Institute, Louisville, KY
Associate Degree with 960 hours in lecture and 960
hours of hands-on training in laboratory.
Nashville State Technical Institute, Nashville, TN
Completed 15 hours toward Associate Degree in
Photography.

Build Your Career Plan Before *You Write Your Resume*

HEART & SOUL TIP

Dream, visualize, develop, and build a career plan before you write your resume!

HEART & SOUL TIP

The Myers-Briggs Type Indicator *(MBTI) and the* Strong Interest Inventory *are excellent instruments to help you in getting to know and understand yourself better, which is useful in writing an in-depth Heart & Soul resume.*

HEART & SOUL TIP

If you don't have a firm grasp of your dreams, passions, interests, and desires, how can you write a resume that accurately describes your heart and soul? Take advantage of whatever resources you have to help you learn more about yourself before you write your resume.

Jeff's resume had no focus, and no special skills or qualifications were highlighted. He had only sent resumes to companies that were listed in the classifieds, and hadn't been very selective about those. He simply didn't have a career plan or goal.

We told Jeff that he had to decide what he wanted to do in order for us to write an effective resume for him. We explained that it was now time to take charge of his life and be proactive in his career search, to develop a career plan rather than simply react to the classifieds.

Jeff was uncertain about his career and wishy-washy about what he wanted to do. In order to help Jeff, we offered in-depth career counseling along with two very valuable career instruments: the *Myers-Briggs Type Indicator®* (MBTI®) and the *Strong Interest Inventory™ (Strong™)*. We have included an appendix at the back of this book that explains these instruments in greater depth and shows how you can use them along with your Heart & Soul resume writing.

Since the Heart & Soul approach to resume writing is an in-depth approach to writing about yourself, we recommend completing these instruments as a way of helping you to know and understand yourself better. Once you've completed them, the career counselor or psychologist administering them will also be able to interpret them for you. They will explore your values, interests, and personality with other life issues that will be relevant in your decision-making process (in this case, your resume-writing process).

Discovering the "right" job for you is all-important, for it will enhance your life. Working in a career that you love is one of the most satisfying and personally fulfilling things you can ever do. The job that is suited to your personality and skills will nourish your inner being—the very heart and soul of your existence. It will allow you the freedom to use your innate strengths in ways that come naturally to you.

Call a local career counselor or career development center for more information. We strongly recommend using these instruments, no matter what your current career situation. The more you know about yourself, the better you will be able to steer your career toward areas where you will be the happiest and most successful. In addition, you'll be able to write a Heart & Soul resume that reflects the person you are. We've recommended some additional reading in the Resources list at the end of this book that we truly believe will be very beneficial in all your career goals.

After Jeff completed the *Strong* and the MBTI, we analyzed and explored many areas of his life that would influence his career decisions. After thorough investigation, career counseling, and interpretation of his scores on the instruments, Jeff was able to identify specific technical, analytical, and mechanical strengths he wanted to develop. We used the results to help write his resume from a Heart & Soul perspective. (When you read the appendix on the *Strong* and the MBTI, you'll understand better how you can use descriptions, certain phrases, and results from the tests to write your own Heart & Soul resume.)

After additional counseling, we helped Jeff identify two good career choices —photography and electronics. He had been dabbling in freelance photography for several years but had never actively pursued this as a full-time career. He had also been freelancing as a handyman and electrician but, again, had taken no active steps toward pursuing his career goal of electronics. These freelance jobs had been buried in his work experience on his old resume and certainly didn't stand out from the other jobs listed. Jeff was happy with the results from the career indicators/tests and admitted that deep down in his heart he had preferred to find a job using his analytical and technical skills, which could be applied to either photography or electronics, but he had felt helpless and at the mercy of the job market. He had felt totally powerless and out of control, unable to do anything about his career. He should have listened to those messages deep down in his heart.

We had to write two different resumes and cover letters for him—one targeted to photography and one to electronics. Figures 2.2 through 2.5 illustrate the difference in the focus for each career and how the focus on both versions greatly improved Jeff's initial resume, shown earlier in this chapter.

In the Electronic Engineering version, we visualized Jeff in an engineering job that would fully utilize his electronic engineering background. From his employment history, we selected the most relevant jobs and emphasized these in the first part of his resume, so an employer could quickly identify Jeff's engineering skills. For example, instead of listing his work with United Parcel Service first (as Jeff had done on his initial resume), we focused on his work as an electronic engineering consultant, since it directly related to engineering jobs. Jeff's technical engineering skills, as well as his quality control and supervision/management experience, were important, since he would be targeting engineering and manufacturing companies.

Like many of our clients, Jeff was interested in more than one career that fully utilized his skills. The next resume illustrates how we targeted his experience and his cover letter toward photography.

In the Photography version of Jeff's resume, it was important first to visualize Jeff as a photographer and then to highlight the experience and qualifications that directly related to obtaining a photography position. So, instead of listing an engineering job first, we focused on his independent photography business and highlighted areas that are important to a commercial photographer. Customer service and business administration, plus sales and marketing, are prerequisite skills for a professional photographer, and we highlighted

■ **FIGURE 2.2**
Electronic Engineering Version of Jeff Whitney's "After" Resume

HEART & SOUL TIP

What a difference! Jeff has been immediately transformed into a well-defined, marketable candidate.

JEFF WHITNEY
715 Anywhere Street
City, State 10000
Phone Number

PROFESSIONAL OBJECTIVE & PROFILE

Highly motivated and goal-oriented electronic engineering specialist is seeking a position that will fully utilize more than 10 years of experience in electronics. Strong leader and supervisor with 8 years of experience in shift management and supervision. Seeking an engineering position that will provide a challenging opportunity to significantly contribute to a company's engineering operations.

SUMMARY OF QUALIFICATIONS

TRACK RECORD OF SUCCESS
Strong analytical, technical, and mechanical abilities with advanced education and training, and more than 10 years of experience providing electrical engineering services for major companies.

SUPERVISION & MANAGEMENT
Managed and supervised shift while working for Martin-Thomas & Owens Plastic Division. Delegated assignments and responsibilities to employees, and monitored overall job performances.

QUALITY CONTROL
Experienced in monitoring plant operations to ensure adherence to OSHA and other federal, state, local, and company policies and procedures.

TECHNICAL QUALIFICATIONS
Basic electricity, solid state, digital, industrial electronics, video, communications, and PRO/CADI.

EDUCATION

ASSOCIATE DEGREE IN ELECTRONIC ENGINEERING
R.E.T.S. Electronic Institute, Louisville, Kentucky

HEART & SOUL TIP

Jeff has a preference for Sensing and Thinking on the MBTI, and for Investigative and Artistic on the Strong. This version incorporates his artistic interests.

PROFESSIONAL EXPERIENCE

ELECTRONIC ENGINEERING CONSULTANT
Electronic Engineering: On a freelance, contract basis, provide electronic engineering services to individuals and businesses. Services include electrical repair of major appliances (washers and dryers, stoves, ovens and microwaves, televisions, and stereo systems). Install telephone and communication systems, plugs, and electrical wiring.

CLIENT RELATIONS
Solicit and obtain clients. Continuously establish and maintain an excellent network of business associates as a result of providing superior service and thorough attention to clients.

QUALITY ASSURANCE
Monitor and review all services to ensure adherence to all federal, state, and local standards, rules, specifications, and regulations.

■ **FIGURE 2.3**
Electronic Engineering Version of Jeff Whitney's Cover Letter

HEART & SOUL TIP

Notice how Jeff's cover letter brings out additional points that were buried in his "before" resume.

JEFF WHITNEY
715 Anywhere Street
City, State 10000
Phone Number

Today's Date

Adrian Carson
Templeton Electronics
201 Hillsboro Road
St. Louis, MO 27215

Dear Mr. Carson:

Are you looking for a highly motivated and goal-oriented electronic engineering specialist? With over 10 years of proven experience, I am confident of my ability to contribute to even your most challenging assignments.

After receiving my associate degree in electronic engineering in Louisville, Kentucky, I went on to build my career with Martin-Thomas & Owens Plastic Division in a supervisory and management capacity. There I monitored all quality control and job performances to ensure adherence to OSHA and other rules and regulations. My electrical engineering skills also include basic electricity, solid state, digital, industrial electronics, video, communications, and PRO/CADI.

I look forward to discussing my background in greater detail and to hearing more about your needs. If you have any interest in my experience and qualifications, please contact me at the above phone number and address.

Sincerely,

Jeff Whitney

■ **FIGURE 2.4**
Photography Version of Jeff Whitney's "After" Resume

HEART & SOUL TIP

All of these skills were buried in, or even withheld from, Jeff's old resume. What a difference a little proactive planning makes for this Heart & Soul resume!

JEFF WHITNEY
715 Anywhere Street
City, State 10000
Phone Number

PROFESSIONAL OBJECTIVE & PROFILE

Highly motivated and goal-oriented independent photographer is seeking a position that will fully utilize more than 4 years of experience in photography. Extremely creative and talented, with experience in commercial and private photography. Seeking a position as a photographer that will provide an opportunity for career growth and professional advancement.

SUMMARY OF PHOTOGRAPHY QUALIFICATIONS

INDEPENDENT PHOTOGRAPHER
Multitalented, creative, innovative photographer with experience using 35mm Minolta X-700 cameras, medium-format Mamiya AB-67 cameras, and Kodak RP X-OMAT processor. Specialize in wedding photography and portraits. Utilize strong technical and analytical skills to produce beautiful photographs.

CLIENT RELATIONS & SERVICES
Establish and maintain an excellent network of business relationships as a result of providing superior service and attention to clients.

SALES & MARKETING
Solicit and obtain clients for independent business. Hold full responsibility for development and nurturance of client relationships, core prospect marketing, all accounting/financial affairs for independent contracting business, competitive bidding, and project management.

EDUCATION

ASSOCIATE DEGREE IN PHOTOGRAPHY
Nashville State Technical Institute, Nashville, Tennessee
(Completed 15 hours toward degree)

ASSOCIATE DEGREE IN ELECTRONIC ENGINEERING
R.E.T.S. Electronic Institute, Louisville, Kentucky

HEART & SOUL TIP

Use the MBTI and Strong results to help you write your Heart & Soul resume. Study the appendix in this book or one of the many related books listed in the Resources.

PROFESSIONAL EXPERIENCE

OWNER & PHOTOGRAPHER
SNS PHOTOGRAPHY, Nashville, Tennessee, 1993 to Present
Specialize in wedding and portrait photography for businesses and individual clients. Utilize Minolta X-700 35mm cameras and Mamiya AB-67 medium-format cameras.

ADMINISTRATION/ OPERATIONS
Direct and manage overall administration and operations of this independent photography business. Responsibilities include all soliciting and obtaining of clients, P&L, marketing, accounting, budget management, and client relations.

CUSTOMER SERVICE & RELATIONS
Committed to providing excellent service to customers by effectively responding to requests and/or concerns.

■ **FIGURE 2.5**
Photography Version of Jeff Whitney's Cover Letter

HEART & SOUL TIP

Try to start your cover letter with a high-impact opening.

JEFF WHITNEY
715 Anywhere Street
City, State 10000
Phone Number

Today's Date

Steven Williams
Williams Photography
527 Harrison Street
Atlanta, GA 54215

Dear Mr. Williams:

Are you looking for a highly motivated and goal-oriented independent photographer? With over 4 years of proven experience, I am confident of my ability to contribute to even your most challenging assignments.

I am currently completing course work for my associate degree in photography, which will supplement my existing associate degree in electronic engineering. I possess the greatest experience in portraits and wedding photography, using 35mm Minolta X-700 cameras, medium-format Mamiya AB-67 cameras, and a Kodak RP X-OMAT processor. I am extremely organized and work well with a wide variety of people.

As I am sure my references would agree, I would be an asset to your organization. If you have any interest in my experience and qualifications, please contact me at the above phone number or address.

I look forward to hearing from you soon.

Sincerely,

Jeff Whitney

these in Jeff's Photography resume in order to make him more marketable. Any employer who viewed his resume could be assured that Jeff would be an asset to the company with these additional skills. In addition, we highlighted that he was pursuing an associate degree in photography. We didn't even list this on the Engineering version, since it wasn't important for an engineering position.

> **HEART & SOUL TIP**
>
> *It is important to stay in tune with your heart's passions and dreams. Stop and listen to those inner heart messages!*

Because Jeff recognized that he needed help with his resume and career pursuits, he came to us and was able to turn his life around. This was his first step toward being proactive, rather than reactive—our second secret to writing a Heart & Soul resume. With some counseling and his results from the *Strong Interest Inventory* and the *Myers-Briggs Type Indicator,* he was equipped to make better decisions. He became more in tune with his true life passions, his heart and soul. His dreams were reinforced and he was more confident in selecting two careers that were right for him and were based on his heartfelt interests, experience, and qualifications. With our assistance, Jeff designed some basic career plans for his future. He also recognized that it was important to continue pursuing his associate degree in photography, since that was one of the areas he had wanted to pursue all along.

We visualized him in these two areas—photography and engineering—and consequently wrote two versions of his resume that were successful in landing him job interviews and several attractive offers. Jeff had actively sent resumes to companies that were of special interest to him and his career goals, whether they were advertising for jobs or not. Jeff was no longer at the mercy of the job market, as he had complained when he first entered our office. Instead, he had become a proactive individual who now had career choices. He was finally listening to his heart messages and using a deeper Heart & Soul approach to his life and career. Finally, after several rounds of negotiations, Jeff accepted a very fulfilling photography position with a well-known, reputable commercial photographer.

Jack of All Trades, Master of None

> **HEART & SOUL TIP**
>
> *You are the most important resource you have in your career search!*

Many people have more than one career that they're interested in. And while this can create a conflict at times, it can also make a person more marketable in the work force. However, we caution you to be very organized if you have more than one career goal, even if the goals are closely related. Keep your focus direct and unwavering in the career you pursue. Be proactive instead of reactive. You are not a victim. You are not helpless or at the mercy of the job market. You and only you can take charge of your life. Only you can get to the heart and soul of your being and your mission in life.

We understand that finding the right career path, or identifying your strengths and heartfelt interests, is not always easy. We also realize that this is the last thing many people ever consider before they write their resume. But it is vital to your success, both short-term and long-term. These seven steps will help you discover your inner heartfelt interests, and then you'll be able to use a Heart & Soul approach in your career goals and in writing your resume.

HEART & SOUL TIP

Strategies for learning as much as you can about the career you want include research, temporary work in that field, and volunteering and interning at the companies where you'd like to work.

For those of you beginning in a new career field, we strongly recommend that you get as much experience as possible through internships, volunteer work, part-time employment, and/or summer jobs to help identify the type of work that's right for you. There is no substitute, when it comes to learning about yourself, careers, and types of industries, for actual on-the-job experience. The good thing about these types of jobs is that there is no long-term commitment. If you don't like the work, you simply move on, with little wasted time or money and no negative feelings from employers. And if you do like the work, you can establish a reputation as a good employee and make contacts for interviews and future long-term employment.

These strategies are examples of being proactive in your career plans. Recognize that being proactive sometimes requires making sacrifices *now* that will benefit you later on. For instance, if a woman chooses to go to medical school and residency training for seven-plus years, she is certainly sacrificing time and money for future gain. A man with a mechanical background who realizes there is a strong demand for diesel mechanics might choose vocational training or a low-paying apprenticeship for two years. A biology major may want to sell pharmaceuticals but learns that he must first sell hospital beds and bedpans for three years to gain the sales experience he needs. All of these examples illustrate the concept of being proactive in your career planning. Being proactive will always pay off. When the biology major with sales experience competes for a pharmaceutical sales position with another biology major who has no sales experience, guess who will have the competitive edge and land the job?

Remember, if you are having trouble planning and strategizing your career goals and are likely to produce a poorly written, unfocused, non-Heart & Soul resume, we urge you to seek help. There are several ways to find career assistance. You can go to your local library and research in-depth career guides, or you can call your local career counselor or career development center for more information. This will be your first proactive step. Remember too that, just as our first secret—creative visualization—is vital to writing a successful resume, so is being proactive rather than reactive in planning your career, which is our second important secret and essential to the heart and soul of resume writing.

So You Want to Be a Brain Surgeon

Being entirely honest with oneself is a good exercise.

SIGMUND FREUD

S O YOU WANT TO be a brain surgeon—but you haven't even applied to medical school yet. Of course, anything is *possible,* but many things are *improbable.* Before writing a resume to get any job, make sure your goals are realistic and that you have the qualifications and skills required for that job. This is the third of the seven never-before-published secrets to creating a successful resume and very important in the synergistic Heart & Soul approach.

It's not that having goals to be a brain surgeon is absurd, but your age, experience, and qualifications might be important factors in making this a career goal. For example, if you've never worked in the health care industry, have no

HEART & SOUL TIP

Be honest and realistic about the possibility of your dreams!

related education, and you're over forty-five years old, a career goal like this one is improbable, but certainly not impossible!

We applaud and encourage lofty goals and ambitions—we encourage dreaming and knowing your inner self—but goals, ambitions, and even dreams must be in sync with reality. If goals are set too high, they can actually inhibit you from finding the job or career that's perfect for you! So we encourage you to spend some time reflecting on your inner self, which can be done with creative visualization/contemplation techniques. Be truly honest and realistic about your job expectations. After all, the Heart & Soul approach is a completely honest approach to your inner self. This is vital to integrating heart and soul—the *essential part of you*—into your everyday existence as well as into your resume writing.

Of course, no one would write a resume targeting a position such as brain surgeon without the qualifications, but it's very possible in less rarefied positions. Getting to the heart and soul—being honest about yourself and your potential qualifications and skill level—is important in setting goals.

Now, please don't get us wrong. We are not suggesting that you stop dreaming or quell your current career ambitions in any way—to the contrary. We maintain that any highly ambitious or lofty goal is best met with a realistic

HEART & SOUL TIP

Objectivity and education are valuable assets when it comes to setting realistic goals and career objectives.

and honest evaluation of your current skill set so you know from where you must build! It's just necessary to be honest about the possibility of your dreams!

Objectivity and *education* are your most valuable assets when it comes to setting realistic goals. If you have ever felt like your career goals aren't in line with your qualifications or expectations, then please read on! First we'll explore why it's important to be objective about your career goals.

Was John Realistic?

One of our clients, John, came into our office and told us, "I want my first job to be a manager's position in a huge corporation, and my salary to be at least $80,000. After getting a college degree, I think I deserve a great job."

"Well," we said, "we're sure you deserve a great job, but what do you have to offer besides your degree? It is very competitive in the corporate world, and at that salary range you'll need to offer much more than just a bachelor of arts degree."

Dumbfounded, he stared blankly at us, as if this hadn't occurred to him. Then slowly he began to tell us his story, none of which included any practical work experience or superior academic performance. While we certainly didn't want to discourage him, John was obviously not being objective about his job expectations or qualifications. John knew what he wanted to do—he had a goal—but he hadn't contemplated the *possibility* of such a career goal based on

HEART & SOUL TIP

Don't let society, peers, the media, family, or friends influence you too much when choosing the career that's right for you. Remember to stay true to yourself and your own dreams!

his current education and qualifications. He hadn't even begun to put a Heart & Soul emphasis on planning his career and writing his resume. As is true for many people, these things had never occurred to him. Getting to the heart and soul of any situation requires total honesty, which is realism in its purist form.

It's very natural for you to want to be successful in your career. Unfortunately, though, goals can be clouded with unrealistic expectations. And when this happens, you can easily veer away from the "heart and soul" honesty and objectivity that are so crucial in planning your career.

Whom Are You Trying to Please?

One of the most fundamental problems in setting career goals is that we often let society define what is "successful" and what is "not successful." By society's standards, some may feel, only the people who earn a great deal of money are considered successful. It's quite common to pick up a popular magazine and read about "The Nation's Richest 100" or "The 25 Most Influential Men and Women of the Year." This can make even the most self-assured people, if only for a moment, feel inadequate about their achievements and question their career goals. It's important, however, to base success on our own individual circumstances without feeling pressured to meet the expectations of society or anybody else!

Ask yourself, whom are you trying to please in your life? And by whose standards do you measure your performance? Only your individual circumstances dictate what you can realistically achieve, and this is what you must be honest about in your career decisions. So, no matter what society, your parents, or your friends say or do, you must first decide to set your own goals and do what you think is best for you. Only then are you really getting to the heart and soul of what you will be happiest doing.

This illustrates the need for objectivity about your career goals, expectations, and qualifications. True success in life is not always based on earnings and most often is composed of a myriad of factors unique to each individual. We all have external forces in our everyday life that push us to be a certain way. Friends, family, colleagues, bosses, peer groups, and the media all influence us greatly, whether we're aware of it or not. And, while trying to please others is a noble gesture, it is much more important to be true to yourself. Being true to yourself is being in tune with your inner self, your heart and soul. And being true to yourself requires objectivity.

John, the college graduate who wanted to earn $80,000 a year, was most influenced by his parents and a very competitive group of friends. For this college graduate it was unheard of to target an entry-level management *training* position as his goal. It wasn't what he, his parents, or his friends expected.

Anything less, he assumed, would mean that he was a failure, and not living up to his potential. Of course, with no professional work experience, internships, or outstanding academic accomplishments, his goal of such a high entry-level income was unfounded. He hadn't been objective or true to his inner self about his goals.

To help John, we offered him the *Strong Interest Inventory* and the *Myers-Briggs Type Indicator,* which was the first step in identifying his career strengths and weaknesses. (For an explanation of these instruments, see the appendix.) We also encouraged him to design a Career Map with specific plans outlining the steps needed to achieve his long-term goal. We'll illustrate how to create a Career Map later in this chapter. We emphasized that his salary expectations may be possible in a commissioned sales position, but it was unrealistic to expect $80,000 a year for an entry-level management training position.

After a careful, objective review of his qualifications, the job market, and his prior unsuccessful bid for a high-paying job, John concluded that he would have to accept a management training position at a lower salary.

HEART & SOUL TIP

Only you can decide what standards you want to live and grow by.

He took an honest, "heart and soul" look at his inner self, his qualifications, and his education, and realized he had to be willing to work and prove himself to a company before he could earn that sizable salary. While his goal was certainly *attainable,* it wasn't immediately *probable* with his limited experience and at such an early stage in his career.

May the Forces Be with You

If you believe the majority of the forces in your life are positive and you agree with them wholeheartedly, then congratulations! *May these forces be with you forever!* However, in this world it would be impossible to have only positive influences in your life. Negative forces clearly exist everywhere. If you feel as though the forces in your life are pulling you in many different directions, and many of them are negative, then it's time to put on the brakes and say *"Stop!"* Only you can decide what standards you want to live and grow by! And that means being true to yourself, being honest and realistic about your qualifications and abilities, and taking a very objective view when designing career goals.

Our world is full of illusions—it is often difficult to distinguish what's *possible* from what's *probable.* Illusions can greatly interfere with creative visualization or tuning in to our inner, higher self—getting to the heart and soul of our being. With all the forces pulling at us from every direction, our vision is often clouded about what we can or can't do in our careers. Objectivity and realism become obscured in the cloak of illusions.

In addition to falling prey to illusions, many people simply aren't aware of the numerous potential careers that are out there in the world. Not knowing what career choices are available is one of the most consistent issues with our clients. They simply lack knowledge about other jobs, professions, and industries, and this limits them greatly when defining career goals. Clients come into our office, throw up their hands in desperation, and say, "I just don't know what's out there!"

Education Is the Key

It is practically impossible to establish and follow a realistic path for a future you know nothing about. For example, how can you become a brain surgeon if you don't know anything about medicine, the health care industry, or medical school? The only way to combat this problem is through education! Education can help you analyze your own potential in the industry. The last thing you should do is jump blindly into a major decision.

To help you decide which job is best for you, we encourage school, training, and in-depth research, along with short-term, voluntary, or temporary employment. Use every resource you have available to you to teach yourself as much as possible about the profession you're considering. Try to do as much preliminary research as you can before committing to any one school or job. We recommend starting with broad-based career guides to help you make a long list of career options. Then we suggest further study on each individual career through periodicals searches and specific books on the profession.

HEART & SOUL TIP

Discover the heart and soul of your career needs through ample research and investigation of different careers and options.

We've worked with many people who went to school or work before conducting preliminary career research, and then later decided that the profession was not for them. Frustrated, they've related to us how they wasted precious years in a certain school or job. We advised them that *any* education is *good* education and that all experiences in life will teach you something important. However, researching your career options will help you invest your time and money more wisely and will clearly help you discover the heart and soul of your needs.

Your career education is only a walk or drive down the road. The public library has volumes of information on every job, profession, and industry you will ever need to make a an ample list of viable career options. And it is all free! The biggest investment you'll ever have to make at the library is your time in learning how to use the different resources. This could be a matter of hours or even days for big projects. Once you do that, you can confidently research and make decisions on any career you're interested in.

Stay objective and realistic about the jobs you're seeking and be honest about yourself. Take the time to journey into your inner self through creative visualization/contemplation and separate the illusions from reality. This is all part of the Heart & Soul approach and more important than ever in today's competitive world. Keep your current situation in perspective with the reality of the marketplace today. Heart & Soul resumes pinpoint specific career goals and are targeted to those employers who offer the jobs that move in parallel with your goals.

Perry Winston

Following is an example of a bright young man who was too unrealistic about his job qualifications. We'll discuss the specific steps required to define and outline his career goals and how we wrote his resume to target these goals.

Perry Winston came into our office with an exaggerated view of his skills and job expectations. He had just received his discharge papers from the military, where he had been a military policeman. Wearing faded army fatigues, Perry sat down in our office and spread out his military papers on the desk. "I was an M.P. in the army, but now I want to be an editor of a wildlife magazine."

Approaching this one carefully, we asked, "Could you tell us why that's your career goal?" While he talked, we carefully perused his military papers to look for writing experience. Throughout his papers were lists and lists of technical information highlighting his skills in weapons training, but nothing about writing.

"I really love the outdoors, and I like to write," Perry said matter-of-factly.

When we asked him if he had any professional writing experience, he said, "No, not really, but I did write lots of poetry in high school and college, and I majored in English in college."

Without discouraging his long-term goal, we explained to Perry that, realistically, it wasn't very likely that he could get a job as an editor of a magazine if he had no prior experience as a writer/editor. Perry had a bachelor of arts degree in international politics and English and assured us that he had good writing skills. However, when applying for any job, a person needs to have more proof of his abilities than just his word.

"But I want a good job as an editor," Perry argued. "I do have a college degree and I am very good in English. Being an editor has always been my dream."

Perry's job expectations were premature. Though Perry had certainly visualized himself as an editor and truly knew "in his heart" this is what he wanted to do, he wasn't being realistic about his short-term career goals. He expected to go from being a military policeman to an editor of a popular wildlife magazine in one giant step. It's very important and necessary to dream about your goals and aim high, but at this stage of his career Perry's short-term, immediate goal was set too high.

We advised Perry that he had to take the practical steps needed to achieve his "dreams" and goals. We told him that the first thing he should do is start writing and compiling a portfolio of writing samples. We advised him that, on any job interview, the employer

HEART & SOUL TIP

You need to design and write down practical career steps to achieve dreams and goals, which can be done on a Career Map. This process gives these goals energy and makes them more real.

would want to see samples of his writing and editing skills. After that, it would be possible to obtain an entry-level position as a proofreader or copy editor. We suggested that he start writing and compiling short stories, articles, poetry, radio and TV commercials—anything that would both illustrate and strengthen his writing skills.

We also urged Perry to use his dream of being an editor as his ultimate goal and to make real-life plans to achieve this goal. We showed him how to create a Career Map and write down the steps needed to reach that ultimate goal. A Career Map can be as simple as a list of your goals, much like a shopping list or a "to do" list, or it can be much more elaborate. One of our clients actually made a collage of photos of people doing the job she wanted to attain! Along the side of the poster, she wrote down ten steps to achieve that dream job!

Writing down your goals is part of the Heart & Soul technique. It enables you to focus on your goals more clearly and directly, and is a very powerful step in creative visualization and in manifesting what you want in life. It is also an important part of being proactive, rather than reactive, in your career planning. This can be a lot of fun, too, as well as an effective and creative tool to use throughout your life. When you actually see the steps written out (or illustrated) before you on paper, your dreams and goals become *real*. Use your imagination to create your own Career Map. You can add pictures, symbols, favorite quotes from your heroes, or anything that will positively reinforce your goals. Also, remember to *visualize* yourself in each step that you write down on the Career Map and practice your positive affirmations, as we discussed in Chapter 1.

Following Perry Winston's Career Map (Figure 3.1) is a blank one for you to use as a guide in creating your own Career Map (Worksheet 3.1). We've listed a few ideas to incorporate into your map—just to get you started. Remember, it's basically nothing more than a "to do" list, and the one we've enclosed is very simple, yet it is a very powerful approach to career planning. Place this Career Map on your bulletin board or refrigerator—anywhere so you can see it each day!

Once Perry wrote his steps down on the Career Map, it was our turn to write the resume he needed for that first job. By now we knew Perry quite well. He had shared his dreams with us and had taken the necessary steps to cast all illusions aside and be honest and objective about his career goals. We were then able to use a Heart & Soul approach to writing his resume by creatively visualizing him in an entry-level position that was right for him at this stage in his career. The goal would be to apply for entry-level positions at magazines that offered opportunities for professional advancement and career growth. Meanwhile, Perry began to write and prepare a portfolio of samples that he could take on interviews.

We probed into Perry's background to find qualities that were relevant to a writing career. We found out he in fact had experience writing and editing

■ **FIGURE 3.1**
Perry Winston's Career Map

HEART & SOUL TIP

Before Perry wrote his Career Map, he wanted to go immediately to the ultimate goal. What about the experience needed to get there?

Step One

Start writing and building a personal portfolio. Write poems, short stories, articles, whatever! Investigate intern positions at newspapers, book-publishing companies, and magazines.

Step Two

Pursue any entry-level job at a magazine or newspaper. Get your foot in the door!

Step Three

Advance from a "get your foot in the door" position to a job as a proofreader. Continue working on portfolio.

Step Four

Submit writing samples to magazines and newspapers, to be considered for publication.

Step Five

Apply for copywriting and editing jobs. Obtain a writing job!

Ultimate Goal
Go for the EDITOR'S JOB!

training materials while in the army. So, instead of developing and summarizing his weapons and infantry training in the resume, we focused on his writing experience. In addition, since he was an avid outdoorsman and desired a position with an environmental or wildlife magazine, we highlighted his background in fishing, hunting, boating, and other outdoor activities.

Take a look at the resume (Figure 3.2) and cover letter (Figure 3.3) we wrote for Perry. Pay particular attention to the "Professional Objective & Profile" and "Summary of Qualifications" sections. We focused on Perry's main areas of interest—writing, editing, and environmental activities.

Notice in Perry's resume how we emphasized everything in his past that involved writing or editing, even a portfolio of writing samples that he was preparing, listing them in the "Summary of Qualifications" section. Employers won't necessarily care if this writing was done for an actual job or not. They

CAREER MAP

HEART & SOUL TIP

The Career Map may be nothing more than a "to do" list, and you can use it to outline the steps you need to take to meet your career goal. Plan out your future and track your progress as you go.

Step One

Step Two

Step Three

Step Four

Ultimate Goal

HEART & SOUL TIP

Practice your creative visualization exercises to imagine yourself in each step.

HEART & SOUL TIP

You could even paste pictures on your map to help you visualize your career steps. Be imaginative!

■ **WORKSHEET 3.1**
Career Map

just want to see tangible evidence of writing skills. As we emphasized to Perry, it's absolutely necessary to have writing samples if you want a job as a writer.

Perry also had skills in computer design, with extensive experience using different computer programs. We pointed out to Perry that this was very important to magazine editors and would help him get interviews.

We deemphasized his training in military/police tactics, since this wasn't the focus of his resume. If he had wanted a position with the metro police force, then we would have focused on his weapons training and infantry field operations. However, for a position as a writer/editor, these skills weren't relevant.

HEART & SOUL TIP

Emphasize all qualifications and experience in a resume that are directly relevant to the job you're applying for.

Since Perry preferred a position with an environmental or wildlife magazine, we further focused on his skills as an outdoorsman. This would be appealing to any editor of a wildlife magazine and might make the difference between choosing Perry over another candidate to interview.

Important for all writers are their research skills and knowledge of the world in general. In this case, we emphasized Perry's research and writing skills he had developed while obtaining a degree in political science. We felt that this background would be a perfect foundation for an entry-level writing job.

Because Perry had come to us and learned how to set high but realistic goals, we were able to write him a successful resume. Perry separated what was *possible* from what was *improbable* and listened to his heart messages. Perry sent out fifty resumes to leading wildlife and environmental magazines around the country and within two weeks landed a job as an entry-level copy editor at one of his favorites!

His journey on his Career Map had just begun!

Wendell Keene

Often people come into our office who want to change careers. For example, Wendell Keene, a well-dressed professional in a navy suit and tie, came in and said that he had been a chiropractor for fifteen years. While discussing his background and career goals, Wendell explained, "I'm tired of my job and want to change careers. I have a friend who is very successful as a pharmaceutical sales representative, and he earns well over $100,000 a year. I don't make that much as a chiropractor, and, well, at forty-four, I'm not getting any younger. I'd like to get a job as a pharmaceutical or medical sales representative."

We asked him if he had any prior sales experience and he said no. He had begun his health care career as a respiratory therapy technician and had then obtained his Doctor of Chiropractic but had never worked in sales. We explained that while it is *possible* that a pharmaceutical company might hire him without sales experience, it's not *probable*. We again emphasized the importance of being objective about career goals and advised that he educate

■ **FIGURE 3.2**
Perry Winston's "After" Resume

HEART & SOUL TIP

This resume is designed to accomplish Step Two on Perry's Career Map.

HEART & SOUL TIP

One of Perry's preferences is Introversion on the MBTI. Notice how his writing skills are combined with his outdoor interests, identified as a Realistic GOT (General Occupational Theme) on the Strong.

PERRY WINSTON
2054 Anywhere Street
City, State 10000
Phone Number

PROFESSIONAL OBJECTIVE & PROFILE

Seeking a position in writing, editing, and/or proofreading that will fully utilize experience and advanced education in English. Experienced in writing and editing training materials for the United States Army. Self-motivated and self-directed. Desire a challenging opportunity that will combine writing skills and a love for the outdoors.

SUMMARY OF QUALIFICATIONS

WRITING, EDITING, & COMMUNICATIONS
Excellent command of the English Language. Strong writing, editing, and communication skills, with experience writing reports, essays, articles, poetry, training materials, and academic documents.

POLITICAL SCIENCE
Wrote, edited, and proofed research articles and essays on the analysis of international politics. In-depth background in academics in the research and analysis of international politics, which provided an excellent basis for interaction with diverse groups, individuals, and foreign cultures.

ENVIRONMENTALIST
Avid outdoorsman with strong skills and background in fishing, hunting, boating, and all types of outdoor activities and sports.

PROFESSIONAL EXPERIENCE

WRITER & TEAM LEADER, SUPERVISOR, & TRAINING INSTRUCTOR

UNITED STATES ARMY—4 YEARS

- *Writing & Editing:* Wrote, edited, and designed training materials that focused on leadership, teamwork, and communications.
- *Computer Design:* Designed graphics by utilizing Microsoft Works, PageMaker, and Lotus 1-2-3.
- *Curriculum/Scheduling:* Assisted in preparing curriculum for enlisted personnel and in scheduling classes. Wrote and prepared training schedules on a daily, weekly, and monthly basis.
- *Investigation & Special Assignments:* In charge of completing special assignments in the military that involved research, investigation, writing reports, and facilitation of orders from police staff.
- *Training:* Instructed individuals one-on-one, and in classroom environment, in all areas of leadership, teamwork, and communications.
- *Program Development:* Responsible for developing educational programs and teaching enlisted personnel in all areas of special military tactics, including procedures and policies of operations. Implemented these programs in field operations.
- *Team Leader—Personnel Supervision:* Supervised, guided, and led groups in field operations. Delegated work assignments and monitored job performances to ensure accuracy and adherence to standards, rules, and regulations.

EDUCATION

BACHELOR OF ARTS DEGREE IN POLITICAL SCIENCE
Areas of Emphasis: English and International Politics
University of California at Berkeley

Portfolio of Writing Samples Available upon Request

■ **FIGURE 3.3**
Perry Winston's Cover Letter

HEART & SOUL TIP

Notice how the cover letter leans toward an entry-level job by asking if they need a "talented young writer." The wording is very concise and the goal is to appeal to companies in search of new talent.

PERRY WINSTON
2054 Anywhere Street
City, State 10000
Phone Number

Today's Date

Courtney Blair
Stiles Public Relations Co.
740 Seaside Drive
Seattle, WA 94210

Dear Ms. Blair:

Are you interested in an enthusiastic, dedicated, and talented young writer? If so, I have enclosed my resume for your review.

In addition to receiving a bachelor of arts degree in political science from the University of California at Berkeley, I have been actively writing, proofreading, and editing short stories and articles throughout my school and professional career. During college I wrote, edited, and proofed research articles and essays on the analysis of international politics.

I served in the U.S. Army for 4 years, where I wrote and edited numerous technical training manuals that focused on leadership, employee relations, teamwork, and communications. I am also proficient in computer operations including all the major word processing and publishing programs.

I would be interested in setting up a personal interview at your earliest convenience, and will be contacting you within a few days to ensure that you received this letter and resume.

Sincerely,

Perry Winston

himself about sales and the pharmaceutical industry, which he could do in any library.

No doubt his health care experience would be an asset, but his lack of sales experience was a real hindrance. Opportunities would be limited to a lower-salary, entry-level position where he would have to prove himself in the field before he could earn a higher salary.

In any business situation, business networking is an important tool in finding a job. Sometimes, "who you know" can significantly enhance your career opportunities. (We will discuss business networking in more depth in Chapter 4 and have included some excellent reference books in our Resources list at the back of the book.) In Wendell's case, it would have helped greatly if he had had a strong business relationship with some higher-up executive inside one of the pharmaceutical companies. Unfortunately, his friend who worked in the pharmaceutical industry was just a sales representative; he could give him a reference, but that was all. Wendell had no immediate networking sources in the pharmaceutical industry.

HEART & SOUL TIP

Business networking is an important tool in finding a job.

"I figured my background in health care would more than make up for not having any sales experience," Wendell responded. "I didn't think I needed any real sales experience."

Wendell showed us his resume that he had been using and asked why it wasn't getting him interviews. It was a good resume for a position as a chiropractor, but it had no "selling" power for a job in pharmaceutical sales. We knew writing a successful resume for him was going to be a challenge.

We first advised Wendell to obtain some type of sales job, even if it was part-time; *anything* to start building his strengths in sales. Even though Wendell's heart was set on being a pharmaceutical sales representative, we helped him recognize the fact that he needed to take certain steps before he could reach his ultimate goal. All dreams must have a plan to make them real, just as all plans must have a dream to make them real! He needed to establish some short-term plans as stepping-stones to reach that long-term goal! When Wendell viewed his situation objectively, he understood that he couldn't realistically jump, in one step, from being a chiropractor to a sales representative earning $100,000 per year.

HEART & SOUL TIP

All dreams must have a plan to make them real.

After thoroughly discussing his background, Wendell confided that a friend of his had started a business that sold a variety of products and that he could begin working with him in order to gain some hands-on sales experience. Wendell hadn't been interested in working with him prior to our meeting because he wouldn't have been able to earn much money initially in this type of business. However, we pointed out that he could use this experience to reach his ultimate, long-term goal.

We showed Wendell how to design a Career Map, which he found helpful in outlining the steps he needed to take. His first step would be to take this sales job and build up some sales experience. From there, he could target pharmaceutical companies, since he already had a strong health care background.

Figures 3.4 and 3.5 are abbreviated versions of the resume and cover letter we wrote and designed for Wendell, which were focused toward obtaining a pharmaceutical or medical sales representative's position.

Because Wendell reevaluated his qualifications and looked at his skills objectively, he became more realistic about his job expectations. Once Wendell obtained some sales experience, we were able to utilize our third secret, "Set high but realistic goals," in writing a successful Heart & Soul resume.

We've only included the first page of Wendell's resume in this book to illustrate how our focus was directly on sales, marketing, customer service, and health care. To obtain a sales position in the pharmaceutical industry, it is equally important to have a background in health care and in sales. Of course, it's possible to obtain a pharmaceutical sales position without having a health care background, but it's not as probable if you're up against another candidate who does have health care experience. Chances are that you won't get the job. So, naturally, we emphasized Wendell's experience in health care as well as his knowledge of pharmaceuticals, health insurance, and maintenance organizations.

Another important area is customer service/client relations. We highlighted this on Wendell's resume. A company will want to know if you have any skills or experience in this area. Building strong business relationships and providing superior customer service is vital to sales.

Because Wendell followed our advice, he looked at his situation objectively and realistically. He then took a very proactive approach in his career strategy and obtained a sales position, even though it wasn't his dream job in sales. He had already been visualizing himself as a pharmaceutical sales representative when he came to see us, but he had to take the proactive step of getting a sales job in a nonpharmaceutical company. It was another step toward his dream job as a highly paid pharmaceutical sales representative.

We can happily add that Wendell is now working for one of the top pharmaceutical companies in the country and earning a six-figure salary!

I'm on the Right Track, but My Train Is Sure Moving Slowly

Remember, not everyone becomes successful in their career by the time they reach midlife. For example, the person who wants to be a brain surgeon has to be patient and plan a slow, steady career path that will lead to the ultimate goal, just as John, the college graduate who wanted to be a manager in a huge corporation, had to realistically begin in a lower-paying position. Plus, both Wendell and Perry had to reevaluate their qualifications and objectively plan a

■ **FIGURE 3.4**
Wendell Keene's "After" Resume

HEART & SOUL TIP

Wendell illustrates his comprehensive science and health care experience as well as his recently developed sales experience.

WENDELL KEENE
1024 Anywhere Street
City, State 10000
Phone Number

Professional Objective & Profile

High-caliber sales representative with an extensive background in the health care industry is seeking a position in pharmaceutical or medical sales. In-depth knowledge of the pharmaceutical industry, including nephrology/renal dialysis, as a result of hands-on experience in the medical field. More than 15 years of experience building and leading integrated health care operations.

Education

Doctor of Chiropractic
Life Chiropractic College, Marietta, Georgia

Bachelor of Science Degree in Biology & Chemistry
University of Tennessee, Knoxville

HEART & SOUL TIP

One of Wendell's motivating forces can be correlated to his Strong GOT of Enterprising. We combined his skills to place him on a better-paying career path.

Summary of Qualifications

Sales & Marketing

Extensive experience in direct sales in the network marketing industry. Expanded sales territory by 75% in 6 months, which increased overall profitability by 65%. Skilled in creating and implementing innovative sales and marketing strategies to increase business and profitability. Facilitated numerous sales seminars and meetings.

Sales Training

Trainer of new sales representatives in all areas of sales, networking, and customer service. Strong motivational speaker and leader, with ability to inspire associates to surpass company goals.

Customer Service/Client Relations

Committed to providing superior service to clients through attention to detail and close follow-up. Personally manage account calls, presentations, and negotiations. Consistently establish and maintain an excellent network of business relationships as a result of excellent service and strong communication skills.

Health Care Expertise

More than 15 years of experience in health care. Comprehensive, diversified background in pharmaceuticals, chiropractic, and business operations as a result of experience as a chiropractor and respiratory therapy technician in a major Nashville hospital.

Health Insurance & Maintenance Organizations

Oversaw the coordination and management of health insurance plans including commercial, private pay, PPOs, HMOs, personal injury, medicare, and others.

■ **FIGURE 3.5**
Wendell Keene's Cover Letter

HEART & SOUL TIP

Wendell's cover letter is specifically targeted to pharmaceutical/ medical sales. In a competitive industry like this one, employers will want to see your commitment, goals, and past experience and qualifications.

WENDELL KEENE
1024 Anywhere Street
City, State 10000
Phone Number

Today's Date

Rachel Michaels
Director of Sales
Astro Merck Pharmaceutical Co.
219 Dutch Street
Philadelphia, PA 27122

Dear Ms. Michaels:

Are you interested in a highly motivated, goal-oriented health care professional? I am submitting my resume to be considered for a pharmaceutical/medical sales position with your company.

My years of health care experience are supplemented by my recent success as a sales representative. After obtaining my undergraduate degree in biology and chemistry, I received my doctorate in chiropractic and proceeded to build a successful private practice. After I decided to change career paths, I developed a track record of success as a sales representative. I am excited about the opportunity to combine my medical science knowledge with a challenging and rewarding sales career in the pharmaceutical industry.

I would like to set up a personal interview at your earliest convenience. I can be reached at the above telephone number and address.

Thank you in advance for your time and consideration. I look forward to hearing from you soon.

Sincerely,

Wendell Keene

career path to achieve their ultimate goals. For all the individuals we've mentioned so far, these goals required diligent patience and perseverance but were very attainable nonetheless. They were all on the right track, even though it seemed that the train was sure moving slowly!

HEART & SOUL TIP

Be patient while working toward your career goals. Sometimes the slow process is the best process!

If you do feel as though your standards and goals are realistic but you are still not achieving them, be assured that it's OK to take slow but sure baby steps. Sometimes the slow process is the best process, and it can allow you to take the extra time to know yourself even better, which is a true Heart & Soul approach.

Your Journey Is as Important as Your Destination

Many folks complain that they are not where they want to be, and worry that they won't be happy until they reach that final destination, whether it's a better job, more money, a bigger house, a better relationship—whatever. They lose their "heart and soul" focus—the focus on their beingness and why they're

HEART & SOUL TIP

Love yourself throughout your journey, and enjoy living in the moment.

here in the first place. They lose focus on living in the moment. These people do not realize that they aren't in tune with their inner self. While we admire these people's drive, we wonder if they will ever be happy. For any given goal, you may spend 95 percent of your time trying to get there, trying to achieve it, and only 5 percent actually being there after you have achieved it,

before you move on to plan your next goal. In life you are always moving—it may be forward or backward—but, as with the cycle of the seasons, you're always moving and changing. Spring doesn't arrive and then just stop; it keeps evolving until summer is here, and then summer keeps moving until autumn arrives, and on and on. It's like that in life. Sure, there may be times when we all feel we are at a stagnant, static point in our life, but that's just an illusion. There is an ebb and flow in life, and everything keeps moving.

HEART & SOUL TIP

Tune in to your heart and soul and there you will find your dreams. Then set your course and begin your journey.

Real satisfaction comes when you tune in to your inner heart and soul and uncover your dreams. You set your course and begin your journey, and then, over the next few months, you begin to make progress. At that time you may find yourself saying, "Yeah, I am doing the right thing. I am on the right track, and it really feels good!"

With such a huge portion of your life spent always working toward something, which in this case is your career goals, you'd better relax and enjoy the journey as much as the destination. So live in the moment and love your journey, for within each step there will be important lessons to learn.

In summary, objectivity and education are two of the most important tools to use when trying to set high but realistic goals. If you're objective about your situation, then you can more clearly distinguish what is real from what is illusory. You can more confidently distinguish what's possible from what's improbable. By tuning in to the heart and soul of your being through creative visualization and contemplation, you're more likely to be true to yourself and to be honest and realistic about your own qualifications. Remember, you have only yourself to please—not society, family, friends, or colleagues. And if you are educated about career choices, then you can more accurately determine which one is right for you. Then and only then can you write a Heart & Soul resume that will reflect a superior candidate on all levels!

4 Attending to Attention

I think the one lesson I have learned is that there is no substitute for paying attention.

DIANE SAWYER

I T AMAZES US THAT people overlook this important detail. Targeting your resume to meet the job's requirements is the fourth of the seven never-before-published secrets to creating a successful resume. We also refer to it as "attending to attention."

Basically, this means knowing how to listen. Knowing how to listen is the trademark of a good communicator. To really listen to someone, you must be aware of the moment. And being aware of the moment means you are tuning in to your inner being, which is essential in writing a Heart & Soul resume and what this book is all about.

Have you ever tried to tell someone something and then have him or her say, "Huh? What did you say? I wasn't listening"? Or poured your heart out to friends about something that's seriously bothering you, and they don't even acknowledge that you've been talking to them? It can be exceedingly frustrating.

Just imagine if you responded to an ad in the newspaper for a job and you didn't mention that you had any of the qualifications that were listed as requirements for the position in the ad. The employer who received your resume would assume that you hadn't even read the ad. The fact is, you probably read the ad, but you didn't pay attention. You didn't listen to what the ad said.

Vital to listening is being aware of the moment, which means keeping your mind on the present, giving it your full "heart and soul" attention. Like the other tools we have discussed, listening is an essential element in your job search. When you read a job advertisement in the newspaper or in a trade magazine, do you really pay attention to the qualifications and skills needed for that job? Do you highlight those qualifications and skills in your resume? We can't emphasize enough to please pay attention when you read an ad or use some other method of pursuing a job. If a friend tells you about a job opening at a certain company, do you pay close attention to what's required in that job? Paying close attention to what an employer wants is one step in helping you succeed in your job search.

HEART & SOUL TIP

"Attending to attention" is vital in researching companies and jobs. The more you know about the job, company, or industry you are targeting, the better your resume will be.

By not paying close attention, you might write a resume that doesn't include the skills and qualifications needed for that job, *even though you possess those skills!* Many people fail to tailor their resumes to a specific job because they simply don't listen to what the employer wants. Later in this chapter we'll demonstrate how we tailored a couple of resumes to match the qualifications and skills that were listed in real job advertisements.

There are other factors involved in "attending to attention" when it comes to being successful, such as attention to detail. If a job advertisement lists specific criteria required for a position, then you need to be able to respond positively to each of those criteria. Only then will you be putting your heart and soul into writing your resume. It will make your resume better and more successful. And, remember, you might only need to go one step further in detail than your best competitor! When all other things are equal, your keen attention to detail will put you over the top.

HEART & SOUL TIP

Listening is being aware of the details—of tuning in to the moment—and an essential part of "attending to attention"!

It's simple. Our message is clear. *If you don't have time to take care of the details, you don't have time to get the better job.* You must situate this as a priority in your life. The marketplace is far too competitive these days, and you simply can't afford to not put your best foot forward. There are no shortcuts. To "attend to attention," you must take the time to really listen, be attentive to detail, and custom-write each resume for the job you're seeking!

Christopher Woodbury

Next is a sample of an advertisement (Figure 4.1) that was listed in the classified section of a newspaper. Following the advertisement are a portion of the resume (Figure 4.2) and the cover letter (Figure 4.3) that we custom-wrote for the position advertised. We'll explain how we looked at the details of the job and tailored the resume to match the criteria listed.

We paid close attention to the description of the job being advertised. Key phrases like "coordinating external audits of hospital financial records, third-party payor audits, and the filing of the Medicare Cost report" describe specific details inherent in the job. The employer would look for these in every resume. Our client, Christopher Woodbury, had experience in these functions, and we were able to highlight them in his resume. If we hadn't paid close attention to the advertisement and asked Christopher about this, we would never have known about that specific experience. Christopher hadn't read the advertisement very closely. He just saw the headline "Internal Auditor" and responded to that. This is typical of many clients who walk into our office; they simply don't pay attention.

Even though Christopher didn't have experience as an internal auditor for a health care company, he did have experience auditing health care facilities as a result of his position as an accountant at a leading accounting firm in Nashville. Therefore, we highlighted his health care experience under "Summary of Qualifications."

Important too in this ad was education. The job required a bachelor's degree in accounting and a CPA license, which we positioned at the top of Christopher's resume so the employer would notice this right away and there would be no questions concerning his educational background. Other accountants who applied for this position without a CPA license or a bachelor of arts degree in accounting would not be chosen over Christopher. Again, attention to detail was the winning ingredient in this Heart & Soul resume.

Christopher possessed account management experience, supervision and recruiting skills, and microcomputer experience, which we emphasized. These skills are valuable assets in this type of job and might be the "extras" needed to win an interview and the job. Plus, we knew that Christopher's long-term goal was to be an internal auditing manager, so we visualized him in that position, even though he had to begin as an internal auditor. He was using this as a stepping-stone to achieve his ultimate goal.

Because we included Christopher's extra skills and experience, the employer would recognize that he had the potential to be groomed for management or supervisory positions, and this could be the determining factor in whether Christopher was called in for an interview over another candidate without

■ **FIGURE 4.1**
Advertisement for an
Internal Auditor Position

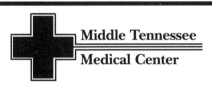

Middle Tennessee Medical Center

INTERNAL AUDITOR

Middle Tennessee Medical Center currently has a full-time position for an experienced Internal Auditor. Responsibilities include: Conducting audits for management and Board of Directors to assess effectiveness of internal controls, accuracy of financial, records, and efficiency of operations, Coordinating external audits of hospital financial records, third-party payor audits, and the filing of the Medicare Cost report. Qualified candidates must hold a Bachelor's Degree in Accounting, CPA license, and three years of healthcare audit experience.

Qualified candidates should send resume
or contact:
MIDDLE TENNESSEE MEDICAL CENTER
Attn: Human Resources
400 N. Highland Avenue
Murfreesboro, Tennessee 37130
Attention: MCO
615-849-4293

*We comply with Title VI, Section 504,
of the Civil Rights Act*

■ **FIGURE 4.2**
Christopher Woodbury's "After" Resume

HEART & SOUL TIP

Notice how the objective ties in exactly with the job posting.

CHRISTOPHER WOODBURY
3047 Anywhere Street
City, State 10000
Phone Number

PROFESSIONAL OBJECTIVE & PROFILE

Accountant at a leading firm in Nashville would like to obtain a position as an internal auditor for a health care company that will provide a challenging opportunity to significantly contribute to the company's efficiency, organization, growth, and profitability.

EDUCATION

BACHELOR OF SCIENCE DEGREE IN ACCOUNTING
Middle Tennessee State University, Murfreesboro

LICENSURE

Certified Public Accountant

PROFESSIONAL AFFILIATIONS

American Institute of Certified Public Accountants
Tennessee Society of Certified Public Accountants
Fellow of the Life Management Institute

SUMMARY OF QUALIFICATIONS

ACCOUNTING & AUDITING EXPERIENCE
Background exemplifies a successful track record of career accomplishments, including more than 14 years of experience as a professional accountant and auditor. Skilled in all areas of technical accounting, auditing, financial analysis, and accounting research. Conduct ongoing analyses to evaluate the effectiveness of internal controls and efficiency of operations.

HEALTH CARE EXPERTISE
Coordinate audits of financial records of various businesses, including hospitals and medical centers. Work includes preparing audits of hospital financial records, third-party payor audits, and the filing of the Medicare Cost report. Extensive knowledge of the health care industry.

ACCOUNT MANAGEMENT
In-depth experience as account manager and as client service executive on major health care accounts. Responsible for overall accounting, auditing, and reporting.

SUPERVISION/RECRUITING
Experienced in all areas of supervision and recruiting, including interviews, hiring, evaluating, and supervision of accountants.

MICROCOMPUTER SKILLS
Demonstrated skills in using microcomputers and in the design of microcomputer applications.

■ **FIGURE 4.3**
Christopher Woodbury's Cover Letter

CHRISTOPHER WOODBURY
3047 Anywhere Street
City, State 10000
Phone Number

Today's Date

Middle Tennessee Medical Center
Attention: Human Resources
400 N. Highland Ave.
Murfreesboro, TN 37130

Attention: Human Resources

Regarding your recent ad for Internal Auditor, I am submitting my resume for your review.

With over 14 years of auditing experience, primarily in the health care field, I feel I am well qualified for your auditor position. I am an active member in the state and national Certified Public Accountant Associations, which allows me to stay abreast of the latest legal and tax accounting changes.

I have expertise in all facets of technical accounting, auditing, financial analyses, and accounting research. I have prepared audits of hospital financial records and third-party payor audits and filed Medicare Cost reports for many years.

I would like to set up a personal interview at your earliest convenience. I can be reached at the above address and phone number.

I look forward to hearing from you soon.

Sincerely,

Christopher Woodbury

HEART & SOUL TIP

Whether you learn about a job from a newspaper, internal company posting, online classified, Web page, job line, referral, informational interview, or networking, pay close attention to what the employer needs and really listen with your whole being. Then, write your Heart & Soul resume to accommodate those needs.

those extra skills. Sure enough, Christopher got an interview with the company, and the employer told him he had a dynamic resume, plus he had management potential. Just what Christopher wanted: a position that would lead to a management job!

Remember to include everything in your resume that is specified in the job advertisement (providing you have those skills), as well as additional qualities that will increase your chances of winning an interview. This is an example of going that extra step, which is also part of the Heart & Soul technique. Any extra step you take—every strategy, every moment you stop and listen to your heart speak—may be the one that gets you to your goal.

Robert Tanner

■ **FIGURE 4.4**
Advertisement for Jobs at an MCO

Figure 4.4 is another sample of a classified ad; we custom-wrote Robert Tanner's resume (Figure 4.5) to match its qualifications. Robert wanted a management position with a managed care organization. He had extensive sales experience but no real managed care experience. We carefully scrutinized the ad and questioned Robert regarding his background. Robert said, "Well, I do have experience selling Medicare supplements and long-term health care plans to retired teachers, and this should directly relate to the qualifications listed in the ad." Robert was right, and we used this as a selling point in his resume.

The advertisement highlighted specific qualifications needed for not just one but several positions in the managed care organization. Robert had direct experience in provider relations and sales and marketing, which were emphasized in the advertisement, so we highlighted these under "Summary of Qualifications." In addition, Robert was skilled in business planning and development and had been successful in expanding sales territories. This managed care organization was looking for individuals who could help grow the business, and we pointed out these particular skills on Robert's resume.

Robert called us about two weeks after he had sent his resume to this ad. "You won't believe it, but I was one of the first people called in for an interview! They really loved my resume. Said it was the best they had received.

"And, you know what else?" Robert continued. "I got a manager's position. I'm going to be leading an entire division in sales."

By reviewing the two previous samples, you have, we hope, learned how to pay attention to detail and how to tailor your resume to match the needs of the job advertisements. However, remember

MANAGED CARE ORGANIZATION

Fast-growing health plan has career opportunities for highly skilled managers and staff with strong managed care experience in:

◆ Finance
◆ Membership services
◆ Provider network development & contracting
◆ Provider relations
◆ Utilization management/Quality assurance
◆ Sales and marketing

Join our team and build our success and reputation while increasing our customer base. We want highly successful people with excellent communication, interpersonal and technical skills, and outstanding futures with their current organizations.

VANDERBILT HEALTH PLANS
Please send resumes to:
Vanderbilt Health Services
1801 West End Ave., Suite 1700
Nashville, TN 37203
Attention: MCO
or fax to 615-320-3175

Affirmative Action Equal Opportunity Employer

ATTENDING TO ATTENTION

■ **FIGURE 4.5**
Robert Tanner's "After" Resume

HEART & SOUL TIP

Robert's Extroversion preference on the MBTI and his Enterprising interests make him an excellent candidate for this position.

ROBERT TANNER

321 Anywhere Street
City, State 10000
Phone Number

Professional Objective & Profile

Highly motivated and goal-oriented sales manager is seeking a management position in a managed care organization that will fully utilize his more than 20 years of building and leading integrated sales operations for diverse companies. Extensive background in and knowledge of health care sales and customer and member service.

Strong general management qualifications in strategic business planning and organizational reengineering. Excellent experience in building underdeveloped territories to achieve maximum profitability.

Summary of Qualifications

Health Care Sales

Extensive experience in selling health care plans, including Medicare supplements and long-term care, while working for United Teachers Associates Insurance Company. In-depth knowledge of the health care industry, sales management, and customer and member service.

Sales Awards & Accomplishments

- Ranked as the No. 1 Sales Representative nationally for 2 years in a row while at United Teachers Associates Insurance Company.

- Sales team produced more than $2 million in premiums during last 2 years of employment at United Teachers Associates Insurance Company.

- National Sales Manager of the Year.

Sales & Marketing

Talented in establishing growth plans for individual accounts and personally managing account calls, presentations, and negotiations. Proven track record of building sales and expanding territories.

Business Planning & Development

Have held full decision-making responsibility for developing annual financial objectives and preparing long-range strategic business plans. Skilled in strategic planning and development of integrated sales, marketing, and business development campaigns targeted to specific markets.

Provider Relations

Direct liaison to health care providers, with expertise in provider relations. Ability to develop and maintain a strong network of business associates as a result of extensive interaction and strong communication skills. Committed to providing superior service, which results in repeat business and referrals.

HEART & SOUL TIP

An aggressive, proactive job search, strong skills, and a well-positioned Heart & Soul resume will give you the quickest and best results!

that you must possess the qualifications. Do not make up your own credentials just so they fit the employer's needs. By reading the first three chapters of this book, you have also already defined your qualifications, job expectations, and goals and visualized yourself in the position you're seeking—all important secrets to writing a Heart & Soul resume.

Always, Always Send a Cover Letter

We assume that you know how important it is to send a cover letter, but maybe you don't. It is another crucial element in "attending to attention" and it's an important detail that many people overlook. Always send a cover letter with your resume! We call it a *power* letter, or *sales* letter, because its purpose is to grab someone's attention and sell you! And, if it's written with a Heart & Soul approach, it will be much more effective as a sales tool.

HEART & SOUL TIP

A cover letter is an essential sales tool and is part of "attending to attention" when you submit a resume.

As in your resume, you must include details in your cover letter that match the qualifications the employer is seeking. Always personalize your letter—that is, address it to the person who will be reading your letter and resume. Of course, many ads will simply list a post office box number or Department of Human Resources, and you may have no choice but to address your letter to a department. We urge you to telephone the company (if its name is listed) and ask the name of the person who will be reading your materials; if you address your letters "To whom it may concern," chances are you won't merit serious consideration. You have only a few seconds to grab someone's attention with a resume and cover letter, so make every second count! Naturally, do not call the company if the ad says, "No phone calls, please!"

HEART & SOUL TIP

When you write a cover letter, address it to someone specifically. Nothing is so bland or boring as a letter addressed "To whom it may concern."

Figure 4.6 is the cover letter we wrote for our client Robert Tanner for the management position in the managed care organization. In this instance, the ad specifically directed the applicant to send the letter to the attention of MCO. It's important to pay attention to even a small detail like this one, which might not seem very significant. Remember, *everything* that's listed in an ad has a reason for being there.

It's always effective to begin your cover letter with something catchy. Most letters will begin with the usual "I am applying for the management position in your company. . . ." *Yawn! Ho-hum!* Be interesting! Nothing pleases a company more than a candidate who knows some morsel of information about the company. Do your research. Research—whether it's your own heart you're researching or a topic in the public library—is a method of getting to the heart and soul of the situation at hand. If you've recently read an article about the company, let them know it, as we did in Robert's letter.

■ **FIGURE 4.6**
Rober Tanner's Cover Letter

ROBERT TANNER
321 Anywhere Street
City, State 10000
Phone Number

Today's Date

Vanderbilt Health Services
Attention: MCO
1801 West End Ave., Suite 1700
Nashville, TN 37203

Dear MCO:

I recently read an article about Vanderbilt Health Services in *The Tennessean* newspaper, and learned that it is in the process of expanding its Managed Care Organization. One of my career goals is to align myself with a company that's developing business opportunities and expanding overall operations, so when I saw your ad for management positions, I wanted to be one of the first to respond.

As you requested, I have enclosed a personal resume that highlights my qualifications. As you will note, I am not a beginner, but rather a seasoned professional with more than 20 years of experience. Specific areas of expertise include the following:

- Skill in developing business opportunities, establishing and nurturing client relationships, core marketing, and project management.

- Excellent management qualifications, which include strategic and tactical planning, organizational reengineering, and quality improvement.

- Provider-relations expertise, with extensive knowledge of and experience in the health care industry, sales management, and customer and member service. Hands-on experience in provider-network development and contracting.

- Ability to be highly successful, with strong interpersonal skills, and to effectively communicate with all levels of management and personnel.

I am confident that, with my experience and career goals, I would be an asset to your organization. I would like to request a personal interview at your earliest convenience so we can discuss how I can significantly contribute to building the reputation, expansion, and success of Vanderbilt Health Services.

I look forward to speaking with you soon.

Sincerely,

Robert Tanner

He knew all about the goals for Vanderbilt Health Services, and we wrote this in the very first sentence.

The organization's ad listed several career opportunities, so we emphasized in the beginning of the letter that Robert was interested in a management position. Next, we wanted to emphasize Robert's qualifications that were relevant to a management position. Even though you don't have to, in this example we used bullets to draw the reader's eye to specific details concerning Robert's background. Often, details can get buried in the cover letter and be hard to pick out. Make it *easy* for the employer to see your accomplishments! You don't want your great qualifications and achievements to be like buried treasure in some lost, sunken treasure chest.

Mind Your Manners: Don't Forget to Say Thank You

Imagine this: You gave your friend a present a couple of weeks ago—nothing expensive, just a nice shirt for her birthday. You didn't have the opportunity to see her open it, so you're not sure if she liked it or if it even fit. You watch the mail expectantly for several days, looking for a note that says, "Thank you for the great shirt!" It doesn't come. You wonder if she knows the gift was from you. Did the name tag get lost in the shuffle? Or does she simply hate the gift and want to avoid discussing it so she can spare your feelings? This is what it's like to not receive a thank-you note for a gift or a deed. It leaves you hanging in the air. You've probably experienced this several times in your life. Most people have. It's only natural to feel disappointed if a person doesn't say "thank you" for a gift.

A thank-you note to a prospective employer is especially important in the Heart & Soul approach. Sending a thank-you note following a conversation or meeting is that little something extra that makes you special. You stand out from those who didn't send one, just as Heart & Soul resumes stand out from the rest.

In your note let the employer know you appreciate the time and effort spent in speaking with you. Emphasize additional qualifications, and add something extra like "I am sure I would fit in well with your team of professionals and would be able to significantly contribute to your company's development plans." An employer will remember the candidates who send thank-you notes. And you *want* to be remembered! Figure 4.7 is the thank-you note we wrote for Robert Tanner after he went on his interview.

HEART & SOUL TIP

Sending a thank-you note after a conversation or meeting with an employer is a way of showing gratefulness and another way of "attending to attention" in your whole job-search process.

■ **FIGURE 4.7**
Robert Tanner's Thank-You Note

ROBERT TANNER
321 Anywhere Street
City, State 10000
Phone Number

Today's Date

Jean Wiggins
Vanderbilt Health Services/MCO
1801 West End Ave., Suite 1700
Nashville, TN 37203

Dear Ms. Wiggins:

I just wanted to say thank you for a productive and interesting meeting last Thursday. As we discussed, I am developing a formal proposal outlining my strategic planning goals and provider-network development ideas. I know my past experience in this area will tie in closely with your needs.

If there is anything I can do for you before your Board of Directors' meeting next month, please give me a call. I look forward to continued discussions!

Sincerely,

Robert Tanner

Here's Another Byte

"Attending to attention" also means being detailed about other aspects of your job search. We suggest managing your job search with your computer. After you write your resume and cover letter, put them on a computer disk as masters, and remember to back up your disk regularly. It will make your life much easier when you custom-write each resume and cover letter.

Always keep a backup copy of your most recent work on hand. If you don't have a computer with a word processor and high-quality printer, find one you can use at a moment's notice. (Many copy centers rent computers for a nominal fee.) Never edit over your master resume or cover letter on the disk, and always make a copy of each resume or letter before you make any changes. We usually scroll to the bottom of the document on the disk, paste a copy of the resume and cover letter on subsequent pages, make the changes, and keep them there for a permanent record of the communication. If your disk or computer file gets too big, simply copy the master resume and cover letter to a new file and begin again.

HEART & SOUL TIP

Find a consistent way to manage your resume and cover-letter writing. During your job search, you may end up with several subtly different versions, with many different cover letters.

Attention to detail is important in keeping your file on disk and in being able to quickly and efficiently tailor your resumes. Having a simple, easy-to-use system in place will save you time! In one simple file you can keep your documents stored and on hand for quick access. That way, you are much less likely to skip the details of tailoring your resume to a specific job.

Heart & Soul Resumes for Your Proactive Job Search

So far in this chapter, we have mainly discussed how to incorporate attention to detail when responding to job postings. While learning how to tailor your resume to match the qualifications listed in an advertisement is an extremely important tool, it is just as important to maintain a proactive career plan. We believe not only in responding to advertisements in newspapers and trade magazines but also in actively approaching companies you'd like to work for *before* they place an ad. We also believe firmly in business networking and using the Internet. Since generally only up to 15 percent of all available jobs are listed in the newspaper, you're greatly limiting your job search by only answering those ads. In addition, search firms (headhunters and recruiting firms) as a whole place candidates in fewer than 10 percent of the executive positions filled. We believe your best resource is *you* when it comes to finding a job.

HEART & SOUL TIP

To be proactive in your job search, use networking and the Internet as tools to find that right job. Don't leave any door unopened, for it may lead to your next great career!

Therefore, while you are responding to key job openings in the newspaper, you should also be aggressively pursuing companies and employers that you would like to work for. You must pay attention to every morsel of information you receive about a company and job openings through networking and/or the Internet. Your in-depth efforts enhance the heart and soul of your resume.

If you have clearly defined your career goals, as outlined in Chapter 3, then by now you have identified which employers and/or companies would be a potential perfect match for you. Using networking and the Internet can help you find these companies and employers. There is a hidden job market out there, with many employment opportunities that are not known to the general public through regular advertising and/or employment agencies. To find these, it's most effective to network with businesses and people you know.

Raina Walraven

One of our clients, Raina Walraven of New York City, told us that she had been networking to try to find a new job in trading, banking, and/or investments. She had called people she had worked with previously and also had contacted companies she was interested in working for. One of her contacts told her about an opening at a prestigious financial company in San José, Costa Rica. Her contact also told her about the special requirements of this job, which involved availability to travel and knowledge of the Spanish language and Latin American culture, as well as experience in trading. Raina had always dreamed of working in Latin America and wanted to send her resume to this company. She carefully listened to all the details needed in this job so she could reflect these in her resume. However, her old resume wasn't very polished and she didn't feel proud of it. Nor did it include any of her experience with the Spanish language and Latin American culture, which were crucial in this position. Let's look at Raina's old resume (Figure 4.8) and the resume we wrote that included attention to detail and a Heart & Soul approach (Figure 4.9). Particularly note the "Professional Objective & Profile." Raina's old resume doesn't have one! Plus, her experience with the Latin American culture is buried and only barely mentioned at the end. We placed it at the very top of her new resume since this was important in getting a job in Costa Rica We also gave it prominent mention in her cover letter (Figure 4.10).

HEART & SOUL TIP

Keep a card file or notepad handy so when you are networking you can write down specific details of the job to include in your Heart & Soul resume.

Because Raina had carefully paid attention to her networking contact and truly *listened,* she was able to communicate to us the details necessary to include in her resume; as a result, she landed an interview and a job offer!

In addition to your networking, you can use the Internet to research companies and find unadvertised jobs. When surfing the Internet for job postings, pay attention the same way you do when perusing the classifieds. It's the same thing. For example, Career Link Worldwide has maintained a global online

■ **FIGURE 4.8**
Raina Walraven's "Before" Resume

HEART & SOUL TIP

Notice there is no proactive career objective—no attention to detail concerning her special skills and talents. Plus, the wording is crunched together and hard to read.

RAINA WALRAVEN
4500 Anywhere Street
City, State 10000
Phone Number

EXPERIENCE

New York National Bank, New York, NY—December 1995 to Present
Vice President: Trader responsible for managing fixed-rate, pass-through, mortgage-backed securities book comprising thirty- and fifteen-year collateral (GNMA, FHLMC, FNMA), balloon securities, and FFIEC CMOs. Duties include selection, positioning, and hedging of all securities. Position limit of 75 million dollars. Maintain excellent relations with primary and regional dealers. Responsible for maintaining a diversified mortgage product inventory and marking all positions to market. Manage sale of all newly originated First American securitized mortgages. Work closely with sales force to fill customer needs for mortgage-backed products. Generate trade ideas and sell trades to sales force and execute trades. Develop and present seminars on the application and use of mortgage-backed products to sales force and institutional clients.

Smith Barney Inc. / Greenwich Street Advisors
388 Greenwich St., New York, NY—August 1993–February 1995
Assistant Portfolio Manager: For one national, eight state–specific, open-end municipal bond funds and one high-yield close-end fund listed on the NYSE. Total assets exceeded 2.8 billion dollars. Responsibilities included identifying and executing trades including bond swaps, derivatives, and private placements. Responsible for credit surveillance of all positions, evaluating bond pricing, and assuring compliance with prospectus and SEC requirements. Communicated with institutional bond dealers and traders throughout the day to evaluate market conditions. Wrote annual and quarterly reports for shareholders and boards of directors as well as marketing bulletins for brokers. Reconciled trading desk accounts at the end of each business day. Traded for Smith Barney National, California, and New York tax-free money-market funds. Total assets exceeded 2.0 billion dollars. Traded daily, weekly, monthly floating rate debt, commercial paper, derivatives, and private placements. Maintained portfolio database, credit ratings, and received offering from dealers. Promoted to long-term bonds funds after one year.

Education: **NORTHERN ARIZONA UNIVERSITY, B.A.,** Flagstaff, Arizona, 1989
UNIVERSITY OF MISSOURI, B.S.—Finance, St. Louis, 1985
FORRESTER INSTITUTO INTERNACIONAL, San José, Costa Rica, Summer 1988

■ **FIGURE 4.9**
Raina Walraven's "After" Resume

HEART & SOUL TIP

We wrote a proactive "Professional Objective & Profile" for Raina, and highlighted pertinent details.

RAINA WALRAVEN
4500 Anywhere Street
City, State 10000
Phone Number

PROFESSIONAL OBJECTIVE & PROFILE

High-caliber financial vice president desires a position in trading, banking, investments, or proprietary trading. Offering 6 years of experience building and leading operations in trading, marketing, product management, and client services. Proficient in Spanish, with an in-depth knowledge of Latin American culture as a result of studying and living with a family in San José, Costa Rica. Available to travel as needed.

PROFESSIONAL EXPERIENCE

HEART & SOUL TIP

It's important to focus on career details.

VICE PRESIDENT OF MORTGAGE-BACKED SECURITIES TRADING
NEW YORK NATIONAL BANK, New York, 1995 to Present

TRACK RECORD OF SUCCESS Began as an investment officer and was promoted to vice president within 1 year as a result of intense study of product and outstanding job performance.

TRADING Hold full decision-making responsibility for directing, managing, and analyzing mortgage-backed securities for an institutional sales force of 20. Trade, position, maintain, and hedge a mortgage inventory with positioning capabilities of $75 million.

PRODUCTION MANAGEMENT— MARKETING Research, analyze, identify, and select dealers. Create markets, determine best price and duration, and sell products to sales staff. Work involves portfolio analysis, generation of trade ideas, and assessment of value in the mortgage-backed sector.

SPECIALTIES Specialize in balloons, FFIECs, 15-year collaterals and CMOs. Assist in ARMs and floaters. .

PROPRIETARY TRADING Provide analytical support to trading desk, which consists of 4 sales representatives.

ASSISTANT PORTFOLIO MANAGER
SMITH BARNEY, INC., New York, 1991 to 1995

COMPANY TRACK RECORD OF SUCCESS Began as an assistant trader and was promoted to assistant portfolio manager after 1 year as a result of intense study of the market and outstanding job performance.

PORTFOLIO MANAGEMENT Held full decision-making responsibility for 1 national, 8 specific open-end municipal bond funds, and 1 high-yield closed-end fund listed on the New York Stock Exchange. Total assets exceeded $2.8 billion.

TRADING Responsible for analyzing, identifying, and executing trades, including bond swaps, derivatives, and private placements. Reconciled trading desk accounts daily.

PROGRAM DEVELOPMENT Developed and initiated Financial Futures Hedging Program.

MARKET ANALYSIS Analyzed markets, including credit surveillance of all positions. Evaluated bond pricing, and assured compliance with prospectus and SEC requirements.

FINANCIAL REPORTING Wrote annual/quarterly reports and marketing news releases.

EDUCATION

BACHELOR OF ARTS DEGREE IN POLITICAL SCIENCE, MINOR IN INTERNATIONAL BUSINESS
Northern Arizona University, Flagstaff
Forrester Instituto Internacional, San José, Costa Rica
Lived with a Latin American family and studied the language, culture, and customs.

BACHELOR OF SCIENCE DEGREE IN FINANCE, MINOR IN SPANISH
University of Missouri, St. Louis

■ **FIGURE 4.10**
Raina Walraven's Cover Letter

HEART & SOUL TIP

This cover letter is tailored to the tips she learned during her networking— attention to detail!

RAINA WALRAVEN
4500 Anywhere Street
City, State 10000
Phone Number

Today's Date

Gonzales Castellanos
One Broadway Street
International Bank of Costa Rica
San José, Costa Rica

Dear Mr. Castellanos:

This letter is in reference to a recent conversation I had with Mr. John Lyles, Vice President of Smith Barney, Inc., in New York. He mentioned that the International Bank of Costa Rica has an opening for a director of finance and investments and suggested that I send you a resume, which I have enclosed for your review.

In addition to having a bachelor of arts degree in political science, with a minor in International business, and a bachelor of science degree in finance, with a minor in Spanish, I also possess six years of aggressive experience that encompasses trading, banking, investments, and proprietary trading. I attended the Forrester Instituto Internacional in San José, Costa Rica, in 1988 and gained valuable experience while living and studying with a Latin American family. Proficient in Spanish, I am confident that I can significantly contribute to your organization and will be a valuable asset.

I would like to arrange for a personal interview at your earliest possible convenience. Please feel free to contact me at my home telephone number or address if you have any additional questions.

Thank you in advance for your time and consideration. I look forward to speaking with you soon.

Sincerely,

Raina Walraven

HEART & SOUL TIP

You must pay close attention to the employer's needs, no matter whether you hear of the job through the newspaper, through networking, or on the Internet, and you must use attention to detail in every aspect of "attending to attention" to write a Heart & Soul resume!

HEART & SOUL TIP

Your public library is a helpful resource to use in researching companies and careers.

computer job database since 1984. It contains 2,500 job openings. Of that number, about 2,100 are jobs in the United States and 400 are overseas. The company adds about 600 new job listings each week. Each job listing shows the job title and job description, just as in a newspaper classified or magazine ad. Career Link Worldwide also includes the hiring company's address and fax number.

If you just want information about companies, you can gain access to annual reports for every public company in America and research any industry you want on the Internet! We have included some excellent books in our Resources list at the end of this book for further reading about business networking and the Internet.

The main thing to remember is this: whether you are responding to an advertisement in a newspaper, contacting a company through networking, or surfing the Internet, you must pay close attention to the employer's needs and tailor your resume to fit those needs! In this way, you are "attending to attention" and implementing the Heart & Soul approach to resume writing.

Libraries Are Not Just for Reading!

Did you know that at your public library you can access lists of thousands of major employers nationwide on CD-ROM for free? You can find detailed information on specific employers in the industry of your choice. It's all right there for the taking! Armed with this information, you can then approach these companies with a telemarketing or mail campaign. What a fantastic way to jump-start your proactive career plan! Also, if you have never done a mail merge on your computer, we highly recommend you learn how. This is a valuable time-saver that helps you maintain a look of professionalism and attention to detail when you are printing a large number of letters simultaneously. Of course, the only things you would change on your resume and cover letter in a mail campaign would be the recipient's address and salutation. The rest stays the same.

Targeting Employers Through the Mail

For a successful mail campaign, you need the following four things:

1. Defined research criteria, so you know that the companies you are targeting all meet your basic needs (location, industry, size, etc.). Remember, each employer will be getting basically the same letter and resume, so make sure the employers are all similar in what they do and in what they would want from you.

2. A lead contact person or decision maker with each employer. Choose one that heads up your area of specialty. When in doubt, choose the president, owner, or CEO.

3. A well-written resume and cover letter that apply universally to each employer you are contacting.

4. A high quality computer and printer (preferably a laser printer) with a word processing program and spreadsheet, such as Word/Excel, WordPerfect/QuattroPro, or WordPro/Lotus. The spreadsheet helps you store and manipulate the data, while the word processing program merges the data into your cover letter. Remember, libraries or copy centers will often provide computers for a nominal fee.

HEART & SOUL TIP

Listening, awareness of the moment, the cover letter, the thank-you letter, classified ads, networking, and using the Internet are all parts of "attending to attention."

Of course you don't have to do a mail campaign. You may choose to contact employers by phone before submitting a personalized resume and cover letter. Either way is fine as long as it is done with diligence and professionalism. Both ways are examples of taking a proactive approach to finding a job, and both will benefit you. Everyone has his or her own particular style of doing anything, even in a Heart & Soul approach, and this is true in your approach to finding jobs, so use whatever method motivates you most!

Everything we've mentioned in this chapter—listening, "awareness of the moment," the cover letter, the thank-you letter, classified ads, networking, the Internet, and even the technical information regarding computers and mail lists—is an important and sustaining part of "attending to attention." No matter which methods you choose to utilize when looking for a job, you simply *must* pay attention to detail and listen to the employer's needs.

5 Doodle Your Way to Details

Writing has laws of perspective, of light and shade, just as a painting does, or music. If you are born knowing them, fine. If not, learn them. Then rearrange the rules to suit yourself.

TRUMAN CAPOTE

BEING ABLE TO WRITE down the details of your life on your resume is essential to the Heart & Soul approach to resume writing. These details reflect who you are—if you can't write them down, then you're not going to be able to write a Heart & Soul resume. To help you in your efforts, we're introducing pre-writing exercises as the fifth of the seven never-before-published secrets to creating a successful resume. These exercises will help you open up those "heart and soul" messages inside you and get those details down on paper.

Writer's Block

Imagine this: You've just brewed a cup of hot tea, and you're now curling up on the sofa. A soft blue hue falls in serene shadows throughout the room. All is quiet in the world except for the rain pitter-pattering rhythmically on the window panes outside. Aha! This is the perfect time to write that resume you've been putting off.

You put your pad of paper on your lap and take your pen in hand. You're ready. This will be a first draft only, you remind yourself. After the draft, you'll take it to the computer and write it in proper form. You stare at the paper and nibble on the pen. Your mind wanders a little bit. *No, mind, stop wandering. Let's start writing this resume,* you tell yourself. And then . . . nothing. *Nothing!* You can't believe it. The words won't come. There are no words inside you. Just a blank screen of nothingness. Where do you start?

HEART & SOUL TIP

Writer's block stops the creative flow from channeling through you—it stops the "heart and soul" messages from your inner being and will inhibit your writing a Heart & Soul resume.

You have writer's block, the chief adversary of writing. We all know it well. It can take us by total surprise and strike at any moment, any time, or any place. Writer's block simply stops the creative flow from channeling through us. It stops the "heart and soul" messages from coming forth. There's nothing more frustrating. It makes you wonder if the words are lodged somewhere in your solar plexus—anywhere but in your mind! If you're experiencing writer's block, you're not going to have much success at writing a resume, let alone a genuine, higher-echelon Heart & Soul resume.

Pre-Writing Exercises

Good writing doesn't come easy, and this holds true even for writing resumes. When you write your resume you become a writer. It may not be the stuff that's going to make you a top-selling novelist, but nonetheless you become a writer. In this chapter we'll illustrate some simple pre-writing exercises to help dissolve your writer's block and ignite that creative Heart & Soul writing process.

The thing about writing is that there are no hard-and-fast rules. Remember when you had to write essays or term papers in school? You created your own protocol for starting the writing process. If you had writer's block, you somehow pushed ahead of it (or left it and came back later) and you wrote that term paper! You created your own method of dissolving writer's block. And it worked. But maybe you've forgotten what you used to do to release the flow. Maybe it's been a long time since you had to write about yourself. Even published authors have trouble when it comes to writing their own resumes. So take heart—this chapter will help you.

Our first pre-writing exercise we call "doodling." That's right. Simple, every-day doodling. Surely you're familiar with the term. Most people like to doodle when they're talking on the telephone or are simply daydreaming at their desk, but you can now use this process to help you dissolve writer's block and write your resume. It's an effective method for unleashing the creative flow within you, which is what Heart & Soul writing is all about. Remember, our goal is not just to write a good resume, but to write a *great* resume, one that reflects your inner "heart and soul" essence.

HEART & SOUL TIP

Doodling is an effective method to help you dissolve writer's block and unleash the creative flow within you.

Take your pad of paper and pen and find a comfortable spot where no one will bother you. It's best to be in a place where you won't be distracted. You might have a favorite park or wooded area where you like to be alone, or you might simply enjoy your own comfy sofa or your office desk. Now, write your name and address at the top of the page. At this point it's very helpful to utilize creative visualization, as described in Chapter 1. Do a contemplation exercise and recite your special word, or mantra. In fact, by creatively visualizing and/or contemplating your life, your job, and your career goals, you may actually be able to prevent writer's block.

A Time to Reflect

Think about how this resume is a partial reflection of your life—the part comprising education, work experience, and qualifications. Start doodling—that is, start writing down your thoughts as quickly as they come to you. Keep your hand moving. Do not stop and read what you've written, just keep going! Once your hand is moving, you do not want to stop the flow of words. These unedited, uncensored words are pouring out naturally from your heart and soul.

HEART & SOUL TIP

While doodling and visualizing your career goals, you are writing down random, mainstream, raw thoughts. These thoughts will later be used to create phrases and sentences for your resume. First thoughts are powerful and original, uncensored by your mind!

Write down the details of your education and what you studied. Write down any qualifications that come to mind—*energetic, highly creative, detail-oriented.* Describe yourself. Describe your thoughts about your jobs and things you thought were important at those jobs. "I'm very good with numbers. I have a great telephone voice. I'm dependable and work well independently, or as a team player. I'm feeling hungry right now, but I have to keep writing. Okay, yeah, that's right, I am good with people. I'm a leader of others and take initiative in my work." Write everything that comes to mind, no matter what it is!

Do not edit yourself during this doodle session. Do not try to be logical or intellectual. Do not stop to correct punctuation, grammar, or spelling. Just keep on writing. Doodle all over the page—go sideways, upside down, round and round. Don't think about what you're writing at this point. Just let it flow. That's the whole idea! Open up the creative flow—the heart flow—within you, and let it out. After all, creativity is a loss of control, so *lose control!* Write all the words and first thoughts out on your paper.

These first thoughts possess extraordinary energy. As Natalie Goldberg said in *Writing Down the Bones,* "You must be a great warrior when you contact first thoughts and write from them." First thoughts, like first impressions, are powerful. They are raw and original, uncensored, and they hold the truth about who we are and what we want to do. They are thoughts that come from the very essence of our being—the heart and soul.

You will know when you are through. You'll feel physically lighter. You will experience a great sense of relief—of accomplishment—as if you had just emptied a lot of heavy baggage from your soul. You might end up with several pages of doodles, which would mean that you were very successful in opening the creative flow—the heart flow—within you.

We have included a worksheet for you to begin your doodling (Worksheet 5.1). You'll probably need several pages, but this is just to get you started. Keep all your work close by because after the next writing exercise you will begin to combine all your doodles into your Heart & Soul resume.

The Match Game

After you finish doodling, the next step is organizing the thoughts you just wrote down. If you're having trouble doing this, we offer a supplemental writing technique that can help. We have developed a simple writing exercise called the "Match Game." The Match Game takes you one step further in the doodling process and is very helpful in recording details about yourself, your jobs, and your career history. It will take you one step further in writing the "heart and soul" details of your life.

Take a sheet of paper and divide it into three columns. In the first column write down ten or more adjectives that are directly related to your career. In the second column, write down ten or more nouns that relate to your job. And in the third column, write down ten or more action verbs that describe you and your work (see Worksheet 5.2). See Figure 5.1 for an example of lists we wrote for a sales representative.

After you are through creating your own lists, select adjectives and nouns and match them with the appropriate verbs (Worksheet 5.3). You can even cut and paste them to help you develop sentences for your resume. Verbs bring life to your jobs, your personality, and your overall career. Be aware of how you use them. Be aware of the power they have and try to use them in fresh, interesting ways. They will bring humanness into your Heart & Soul resume. The same is true of adjectives. They add a touch of color—a touch of soul and depth—which is vital in a Heart & Soul resume.

HEART & SOUL TIP

Incorporate descriptive words and phrases from your MBTI "Type" and your Strong Interest Inventory results in the Match Game (see Appendix). Read books on the Resource list for more ideas.

DOODLE PAGE

Write anything you can think of! Let your heart open!

Describe yourself, writing down any qualifications that come to mind. Do not stop to read what you've written or to edit yourself. Just keep going!

THE MATCH GAME

Adjectives	Nouns	Action Verbs
•	•	•
•	•	•
•	•	•
•	•	•
•	•	•
•	•	•
•	•	•
•	•	•
•	•	•
•	•	•
•	•	•
•	•	•
•	•	•
•	•	•
•	•	•
•	•	•
•	•	•
•	•	•
•	•	•
•	•	•

■ **WORKSHEET 5.2**
Play Your Own Match Game

To show you how this works, we have provided some examples in Figure 5.2. Notice how we have built partial sentences by placing adjectives in front of nouns and used these to describe skills and qualifications of the candidate. Mix them up if you'd like to exercise your creativity! Take risks. Be creative in the way you connect verbs and nouns. You might discover some very innovative approaches to describing yourself that pique interest and grab attention!

■ **FIGURE 5.1**
The Match Game

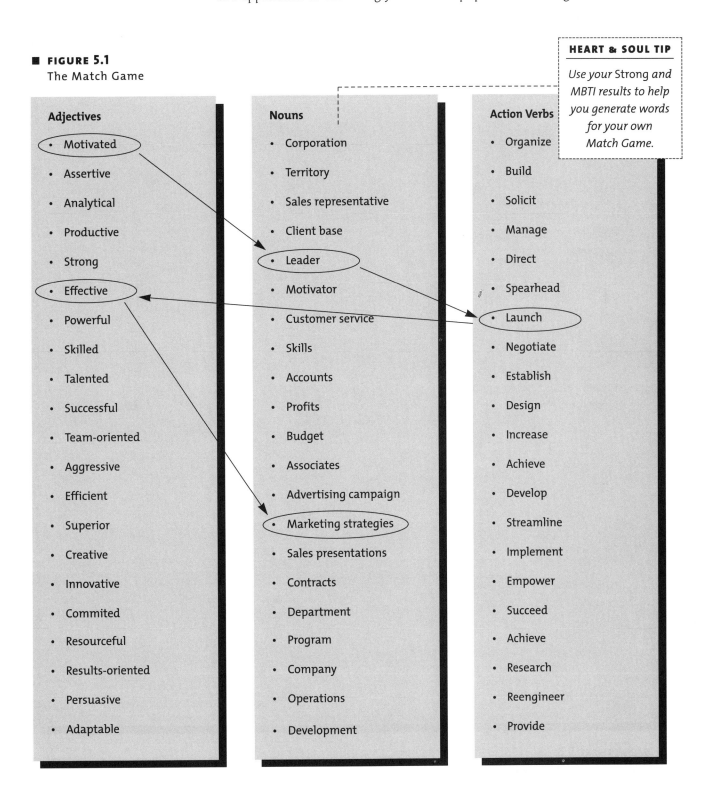

HEART & SOUL TIP

Use your Strong and MBTI results to help you generate words for your own Match Game.

MATCHING ADJECTIVES AND NOUNS WITH VERBS

Select adjectives and nouns from your lists in Worksheet 5.2 and combine them with the appropriate verbs to help you develop sentences for your resume.

-
-
-
-
-
-
-
-
-
-
-
-
-
-
-
-

■ **WORKSHEET 5.3**
Match Your Adjectives and Nouns with Your Verbs

■ **FIGURE 5.2**
Matching Adjectives and Nouns with Verbs

- Motivated leader launched effective marketing strategies

- Negotiated successful contracts

- Organized resourceful, aggressive sales representatives

- Reengineered programs to streamline operations and implement marketing strategies

- Talented, results-oriented sales representative built and expanded territory

- Committed to providing superior customer service

- Strong motivator who empowers associates to achieve their maximum potential

- Spearheaded development of innovative advertising campaign

- Utilize strong analytical skills in developing and implementing marketing campaigns

- Aggressive leader with persuasive skills led company to achieve its highest earnings

- Design and implement adaptable marketing strategies

- Establish accounts and manage sales presentations

- Build and increase client base

This is a simple but fun writing exercise that will supplement your doodle page and help you streamline your thoughts. Study the examples and then try the Match Game for yourself!

Notice how the five elements we circled in Figure 5.1 were combined to create the first phrase in Figure 5.2. Use your imagination to see how many phrases you can come up with. When you're finished, select the ones you like best, or those most appropriate, to include in your resume and cover letter!

Now, take your doodles and your phrases from the Match Game and start arranging them on a clean piece of paper, or use Worksheets 5.4 and 5.5 as a guide. Structure your page by organizing the information into different sections: "Professional Objective & Profile," "Education," "Summary of Qualifications," and "Summary of Accomplishments." These are the categories you'll highlight on your resume. Start filling in each section with information you compiled from the Match Game. As you do this, you will notice that everything falls into place much more easily than before, when you couldn't think of anything to say!

OBJECTIVE & PROFILE/SUMMARY INFORMATION

Organize your "Objective & Profile" and "Summary" information first!

Your Name:

Your Address:

Your Phone:

Professional Objective & Profile

Education

Summary of Qualifications

-
-
-
-
-
-

Summary of Accomplishments

-
-
-
-
-

■ **WORKSHEET 5.4**
Organize Your "Objective & Profile" and "Summary" Information

PROFESSIONAL EXPERIENCE

Organize your Employment History next!

Most Recent Position
Company:
City, State:
Dates of Employment:
Job Description Highlighting Accomplishments and Relevant Skills:

Next Most Recent Position
Company:
City, State:
Dates of Employment:
Job Description Highlighting Accomplishments and Relevant Skills:

Next Most Recent Position
Company:
City, State:
Dates of Employment:
Job Description Highlighting Accomplishments and Relevant Skills:

HEART & SOUL TIP

Use as many pages as you need. Then design your resume so that it's pleasant to look at and easy to read.

■ **WORKSHEET 5.5**
Organize Your Employment History

If You Listen, You Will Hear . . .

After the Match Game exercise, you should have conquered that stubborn writer's block. However, while playing with your lists of words and organizing your doodles, remember to listen. It's another method of conquering writer's block and complements the whole writing process—the ability to listen inwardly. We discussed listening and how important it is to attention to detail in the last chapter. It is just as important to be attentive to the details you wrote down on that pad of paper while doodling. Listening, in this context, is being able to receive information—being able to perceive in full awareness what truly is in the moment. When the creative energy is flowing through you, listen to what it's saying.

HEART & SOUL TIP

When creative energy is flowing through you, listen to what it is saying.

Listening is being able to absorb the reality of your outflow, your doodling, without judging it. It's knowing that this is who you are, what you have achieved, and what your dreams are made of. They are the details of your life, so be sure to listen while you're arranging your scribbled notes and matching words in the Match Game.

We use doodling as a method to write down notes about clients while talking to them. It allows us to be freer and more creative in our note-taking process, and we get to know the individual on a more personal basis. We're aware that some resume-writing companies have their clients fill out forms, but we've always felt that was very unfriendly and impersonal. There is no way we could write a Heart & Soul resume if we didn't get to know our client. Our resumes reflect the very essence of a person, not merely a compilation of data, which is one reason they're so successful.

Jenna Jackson

Following is an example of how we used doodling to write a client's resume. Jenna Jackson had just flown in from Philadelphia to visit family and friends. She had been referred to us by a family member and called to set up an appointment. Our first impression of her when she walked in the door was that she was vivacious, charming, and bright. Jenna didn't have a resume and had never been to a professional resume-writing service before. "I don't really know where to start," she said. "I've been a model on the home shopping television network and produced my own TV shows for an independent TV station, but I have no idea how to put a resume together."

HEART & SOUL TIP

When doodling, don't stop to correct your grammar. It will stifle the creative flow.

While talking with her, we doodled on several pages of paper, quickly scribbling notes about her. We scribbled all over the page and didn't stop and edit ourselves or try to correct punctuation. We didn't worry if it was neatly written or messy. It would have stopped the creative flow and the whole Heart & Soul process. We wrote as fast as we could, and when we were finished, we had eight pages of notes. Through this process, we became friends with Jenna and got to know her as a person—not just as a client. We could have used the Match Game to build powerful sentences if necessary, but in this case our doodled notes were sufficient.

Sometimes, the first doodle exercise is all you'll need to do. Other times, you may find that the Match Game helps organize your thoughts better. In both instances, just remember to listen to that inner voice and pay attention to the details.

The type of resume we designed for Jenna is called a "brochure" resume, which consists of a two-page resume and a cover page, all copied on an 11- by 17-inch sheet of paper and folded (see Figures 5.3 and 5.4). Figure 5.5 shows Jenna's cover letter. We delve into more details regarding this and other resume formats in Chapter 7.

Please understand that these doodled notes are simply to give you an *idea* of how to dissolve writer's block. It's free-form writing at its best, and it allows the creative source within you to open up.

■ **FIGURE 5.3**
Designing the Brochure Resume

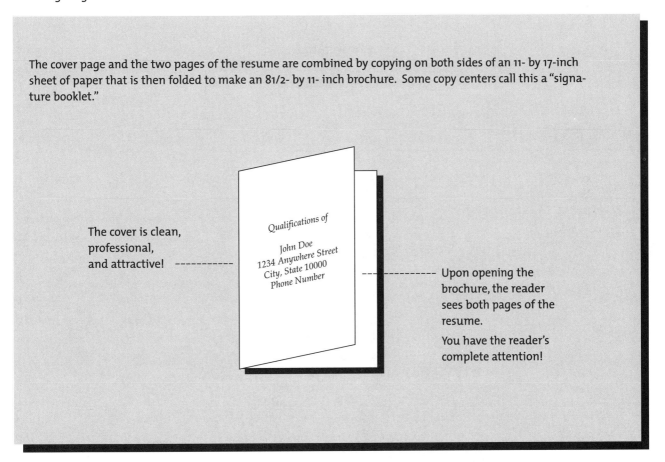

The cover page and the two pages of the resume are combined by copying on both sides of an 11- by 17-inch sheet of paper that is then folded to make an 81/2- by 11- inch brochure. Some copy centers call this a "signature booklet."

The cover is clean, professional, and attractive! ----------

Qualifications of

John Doe
1234 Anywhere Street
City, State 10000
Phone Number

----------- Upon opening the brochure, the reader sees both pages of the resume.

You have the reader's complete attention!

■ **FIGURE 5.4**
Jenna Jackson's Brochure Resume (Cover Sheet)

JENNA JACKSON

A Presentation
of
Professional Broadcast Credentials

1111 Anywhere Street
City, State 10000
Phone Number

■ **FIGURE 5.4 CONTINUED**
Jenna Jackson's Brochure Resume (Page 1)

HEART & SOUL TIP

Start with your Doodle Page, follow up with the Match Game, and then compile your Heart & Soul resume. It will almost write itself.

JENNA JACKSON
111 Anywhere Street
City, State 10000
Phone Number

Professional Objective & Profile

An extremely creative, highly professional, experienced producer, director, writer, and on-air talent is seeking a career opportunity in communications, television, and video production. More than 14 years of experience leading integrated broadcast operations, which includes all facets of management, program development, writing, production, and directing.

Summary of Qualifications

Track Record of Success

Background exemplifies a successful track record of career accomplishments that encompasses positions such as president, owner of Running Productions, television model and on-air talent, director and producer, and vice president of special projects.

Broadcast Production & Creative Program Development

Conceptualized, created, and developed programming for major television networks. Hold high-visibility position as president, owner, and manager of broadcast production company. Responsible for directing and guiding all facets of video and film production for TV commercials.

Strengths & Characteristics

Creative, with exceptional sense of style, fashion, and image. Dynamic and personable, with superior communication skills. Self-motivated, with ability to create and develop innovative television formats and programs. High-energy, positive, and supportive. Committed to excellence, which results in success.

Business, Artist, & Entertainment Relations

More than 14 years of experience building and maintaining an exemplary network of business relationships with major artists, celebrities, entertainment and production companies, television networks, and executive entertainment staff members. Ability to effectively communicate with all types of individuals in both small and large corporate business environments.

International & Domestic Experience

Experienced in working with foreign businesses, entertainment facilities, and organizations to organize, coordinate, and produce television specials. Have been in charge of video and film productions throughout the U.S. and in London, England.

Employee Relations—Leadership

Ability to effectively guide and lead associates in all areas of production. Encourage and support a team-like work environment, which increases efficiency and overall production.

■ **FIGURE 5.4 CONTINUED**
Jenna Jackson's Brochure Resume (Page 2)

Broadcast, Advertising, & Media Experience

Vice President of Advertising
JULIENE'S, INC., Philadelphia

- *Writing & Video Production:* Wrote and produced radio and TV commercials and advertising print. Talent for voice-overs. Production involved auditioning and selecting talent for spots and scheduling all video shoots. Also produced and directed live fashion shows.

- *Advertising & Program Development:* Created and implemented innovative, artistic advertising campaigns, visual displays, and programs to promote business and increase revenue.

Freelance Model & On-Air Talent
QVC, INC.—HOME SHOPPING NETWORK, Philadelphia

- *On-Air Talent:* On-air talent for QVC, including modeling and interacting with hosts to sell products on broadcast television.

- *Auditions & Evaluations:* Organized and coordinated adult and child model auditions for QVC. Evaluated and recommended models.

President, Owner, & Manager
RUNNING PRODUCTIONS, Philadelphia

- *Broadcast Consultant:* Assisted in coordinating all facets of video production for clients and consulted with television broadcast officials concerning formats, set design, programming, scripts, on-air talent, and production.

- *Management:* Directed overall administration and operations of this company. Managed adult and child modeling staff for on-air television productions.

- *Writing:* Wrote television scripts, commercials, and promotional spots.

- *Training & Instruction:* Conducted training classes and trained new models in all areas of television modeling and performance. Worked closely with modeling agencies to evaluate and assess models' overall job performances.

Vice President
ENTERTAINMENT PROGRAMMING, Philadelphia

- *Executive Producer:* Served as department head of Entertainment Programming. Responsible for all facets of video and film production for television commercials, network series, promotional spots, and music videos. Provided programming content for major television networks.

- *Artist & Entertainment Relations:* Interacted extensively with major artists, celebrities, entertainment and production companies, record labels, television networks, and executive entertainment staff members. Continuously established and maintained an excellent network of business relationships as a result of superior communication skills.

- *Budget Management:* Analyzed and administered operating funds allocated for production and general expenditures. Designed budget forecasting and analysis plans.

EDUCATION
Bachelor of Science Degree in Broadcast Communications
Belmont University, Nashville, Tennessee

■ **FIGURE 5.5**
Jenna Jackson's Cover Letter

HEART & SOUL TIP

Use imaginative, attention-grabbing first sentences like this to begin your cover letter.

JENNA JACKSON
1111 Anywhere Street
City, State 10000
Phone Number

Today's Date

Don Templeton
Executive Director
Westchester Communications
1212 West 57th Street
New York, NY 10009

Dear Mr. Templeton:

Creative . . . multi-talented . . . experienced broadcast producer, director, and on-air talent . . . These are just a few of the many qualities I can offer your broadcast company.

It has been brought to my attention that Westchester is in the process of expanding its production facilities, and I would like to be instrumental in the growth and development of this division. Please carefully review my resume to see how I can best contribute to Westchester Communications' team of professionals. My areas of expertise and qualifications include the following:

■ Innovative leadership in creating, developing, and producing programming for commercial broadcast television.

■ High-visibility positions, with more than 14 years of hands-on experience in writing, directing, and producing television commercials, entertainment shows, and music videos.

■ Dynamic, personable communication skills, with ability to successfully network with leading executives as well as with all levels of management and personnel.

■ Strong client-relations skills, with special talents in international relations. Coordinated numerous productions in England as well as in the U.S.

■ High energy, with positive attitude. Supportive of collaborative efforts.

I am confident that, with my background and career goals, I would be an asset to Westchester Communications. I would like to arrange a personal interview with you at your earliest convenience. I will follow up with a phone call in a few days to schedule a meeting.

Thank you in advance for your time and consideration.

Sincerely,

Jenna Jackson

HEART & SOUL TIP

Getting in touch with your inner self will help you feel in tune with life.

Now imagine this: You're still curled up on your sofa and totally relaxed. You feel good. You have accomplished a lot this day, and you lift your arms and stretch contentedly. Getting in touch with your inner self has left you feeling remarkably in tune with life. The pitter-pattering rain has stopped and the sun is now casting a warm yellow glow across the room. The world is beckoning for you to come outside. You can go guilt-free because you've just successfully completed the first Heart & Soul draft of your resume!

The Attitude of Gratitude

*Nothing can stop the man with the right mental attitude
from achieving his goal; nothing on earth can help the
man with the wrong mental attitude.*

THOMAS JEFFERSON

OUR THOUGHTS MAKE US what we are. They direct our mental attitude, which is one pivotal factor that determines our fate. Our mental attitude can be positive or negative. With an "attitude of gratitude" you'll maintain a positive attitude toward life. If you have the right attitude, you'll be able to more easily highlight your accomplishments without sounding boastful and will, in general, produce a more pleasing, effective resume. This is the sixth of the seven never-before-published secrets to creating a successful resume.

An attitude of gratitude is a feeling of thankful appreciation, of being grateful for what we have, instead of complaining about what we don't have. Our

HEART & SOUL TIP

The attitude of gratitude is a positive attitude toward life. It's being grateful for what you have.

HEART & SOUL TIP

It is important to incorporate gratitude into the tone of your Heart & Soul resume.

HEART & SOUL TIP

Your attitude is projected in your resume. An attitude of ingratitude *will stand out. The employer may not consciously recognize it, but he or she will feel its negative vibrations.*

attitude is the core of our personality—it's everything we are—and it's reflected in our writing. To maintain a true Heart & Soul approach to writing a resume, it is absolutely necessary to incorporate an attitude of gratitude. This takes some skill and careful wording, but it is very effective. In this chapter, we'll explore ways to highlight your accomplishments without sounding too boastful, and illustrate how to incorporate gratitude into the tone of the resume.

If you've read the first five chapters of this book, then you should have a good start for integrating the attitude of gratitude into a genuine Heart & Soul resume. You've practiced creative visualization and imagined the kind of job you desire. You have repeated affirmations to help you visualize this job and to reinforce the positive side of your nature. You have taken responsibility for your career and maintained a proactive approach toward finding the job that's right for you. You've been realistic about your goals and have developed a strong Career Map to follow, with career steps carefully outlined. You've paid close attention to job advertisements, business networking, and the Internet, and carefully integrated into your resume any specific details needed for a job. You have learned how to be aware of the moment and listen inwardly with your whole being and all of your senses. And, finally, you've overcome writer's block and honed your writing skills with our doodling exercises. Now you're ready to study this sixth secret and fine-tune your resume so it's nearly Heart & Soul perfect.

An employer probably won't consciously recognize a resume with a bad attitude or one that's ungrateful or too boastful. He or she may not immediately say, "Oh, I don't like this candidate. He's full of himself!" The fact is, the employer may not even realize that he or she is thinking this. However, he or she will *feel* it. Remember, your *attitude* is an *energy* that's present in everything, even in a resume, and its presence can affect the way an employer feels when he or she is reading it.

One of the first ways to make sure you have the right attitude is to make a list of the things you're grateful for. This may seem like an elementary, unimportant thing to do, and even like a waste of time, but trust us—it's not. You see, if you are discouraged in the job market and feel like you're not being given a fair chance, then you may try too hard to convince the employer that you are worthy of a good job, and your resume may end up sounding boastful. It's as if you're doing cartwheels to get noticed—trying *too hard* to get someone's attention, hoping he or she will appreciate your talents. To put it another way, did you ever have a date with someone, or meet someone for the first time, who tried so hard to impress you and please you that it turned you off? The same psychological process takes place when someone is reading your resume. When you try too hard, you push people away! It's a fine-tuned balancing act to set the right tone—to get the right attitude of gratitude into the resume without coming across too strong or boastful.

You might be saying, "Hey, I don't feel very grateful now. I don't have a job. I have no prospects, and I have no money. I don't have much going for me in my life and I don't want to write any stupid list about things I'm grateful for because I don't have anything." Actually, this is a typical attitude. We grow up in a negative world and, unfortunately, we've been programmed all our lives to be negative, so it's very easy to slip into old programmed habits of being negative when things are going wrong: those habits are familiar to us. They are comfortable, even if they aren't pleasurable. Sure, it's easy to have a great attitude and be positive and upbeat when things are going great, but the real test comes when life isn't so smooth.

HEART & SOUL TIP

Attitude is an energy that is reflected in your resume.

If you try to write your resume while you're feeling negative and ungrateful, your feelings will come through in the resume, just as they come through in everything else you do, and with the people around you. After all, like attracts like, so negative energy attracts negative energy, and when the employer reads your resume, he or she will feel the negative vibrations, consciously or not. The result is that your resume will probably be tossed into the trash.

Marty Clemons

Marty Clemons is a musician who came into our office feeling very upset about his circumstances. "I can't get a fair shake in this town," Marty said as he thrust his resume on our desk. "I'm at the end of my rope. I just can't get anyone to let me audition."

Yikes! Marty's attitude surely needed an adjustment! We wondered what his resume looked like: sure enough, his bad attitude was reflected throughout his writing. The resume was poorly written and was more boastful than necessary. He was obviously bending over backward to try to impress those people who could hire him. When asked what he was grateful for in his life, he couldn't think of anything at all until we coaxed him.

If you feel as though you are lost and have no idea what to be grateful about, then look at the Grateful List we composed for Marty (Fgure 6.1). Again, we realize how simple and elementary this looks, but its effects are enormous. By writing down things you're grateful for, you will be actively changing the energy that currently envelops you in a world of negativity and recharging yourself with the positive energy that's so important to integrating your heart and soul into your resume. Make your own Grateful List (use Worksheet 6.1) and review it every time you feel that habitual tendency to revert to those old negative (albeit comfortable) attitudes.

By the time we were finished writing this Grateful List, we saw a real change in Marty's attitude. It was a remarkable transformation. He was

■ **FIGURE 6.1**
Marty Clemons's Grateful List

HEART & SOUL TIP

Marty's attitude greatly improved when he wrote out his Grateful List. It helped him see what was truly important in his life.

1. I am grateful for my health and the fact that I am very seldom ill.

2. I am grateful that I have a college degree.

3. I am very grateful that my parents could afford to send me to school and that I didn't have huge college loans to pay back.

4. I am grateful that I am married and have three beautiful children.

5. I am very grateful for my wife and her patience with me. Not many women would tolerate a musician's lifestyle. My family is healthy and strong and very intelligent, and I like that.

6. I am grateful that my children are musically inclined and are learning how to play music at an early age .

7. I am grateful that I've had opportunities to work for some leading entertainers.

8. I am grateful for the talents I was born with. Not everyone can play music the way I can.

9. I am grateful that I have a nice home with an affordable house payment.

10. I am grateful that my parents are still alive and that we have a good relationship.

11. I am grateful that I live in an area that doesn't have severe winters, and that it's warm most of the time.

12. I am grateful that I've had the opportunity to travel throughout Europe.

HEART & SOUL TIP

Writing a Grateful List will open your heart and your awareness to the riches that already exist in your life. It can change negative thinking to positive thinking.

surprised that writing this simple list could affect his mood so profoundly.

The physical act of writing down things you're grateful for will bring you pleasant thoughts and good memories, and these good memories will help change your attitude. In other words, this Grateful List will open your heart and your awareness to the riches that already exist in your life. And when this happens, you will become filled with so much love that there's little room for negativity.

Appreciating what you can *give* to life is one way to be grateful for what you have. The better you feel about yourself and the more you acknowledge your self-worth, the happier you will be, and this will reinforce a positive attitude in yourself. Once this takes place, you are integrating the attitude of gratitude into your everyday life and can then take this one step further and incorporate it into your resume.

One reason our Heart & Soul resumes are so successful is that we make people feel good about themselves. We recognize their value and contributions in life, and we reflect these in the resume—as you should, too! After we write a resume, the client often says, "Wow! I didn't realize I had so much to offer!" If you adjust your attitude and write down all the things you're grateful for,

WHAT ARE YOU GRATEFUL FOR?

HEART & SOUL TIP

Write out what you are grateful for to help you change your attitude to one of gratitude and to gain a better perspective on what is really important to you.

1.

2.

3.

4.

5.

6.

7.

8.

9.

10.

11.

12.

13.

14.

15.

■ **WORKSHEET 6.1**
What Are You Grateful for?

then you'll find yourself saying the same thing. Go on—say it again, just for the positive effect it has on your life: *"Wow! I didn't realize I had so much to offer!"*

Appreciating your qualities is all-important, but keep your ego in check. It's one thing to be proud of your accomplishments, and it's quite another to be boastful. An employer will be turned off by a resume that *brags, brags, brags, brags.*

Marty had been suffering from low self-esteem and had been far too critical of his own talents and abilities. We pointed out to Marty that he had tried *too hard* on his resume and, as a result, had boasted about his accomplishments. Sometimes, when a person feels bad about himself and has developed low self-esteem, as Marty had, he can overcompensate by bragging about his talents.

HEART & SOUL TIP

If you try too hard, you may sound boastful on your resume. This can come from low self-esteem and result in overcompensating by bragging about your talents.

"But," Marty said to us when we explained this, "aren't I supposed to highlight my accomplishments?"

We explained that there is a very thin line between writing a resume that *boasts* about talents and accomplishments and a resume that *highlights* them. The difference is in the attitude.

Marty's old resume (Figure 6.2) had problems everywhere. It wasn't complete and it was full of boastful statements. Marty tried to write a positive biography of his musical career in his Objective, but he ended up sounding conceited. He told us that, when he hastily put this resume together, he had been mad that no one would give him a job as a harmonica player, even though he felt that his qualifications were just as good as anyone else's. He had taken this resume to several music studios, but no one had called him for an audition. A friend of his had advised him to seek help from some career professionals, and that's how he ended up at our door.

After writing a Grateful List, Marty felt different about himself and life in general. He truly felt grateful for things that he had been generally taking for granted. Writing the Grateful List opened his heart and booted that old negative feeling right out the door!

We sat and talked with Marty, learned about his "heart and soul" dreams, doodled notes about his background, and then wrote a two-page Heart & Soul resume (Figure 6.3). When writing a creative resume, especially for entertainment artists, we always include a Music Career Profile highlighting the musician's music career. In Marty's case, we also added a sheet of Career Accomplishments.

HEART & SOUL TIP

Incorporating a tone of "service" into a resume implies gratefulness and is very attractive to any employer.

In Marty's cover letter (Figure 6.4), we were direct and to the point, and careful to highlight noted musicians he had toured with.

In the resume, we wrote a Music Career Profile, a biography of the musician's background, and an added page of Music Career Accomplishments. The fact that Marty was willing to work on a part-time basis, and to travel as needed, shows flexibility and an eagerness to accommodate the employer's needs. Just a few words was all it took to incor-

■ **FIGURE 6.2**
Marty Clemons's "Before" Resume

HEART & SOUL TIP

Don't write your resume in the first person and don't brag about yourself like this! You want to highlight your accomplishments but not brag about them.

Marty Clemons
608 Anywhere Street
City, State 10000
Phone Number

OBJECTIVE
I am looking for a job as a harmonica player. I am a dynamite harmonica player and I think I am the best in the United States. I began playing the harmonica when I was 14 years old and I was so good that I toured with several bands, including the South Texas Boys. I got a contract to endorse Hammer Harmonicas, and *Music and Sound* magazine took pictures of me and wrote about me. They said I was very handsome and very talented. Everywhere I play, women come up to me and want my phone number.

I played the harmonica on a CBS special and I've played with famous stars like Tanya Washington, Reba Montgomery, and many others. I've recorded lots of CDs, too.

I think I deserve a job as a harmonica player with your band.

EDUCATION
B.S., UT, Knoxville, Tennessee

AFFILIATION & HONORS
Voted the Best Looking Male in high school

Voted the Most Likely to Succeed in high school

Won Mr. Universe Pageant in college

Local Musician's Union

Music City Blues member

REFERENCES
Available upon Request

■ **FIGURE 6.3**
Marty Clemons's "After" Resume (Page 1)

HEART & SOUL TIP

Notice how the whole tone of the resume took on a different attitude and feeling after Marty wrote his Grateful List.

MARTY CLEMONS
608 Anywhere Street
City, State 10000
Phone Number

Professional Objective

Multitalented harmonica player is seeking a full-time position with a music studio. Desire an opportunity that will provide a creative challenge to play with leading Nashville musicians and to progress professionally as an entertainment artist. Willing to work on a part-time basis. Available to travel as needed.

Music Career Profile

Very dedicated and committed to the enlightenment and uplifting of society through music, Marty Clemons is in the entertainment business because he loves music and loves playing the harmonica. Born and raised in Texas, he is hardly a beginner when it comes to music. When Marty was only 14, a friend introduced him to the harmonica. His love affair with the harmonica continues today.

Marty spent several years playing with local bands in Texas, including the Wild Bunch and the Texas Crooners. After winning several state music contests, Marty moved to Nashville and started his own band, the Nashville Honky Tonks.

Since moving to Nashville, Marty has been hired to endorse Hammer Harmonicas and was featured in *Music and Sound* magazine. He has toured with Tanya Washington, Reba Montgomery, John Michael Morrison, and others. In addition, Marty performed live on a CBS television special and has recorded several CDs. Versatile, adaptable, and creative in his style and technique of harmonica playing, this is only the beginning for Marty Clemons.

Professional Affiliations & Honors

Hammer Harmonicas endorser
Local Musicians' Union
Music City Blues Society member
Featured in *Music and Sound* magazine

Education

Bachelor of Science Degree in Music Education
University of Tennessee, Knoxville

MARTY CLEMONS   Page 2

Music Career Accomplishments

Following is a sample list of music accomplishments with other artists, on tours, and for broadcast.

Featured Artist

Selected to be featured on a Blues Summer CD, *The Whiskey Blues*, released in London. Sold over a million copies worldwide.

Reba Montgomery

Toured with Reba throughout the United States. Played harmonica on her latest album.

John Michael Morrison

Toured with John Michael throughout the Southeast and was featured solo harmonica player during live performances.

Alan Johnson

Toured throughout the U.S. and Europe with Alan on special holiday tour.

Broadcast

Featured in soft-drink television commercial
Featured on Easter Seals Telethon, CBS television special
Featured in blue jeans label radio commercial

Dance Mixes—cds

Tanya Washington
Mark Chesterfield
Lori Morrison

Blues Artists

Sam Layson
Fred Jamison

Bands

The Nashville Blues Boys
The Wild Hitchcock Band
Western Country Music Band
Texas Stompers Band

Marty Clemons's Cover Letter

HEART & SOUL TIP

The cover letter highlights his accomplishments without boasting and reflects an "attitude of gratitude" in the way it's written.

MARTY CLEMONS
608 Anywhere Street
City, State 10000
Phone Number

Today's Date

Billy Anderson
Vice President
Quadrophonic Music Studio
2002 Music Row
Nashville, TN 37205

Dear Mr. Anderson:

I am interested in auditioning for a full- or part-time position as a harmonica player in your music studio. For your review, I have enclosed a personal resume/bio, which will provide you with basic details concerning my credentials.

As you will note, I am not a beginner, but rather a seasoned professional with more than 10 years of experience playing with leading artists. My career has included performances as a featured artist with Reba Montgomery, John Michael Morrison, and Alan Johnson. In addition, I have appeared in national television commercials for leading beverage and clothing companies.

In order to continue advancing professionally, I would like to play consistently with leading Nashville musicians in a studio environment. I am confident that, with my creativity, experience, and career goals, I would be an asset to your team of studio musicians.

I would like to request an audition at your earliest convenience and will contact you within the next couple of days to ensure that you received my demo tape and resume.

Thank you in advance for your time and consideration.

Sincerely,

Marty Clemons

porate a tone of service into the resume, implying gratefulness, which is very attractive to any employer.

In Marty's resume, he had sounded boastful about being the best harmonica player around. Plus, he thought it was important to highlight that he had been voted Best Looking Male in high school, and that he had won the Mr. Universe pageant in college. We told him that, unless he was trying out for another Mr. Universe title, that bit of information would probably turn off every person he handed his resume to. No wonder he wasn't getting auditions!

Marty loved the resume we wrote for him, and he called us back within two weeks to let us know he had landed a part-time job in a studio as well as a part-time job on television as a regular harmonica player for one of the top-rated TV entertainment shows in Nashville!

By compiling a Grateful List, Marty opened up his heart and changed his negative thinking to a positive attitude. Being more grateful about his life made Marty more appreciative of his skills and talents. And, being more appreciative, he became more service-oriented.

Min Seo

Another client, Min Seo of Portland, Oregon, originally of Seoul, Korea, asked for our help. Min had an excellent education and work experience but was having difficulty getting an interview for a management position. After we looked at her resume, we understood why. Min had felt very insecure about herself even though she had an excellent background. She had grown up in a family with six older brothers who had excelled in their careers and she had always felt inferior to them. Overcompensating for her feelings of inadequacy, she wrote too many boastful statements in the Objective section of her resume. Plus, she included her salary requirements on the resume, which is not advisable. Min felt underpaid in her current position and wanted to make sure she got a better salary at her next job. We informed her that this wasn't the way to get that better salary. It is best to wait and get the interview first! Once you have succeeded in the interview, let the employer make an offer, and be prepared to negotiate salary requirements.

HEART & SOUL TIP

Never list your salary requirements on your resume.

We asked Min to write down a Grateful List, which gave us more insight to her inner self. Like Marty, she then noticed that her heart opened. She felt softer and gentler, and much more appreciative of her life and career goals. As a result, we were better prepared to write a more in-depth Heart & Soul resume, the way we had for Marty.

As we began preparing Min's resume, we toned down the statements in her Objective and rewrote the rest of her resume, highlighting areas of accomplishment and expertise. We didn't have to brag. Her background spoke for itself. She happily reported to us within three weeks that she had two very viable job

■ **FIGURE 6.5**
Min Seo's "Before" Resume

HEART & SOUL TIP

Min boasted unnecessarily in her resume. She didn't need to try so hard to prove herself. She has great experience.

Min Seo
808 Anywhere Street
City, State 10000
Phone Number

OBJECTIVE:
A fantastic, superior health care supervisor is seeking a position that will fully utilize skills in management, foreign languages, health care operations, and a track record of winning awards and commendations throughout career. Known as the "most intelligent leader in the hospital." Due to high intelligence able to perform in many areas of hospital and experienced in many different units including management and quality assurance. Able to get employees to work as many hours as needed to get the job done. Able to win approval from top industry leaders and executive management team. Able to make others see things "my way."

WORK EXPERIENCE:

Health Systems User Analyst, PORTLAND UNIVERSITY MEDICAL CENTER, Portland, Oregon—1994 to Present
Awarded position of being Team Leader of the Health Systems User Analyst Group as a result of being able to continuously improve operations. Supervise employees. Ensure compliance with rules and regulations. Train doctors in computer systems.

Clinical Nurse Analyst, I.S., Critical Care Nursing Supervisor, WESTERN RESERVE CARE SYSTEM, Youngstown, Ohio—1988 to 1994
Main person in unit with total administrative and staffing responsibilities. Trained nurses, ward clerks and registration staff on how to use computers.

Assistant Head Nurse & Staff Nurse, Emergency Center & IV Therapy, ST. ELIZABETH HOSPITAL MEDICAL CENTER, Youngstown, Ohio—1986 to 1988
Worked in the Emergency Center & IV Therapy.

Registered Nurse, IV Therapy, TORONTO HOSPITAL, Toronto, Canada—1980 to 1986

Assistant Coordinator, Emergency Department, WEST HOUSTON MEDICAL CENTER, Houston, Texas—1976 to 1980

EDUCATION:
B.S., Nursing, PORTLAND UNIVERSITY, Portland, Oregon
B.S., International Trade, SOOK MYUNG WOMEN'S UNIVERSITY, Seoul, Korea
Diploma in International Languages, DAEWON FOREIGN LANGUAGE SCHOOL, Daewon, Korea

Licensed in Oregon

Professional Achievements

- **Lead User Analyst** - Order Entry Implementation.
- Coordinated, set up and implemented **Emergency Equipment and medications** for the Oregon Preventive Medical Center.
- **Founder of the West Oregon Dental Association**, organization for area dentists and staff.

SALARY REQUIREMENTS:

$80,000 Annually

■ **FIGURE 6.6**
Min Seo's "After" Resume (Page 1)

HEART & SOUL TIP

We have taken out the boastful statements and rewritten her resume with a sensitive, "attitude of gratitude" approach, which is essential in a Heart & Soul resume!

MIN SEO
808 Anywhere Street
City, State 10000
Phone Number

Professional Objective

High-caliber health care supervisor and project leader with 20 years of experience building and leading integrated health care operations for medical centers/hospitals is seeking a position that will fully utilize an extensive background in health care. Cross-cultural background and advanced study in both South Korea and the United States. Offering hands-on clinical experience in ER, as well as in management, quality assurance, and health systems user analysis. Strong managerial skills emphasizing use of analytical tools in optimal decision making and a participative, team-oriented approach to issue resolution. Goal-oriented, with a strong focus on quality results.

Summary of Qualifications

Track Record of Success

Background exemplifies a successful track record of career accomplishments, including 20 years of experience in health care. Continuously advanced throughout career to positions of higher levels of responsibility and authority. Positions have included: health systems user analyst, critical care nursing supervisor, assistant head nurse, charge nurse, and staff nurse in the Emergency Department.

Management Expertise

In-depth background in managing and directing overall operations for various departments within health care centers, working as critical care nursing supervisor, head nurse for an oral surgeon, and charge nurse. Experienced working in pediatrics and in oral surgery. Management experience includes interviewing, hiring, training, and supervising staff members.

Emergency Expertise

Hands-on clinical experience in the Emergency Room as a charge nurse/assistant coordinator and quality assurance coordinator. Coordinated all functions of the Emergency Room for the evening shift, assisting up to 175 patients per shift. In-depth experience with medical/surgical emergencies, EKG monitoring, and pacemaker insertion.

Quality Assurance

Background includes managing quality assurance in Emergency Department. Moni-tored and reviewed facilities and procedures to ensure compliance with federal, state, local, and JCAHO regulations and standards.

Budget Management

Completed administrative practicum with focus on budget, payroll, staffing, and quality assurance.

Computer Operations & Systems

Developed and designed clinical computer systems to streamline operations and increase efficiency, including order entry, COR, Physician's View, Invision software, and Shared Medical Systems. Also knowledgeable in Basic OAS, Service Master, and Charge Description Master File.

Training & Education

Skilled in developing and implementing educational curriculum and in training physicians, residents, and professional staff members in all areas of clinical computer systems and operations.

■ **FIGURE 6.6 CONTINUED**
Min Seo's "After" Resume (Page 2)

MIN SEO   Page 2

Professional Experience

Health Systems User Analyst
PORTLAND UNIVERSITY MEDICAL CENTER, Portland, Oregon, 1994 to present

■ *Project Management*: Team leader of the Health Systems User Analyst Group.
■ *Health Systems User Analyst*: Troubleshooter: Evaluate services and systems and continuously improve all phases of operations. Review, analyze, evaluate, and identify problems within computer systems. Set up, customize, and upgrade systems to streamline operations and increase efficiency.
■ *Supervision & Management:* Interview, train, and supervise staff members. Monitor overall job performances to ensure adherence to standards, rules, policies, and procedures.
■ *Education/Curriculum Coordination:* Align the objectives of staff members within educational curriculum, then develop and implement instructional programs accordingly.
■ *Physician Training Coordination:* Train physicians in computer systems and operations, including training professional staff in Guest Relations Department.

Clinical Nurse Analyst I.S., Critical Care Nursing Supervisor
WESTERN RESERVE CARE SYSTEM, Youngstown, Ohio, 1988 to 1994

■ *Supervision & Management:* Hospital critical care nursing supervisor with total administrative and staffing responsibilities.
■ *End User Education:* Trained nurses, ward clerks, and registration staff in computer systems and operations.

Assistant Head Nurse & Staff Nurse
ST. ELIZABETH HOSPITAL MEDICAL CENTER, Youngstown, Ohio, 1986 to 1988

■ *Management:* Assisted in the management of operations and provided support in the Emergency Center and in IV therapy. Responsible for scheduling and training staff members.

Registered Nurse—IV Therapy
TORONTO HOSPITAL, Toronto, Ontario, Canada, 1980 to 1986

Education   *Bachelor of Science Degree in Nursing*
Portland University, Portland, Oregon

Bachelor of Science Degree in International Trade
Sook Myung Women's University, Seoul, South Korea

Diploma in International Languages
Daewon Foreign Language School, Daewon, South Korea

Licensure

Oregon, Ohio

Professional Achievements
■ Coordinated, set up, and implemented emergency equipment and medications for the Oregon Preventive Medicine Center.
■ Founder, West Oregon Dental Association, organization for area dentists and staff.

■ **FIGURE 6.7**
Min Seo's Cover Letter

HEART & SOUL TIP

As in the resume, we have highlighted accomplishments without sounding boastful. The bullets help draw the eye to specific points we want noticed.

MIN SEO
808 Anywhere Street
City, State 10000
Phone Number

Today's Date

Attn: Personnel Director
Coopersmith Hospital
200 West Street
Seattle, WA 87000

Dear Personnel Director:

I am interested in applying for a position in your company that will fully utilize my skills and experience in information systems and health care. I have enclosed a personal resume so you may review my qualifications.
As you will note, I am not a beginner, but rather a well-seasoned professional with 20 years of experience building and leading integrated health care operations in medical centers and hospitals. My areas of expertise include the following:

■ Ability to manage multidisciplinary operations in a health care environment.

■ In-depth experience, encompassing such positions as critical care nursing supervisor, charge nurse, assistant head nurse, clinical nurse analyst, and staff nurse.

■ Hands-on experience in the Emergency Department as well as supervisory experience during the evening shift.

■ Excellent skills in speaking Chinese and English, with ability to communicate with people from foreign cultures and with diverse individuals.

■ Demonstrated leadership, communication, and negotiating skills.

■ Experience in training physicians and residents in computer systems and operations.

■ Proven ability to define issues, propose solutions, and implement changes.

■ Advocacy of proactive health care administration.

I sincerely believe that, with my experience and career goals, I will be an asset to your company. I would like to discuss this position with you at your earliest convenience.

Thank you in advance for your time and consideration. I look forward to speaking with you soon.

Sincerely,

Min Seo

offers and was ecstatic with the results of the resume we had written for her. She said, "My dreams for a well-paid management position are finally coming true!" We have included her old resume and our new version, along with a cover letter to illustrate the "before" and "after" effects of writing a Heart & Soul resume (see Figures 6.5 through 6.7).

Learning how to feel good about yourself and communicate this without boasting about your accomplishments is very important in Heart & Soul resume writing. You must value yourself and know that you have something special to offer the world. You are unique— no one else in the world is like you. If you don't feel good about yourself, write a Grateful List, and this will open up your heart so you can maintain an attitude of gratitude. Sometimes this is all it takes to get that special interview for the job you've been dreaming of! Like Marty and Min, you too can be successful in making your dreams come true!

HEART & SOUL TIP

It is important to value yourself and know that you have something important to contribute to the world.

7 *Appealing to the Heart*

When dealing with people, let us remember we are not dealing with creatures of logic. We are dealing with creatures of emotion. . . .

DALE CARNEGIE

WHAT MAKES SOMETHING APPEALING to the heart? How do you know if it does appeal to the heart, and why is that a good thing? Like a movie or a book, can't it be just as good if it doesn't? We don't think so. Going beyond visual attraction to emotional appeal—in other words, appealing to the heart—is the seventh of the seven never-before-published secrets to creating a successful resume. This secret sums up everything in this book and is the hallmark of a Heart & Soul resume.

We all know what the heart is, or at least we think we do. It's that intangible, fragile thing that poets and dreamers throughout the ages have written about and pondered over. It's that thing we draw on our greeting cards to say "I love you." It's that very thing that makes us sigh when we read a great novel or watch an inspiring movie. It separates good books from great books. Anything that's written or produced from the heart will have a distinctive appeal, and that includes resumes.

You might say at this point, "I expect to be emotionally touched when I read a novel or watch a great movie, but I never expected a resume to bring out any emotional feelings one way or the other." No one does. It's not something that most people are cognizant of. Who would ever think it was important to write a resume from the heart? Why, some might even laugh at this notion! Others might get embarrassed, shuffle their feet, and look down at the floor while trying desperately to avoid the topic. After all, the heart is something romantics and poets talk about—not everyday, regular people. Yet it's one of the most important things to understand if you truly want to be successful.

HEART & SOUL TIP

True Heart & Soul resumes are written from the heart and, in turn, appeal to the heart.

"Eye appeal" is an important factor involved in presenting an outstanding, appealing Heart & Soul resume. In this chapter we will highlight the tangibles and intangibles that will make a potential employer want to read your resume. To begin, pay attention to how you feel when you look at someone else's resume. Don't read it. Just scan over the presentation. Does it appeal to you? Does anything about it make you want to read more? A good resume will draw you in, like a good book. A nice book jacket and design will lure you into buying the book, but once you start reading it, you'll lose interest if it's not written well. The same is true for the resume. With one quick glance, a great-looking resume will pique your curiosity and make you eager to know more. But once you're drawn in, the writing must be impeccable and written from the heart in order to keep you interested.

HEART & SOUL TIP

Authentic Heart & Soul resumes are not only well written but are also professionally and attractively formatted.

Eye appeal generally encompasses all the physical characteristics of the resume, like the texture of the paper, size, titles, letter font, spacing, paragraph indention, alignment, bolding, italics, and underlining. Many first-time writers make the grave mistake of using too many different text and paragraph styles. Conversely, many experienced writers assume a simple, bland typewritten page is more than enough. We consistently recommend a conservative balance between the two, which we'll explain in more detail later on in this chapter. We emphasize *conservative* for a reason—unless you are in a highly creative and expressive career field, the resume is not the place to be funny, artistic, or whimsical.

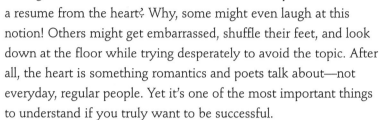

HEART & SOUL TIP

Your Heart & Soul resume is your sales tool, so make every line count! Remember, you have only about ten seconds to grab someone's attention!

Your resume is your sales tool, so you want to capture the reader's eye while remaining tasteful and professional. You have only about ten seconds to grab someone's attention, so make every second count. You must make the reader interested in reading more, and he or she must take you seriously! Read on to see how beautiful, professional, "appealing to the heart" resumes are prepared!

Carl Snyder

"Wow! What a nice resume!" Ben Charles commented to himself as he picked up the resume before him. Enclosed in a crisp, dark green folder, with gold-embossed lettering that read "Confidential Resume," the portfolio stood out among the stack of ordinary-looking resumes on his desk. Mr. Charles carefully opened it. He had never seen a resume like this in his twenty years as director of personnel at a major travel agency in Denver, Colorado.

Three sheets of resume paper had been combined to present an 8½- by 11-inch brochure. The wording was impeccable, and the design was very pleasing to the eye. Well written and easy to read, it was a beautiful resume. Before he had even finished reading it, Mr. Charles reached for the phone and dialed the number.

"Carl Snyder, this is Ben Charles at the corporate office in Denver. I just received your resume and I think it's fantastic."

HEART & SOUL TIP

Beautifully written and well-designed resumes stand out among all the others.

You want this same kind of response when you send someone a resume. The following describes how we prepared Carl's Heart & Soul resume, which landed him some very desirable interviews and several attractive job offers.

When Carl came into our office he looked very professional, dressed in a navy blue suit with a starched white shirt and striped tie. Carl was a successful corporate travel manager on a fast career track, with a clear career focus and an excellent work history to support his goals. Given his drive, sense of purpose, and knowledge of the job market, we didn't have to spend much time working with him on some of the topics we discussed earlier in this book. With self-assurance and confidence, Carl was very proactive in his career and had already visualized himself in a higher career position as a corporate travel manager. He had a great attitude about himself and life. Plus, he had already completed several stages of his career goals. He told us that during his early years as an office manager at a travel agency he had repeated positive affirmations every day: "I am a successful corporate travel manager." He clearly visualized himself at the top of the corporate world.

Because Carl had already incorporated most of the steps outlined in this book, our job was much easier. All we needed to do was prepare the best resume package possible. We started by drafting his resume (Figure 7.1). We emphasized the "Summary of Qualifications" and "Summary of Accomplishments" sections, which were significant. Knowing that any target company would be interested in his ability to generate profitability and growth, we highlighted the "Revenue & Profitability Growth" subsection. We also highlighted, in a section called "Operational Improvements," how Carl had initiated a plan to install a satellite computer and ticket printer that successfully expedited service at the travel agency. We carefully distributed and highlighted achievement and accomplishment statements throughout the resume in order to demonstrate parallels between his record of success and the potential employer's needs. These kinds of statements also help to reveal the heart and soul of a person—his or her ambitions, attitudes, and character. We used bullets to draw the reader's eye to specific details about his career. You don't have to do this, but sometimes it can be effective.

HEART & SOUL TIP

Achievement and accomplishment statements are effective in illustrating the heart and soul of a person.

As you are aware by now, attention to detail is important in all aspects of preparing a Heart & Soul resume, even down to the type of font that's used. In Carl's resume, we used an easy-to-read font and kept the bolding and underlining to a minimum. Your resume will look much more professional when it is designed on a computer connected to a laser or other high-quality printer, but a good typewriter will suffice if you do not have access to a computer.

We designed Carl's resume so there would be plenty of white, uncluttered space. A resume that's too crowded with words is hard to read. It will make the reader tire very quickly, and you don't want that to happen!

Carl wanted us to prepare an entire Executive Career Package, so once the resume was completed, we wrote Carl's cover letter, reference page, salary history, follow-up letter, and thank-you letter (Figures 7.2 through 7.6). On the basis of Carl's experience and track record of success, we recommended the best presentation we could offer: the "brochure" resume (see Chapter 5).

Carl said he loved the brochure format and would use it for special target companies and interviews, but he wanted a one-page resume (what we call an "executive summary" resume) to give to the headhunter he was working with. He was also executing a mass mailing campaign and preferred the one-page executive summary resume for that, too. This would save him time and money, since he was planning on mailing his resume to over five hundred companies nationwide.

HEART & SOUL TIP

A one-page executive summary can be used in direct mail campaigns to generate initial interest from employers.

When clients use the executive one-page summary in mail campaigns, we urge them to take the brochure resume to interviews and to send them to specific companies they want to wow. The executive summary is efficient and can be used to generate initial interest. In addition, it can be followed up with the more extensive brochure resume if the potential employer is interested in more details. Carl's executive one-page summary is shown in Figure 7.7.

Carl's cover letter was prepared as a simple letter of introduction. We put all his documents on a computer disk so he could use it later to custom-tailor each letter to an individual company. And, as already mentioned, we wrote Carl a follow-up letter and a thank-you letter. It's important to send a follow-up letter if you don't get a response from your original cover letter. Up to 95 percent of job candidates never send a follow-up letter, so you'll stand out above the rest if you do. Remember, you want to do all those little extra things that will define you as special. Being special is a trait of a Heart & Soul resume, just like the attitude of gratitude and "attending to attention." You want this specialness trait to shine through when you're seeking a job!

HEART & SOUL TIP

Send a follow-up letter if you haven't had a response from the initial resume, and a thank-you letter after an interview, so you'll stand out from all the other candidates. After all, you want to reflect your special, unique self, the way your Heart & Soul resume reflects you!

We put references and salary history on separate pages. This allowed Carl to include this information only for those companies that specifically requested it. As for the references, we usually prefer professional references over personal ones, and generally no more than a total of six. We don't recommend sending references with each resume, but it's OK if you want to, especially if yours are outstanding.

Notice that Carl's salary history is simply a breakdown of the annual income for his previous jobs. We think it's important to add employee benefits, bonuses, etc., because these can greatly enhance annual earnings. It isn't necessary to send a salary history unless a company specifically asks for it. However, if it is requested, you must enclose one. Otherwise, you won't be considered for the job. Again, it's important to pay attention to the details! If a company asks for salary requirements, this is different from your salary history. If you are asked for salary requirements, just add a line on your cover letter like "Salary negotiable." You don't want to overprice or underprice yourself. Always let the employer mention salary figures first. Finally, we advised Carl to mail everything in a 9- by 12-inch envelope. Never fold your resume: this looks unprofessional. Following is the complete Executive Career Package we put together for Carl.

■ **FIGURE 7.1**
Carl Snyder's Brochure Resume

HEART & SOUL TIP

Prepare a master copy of your resume, cover letter, reference page, salary history, and follow-up letter. You can tailor them to specific situations as needed.

A Presentation of Qualifications

CARL P. SNYDER, CTC

145 Anywhere Street
City, State 10000
Phone Number

■ **FIGURE 7.1 CONTINUED**
Carl Snyder's Brochure Resume (Page 1)

PROFESSIONAL OBJECTIVE & PROFILE

To obtain a position as a corporate travel manager utilizing experience in hotel, car rental, and travel agency negotiations. (A more extensive portfolio available upon request.)

SUMMARY OF QUALIFICATIONS

- 16 years of corporate travel experience, both in a travel agency and in a corporate setting.
- Experience managing a corporate travel budget of $2.4 million, including the organization and negotiation of regional and central conventions/meetings.
- Over 6 years of experience as a travel agency manager, building contacts throughout the industry. Proficient with SABRE & SYSTEM-ONE.
- Bachelor of science degree in finance; Certified Travel Consultant.
- Excellent organization and negotiation skills. Work well with peers. Team-oriented. Strong public speaking/presentation skills.

SUMMARY OF ACCOMPLISHMENTS

- *Administration:* Revised corporate travel policy to better monitor travelers' flights without changing travelers' routines. New policy is credited with saving the company over $75,000 per year.
- *Operational Improvements:* Initiated a plan to install a satellite computer and ticket printer to expedite service from the travel agency.
- *Computer/Systems Administration:* During employment at travel agency, planned, initiated, and executed a complete overhaul to a new computer system, SABRE. This was done with virtually no downtime for our customers.
- *Leadership:* Recognized as most valuable employee in 1989, mostly as a result of organizing and negotiating a meeting in Las Vegas that drew nearly 3,500 attendants.
- *Revenue & Profitability Growth:* Implemented a plan to market travel agency services outside Nortel. Hired an outside sales force, and within two years non-company travel business accounted for 10% of volume ($1 million per year).
- *Problem Solving:* Quickly resolved racial issues that arose within the travel agent pool. Implemented sensitivity training and terminated problem employees without any recourse to the employer.

■ **FIGURE 7.1 CONTINUED**
Carl Snyder's Brochure Resume (Page 2)

PROFESSIONAL EXPERIENCE

July 1986 to
Present

CORPORATE TRAVEL MANAGER
NORTEL, Nashville, TN
Fully responsible for a $2.4 million travel budget to include four regional meetings per year and one nationwide annual meeting. Supervise a support staff of two people. Revamped the corporate travel policy to better monitor travel. Consolidated travel to two airlines, three hotel chains, and two auto rental companies. Increased volume to travel vendors, which improved negotiating power and cost savings. Review and consolidate all weekly, monthly, quarterly, and annual travel reports submitted from all vendors. Monitor travel patterns to make sure they are in line with company policies. Assist regional offices in designing and implementing their corporate travel strategies.

November 1979 to
July 1986

TRAVEL COORDINATOR
NORTEL, Nashville, TN
Assisted travel manager in all aspects of the travel department. Followed up on administrative problems with vendors. Headed up regional conventions, with the supervision of the travel manager.

July 1975 to
October 1979

OFFICE MANAGER
UNIGLOBE ESQUIRE TRAVEL, Nashville, TN
Originally hired as a travel agent. Promoted to manager within the first year. Office grew from $1 million per year to $5 million per year after an aggressive corporate marketing strategy was designed and implemented with the owner. Clients included South Central Bell, First American Bank, and leisure businesses.

EDUCATION

TRAINING, WORKSHOPS, & ONGOING EDUCATION
• Managing a telephone service center, Nashville, TN
• SABRE Advanced Booking, Dallas, TX
• Dale Carnegie Course, Houston, TX
• Leaders in Travel Agency, Vancouver, BC

CERTIFIED TRAVEL CONSULTANT, ATLANTA, GA
Licensed August 1979

BACHELOR OF SCIENCE DEGREE IN FINANCE
University of Tennessee, Knoxville
Graduated with Honors
President, Kappa Kappa Gamma

■ **FIGURE 7.2**
Carl Snyder's Cover Letter

CARL P. SNYDER, CTC

145 Anywhere Street
City, State 10000
Phone Number

Today's Date

William Shufer
Executive Director
Worldwide Travel Agency
215 Blair Avenue
Sacramento, CA 95032

Dear Mr. Shufer:

I am interested in the possibility of joining your organization as a corporate travel manager.
The enclosed resume will provide you with information about my background and education.

For over 11 years, I have been directly involved with the administration and management of the
demanding corporate travel environment. My success is due largely to my ability to excel in a fast-
paced, high-pressure environment. My contacts are as diverse as they are authoritative, which lends
itself well to increasing my negotiating power. My strengths are in monitoring corporate travel policies and managing large meetings/conventions. My professional growth is at a standstill at my
current position, where the travel budget is slated to decrease 10% over the next 5 years. I am therefore seeking out professional organizations such as yours to continue my career progress.

I would appreciate the opportunity for a personal interview. If you need further information, I will
gladly respond upon request.

Thank you for your time and consideration. I look forward to hearing from you soon.

Sincerely,

Carl P. Snyder, CTC

■ **FIGURE 7.3**
Carl Snyder's Reference Page

CARL P. SNYDER, CTC

145 Anywhere Street
City, State 10000
Phone Number

REFERENCES

Winston Meredith
Controller
Nortel
1 Metro Center Boulevard
Nashville, TN 37217
Phone Number

Nancy Griffith
Attorney
123 3rd Avenue North
Nashville, TN 37212
Phone Number

Kimberly Winchester
Owner, American Travel
45 5th Avenue North
Washington, D.C. 22047
Phone Number

HEART & SOUL TIP

Use only 3 to 6 references. Try to use people who can speak for your professional work.

■ **FIGURE 7.4**
Carl Snyder's Salary History Page

CARL P. SNYDER, CTC

145 Anywhere Street
City, State 10000
Phone Number

SALARY HISTORY

NORTEL
Corporate Travel Manager
July 1986 to Present
$36,000 to $43,500 annual salary
plus bonuses, expense account, and employee benefits

NORTEL
Travel Coordinator
November 1979 to July 1986
$28,200 annual salary
plus bonuses and employee benefits

UNIGLOBE ESQUIRE TRAVEL
Office Manager
July 1975 to October 1979
$19,000 to $22,000 annual salary
plus employee benefits

HEART & SOUL TIP

*Never send your
salary history unless
it is specifically
requested by the
employer.*

■ **FIGURE 7.5**
Carl Snyder's Follow-Up Letter

CARL P. SNYDER, CTC

145 Anywhere Street
City, State 10000
Phone Number

Today's Date

William Shufer
Executive Director
Worldwide Travel Agency
215 Blair Avenue
Sacramento, CA 95032

Dear Mr. Shufer:

Approximately two weeks ago, I submitted a resume for your review. Having received no reply, I am enclosing a second copy in case my previous correspondence is lost or missing.

As indicated on the resume, I am interested in a position as a corporate travel manager. With over 11 years of directly related experience and excellent managing skills, I feel I would be an excellent candidate for your organization. I have controlled costs on a $2.4 million budget. I have revamped the corporate travel policy and negotiated better rates with vendors through a consolidation of business.

I would like to request a personal interview at your earliest convenience. Please contact me at the above address or telephone number.

Thank you for your time and consideration. I look forward to hearing from you soon.

Sincerely,

Carl P. Snyder, CTC

■ **FIGURE 7.6**
Carl Snyder's Thank-You Letter

CARL P. SNYDER, CTC

145 Anywhere Street
City, State 10000
Phone Number

Today's Date

William Shufer
Executive Director
Worldwide Travel Agency
215 Blair Avenue
Sacramento, CA 95032

Dear Mr. Shufer:

I would like to take this opportunity to thank you for meeting with me concerning a position as corporate travel manager. It was a pleasure meeting you and discussing career opportunities.

As I mentioned to you in our interview, I have over 11 years of directly related experience and have developed excellent management skills. Extremely cost-conscious, I have successfully controlled costs on a $2.4 million budget and have increased the company's overall profitability while at Nortel. With this in mind, I am confident that, with my experience and career goals, I would be an asset to your company.

Again, thank you for meeting with me. Please contact me at my home or telephone number if you have any additional questions. I look forward to another meeting.

Sincerely,

Carl P. Snyder, CTC

■ **FIGURE 7.7**
Carl Snyder's Executive One-Page Summary

CARL P. SNYDER, CTC

145 Anywhere Street
City, State 10000
Phone Number

PROFESSIONAL OBJECTIVE

To obtain a position as a corporate travel manager utilizing experience in hotel, car rental, and travel agency negotiations. (A more extensive portfolio available upon request.)

SUMMARY OF ACCOMPLISHMENTS

ADMINISTRATION Revised corporate travel policy to better monitor travelers' flights without changing travelers' routines. New policy is credited with saving the company over $75,000 per year.

OPERATIONAL IMPROVEMENTS Initiated a plan to install a satellite computer and ticket printer to expedite service from the travel agency.

COMPUTER/SYSTEMS ADMINISTRATION During employment at travel agency, planned, initiated, and executed a complete overhaul to a new computer system, SABRE. This was done with virtually no downtime for our customers.

LEADERSHIP Recognized as most valuable employee in 1989, mostly as a result of organizing and negotiating a 3,500-member meeting in Las Vegas.

PROFESSIONAL EXPERIENCE

July 1986 to
Present

CORPORATE TRAVEL MANAGER
NORTEL, Nashville, TN
Fully responsible for a $2.4 million travel budget to include four regional meetings per year and one nationwide annual meeting. Supervise a support staff of two people. Revamped the corporate travel policy to better monitor travel. Consolidated travel to two airlines, three hotel chains, and two auto rental companies. Increased volume to travel vendors which improved negotiating power and cost savings. Assist regional offices in designing and implementing their corporate travel strategies.

November 1979 to
July 1986

TRAVEL COORDINATOR
NORTEL, Nashville, TN
Assisted travel manager in all aspects of the travel department. Followed up on administrative problems with vendors. Headed up regional conventions, with the supervision of the travel manager.

EDUCATION

TRAINING, WORKSHOPS, & ONGOING EDUCATION
Managing a telephone service center, Nashville, TN, 1990
SABRE Advanced Booking, Dallas, TX, 1986

CERTIFIED TRAVEL CONSULTANT, ATLANTA, GA
Licensed August 1979

BACHELOR OF SCIENCE DEGREE IN FINANCE, May 1975
University of Tennessee, Knoxville
Graduated with Honors

The One-Page Myth

We can't tell you precisely how long a resume should be. One page, two pages, as many pages as it takes—there are simply no concrete rules! You can prepare a Heart & Soul resume with however many pages you want to use. One thing is sure: for every person you ask, you will get a different opinion. The most common myth we hear is that a resume should never be more than one page. Not true! In fact, most employers expect professionals to have at least a two-page resume. At a glance, an employer might think that you don't have much experience if you submit only one page.

Your resume format will depend on your individual objectives and circumstances. You can control the reader's eye by how you design your pages. You should create an "Objective" and/or "Summary" section at the top of the first page, to give the reader the overview he or she needs for those crucial first few seconds. The remaining length is determined by how much needs to be incorporated into the resume; that varies with each individual. As we mentioned earlier with Carl's resume package, he wanted a one-page executive summary to give to his headhunter and to distribute in his mail campaign, which is sufficient. Plus, we emphasized that he had a more extensive portfolio available upon request. Carl used the brochure resume for special companies and for high-powered interviews.

HEART & SOUL TIP

A Heart & Soul resume will capture the employer's attention and get you that interview!

The only absolute we accept is that you will have only about ten seconds to capture the reader's attention. You must pay close attention to detail, incorporate all the information we've discussed regarding design, fonts, and resume content, and finally, write the resume from the heart! A Heart & Soul resume will capture the reader's attention and get you that interview! Figure 7.8 illustrates some popular resume formats and discusses the pros and cons of each.

The Brochure Resume

The brochure resume is a very powerful visual and professional presentation. Without a doubt, we get the most positive feedback and impressive success stories from this style of resume. While your own circumstances may be unique, we highly recommend this format. Again, see Chapter 5 for complete instructions on preparing a brochure resume.

■ **FIGURE 7.8**
Popular Resume Formats

POPULAR RESUME FORMATS

Executive One-Page Summary

Pros

- Easiest to prepare, fax, and send in mail campaigns.
- Best for quick introductions. Good for entry-level applicants.

Cons

- Very common; can easily get lost in the shuffle of all the other one-page resumes.
- Less room; limits depth of content and suggests a person has limited experience.

Two-Page Resume

Pros

- Plenty of room for detail.
- Captures attention and provides support.

Cons

- Second page can get lost.
- Cumbersome; difficult to read and hold both pages.

Three- (or More) Page Resume

Pros

- Very detailed.
- The most thorough, detailed resume possible.

Cons

- Too detailed; might bore the reader.
- Can convey too much unnecessary information.

Brochure-Style or Signature-Booklet Resume

This is effectively a two-page resume with a cover page. All pages are combined to make an 81/2- by 11-inch presentation.

Pros

- Attractive "no clutter" cover sheet is eye-catching and appealing.
- Opens like a book so the reader can see both pages simultaneously.
- No chance of the reader losing any page of the resume.
- Easily expandable with printing on back page or inclusion of inserts.
- Stands out in a stack of one- or two-page resumes.
- By far the most popular and successful for the discerning professional.

Cons

- May be considered "too nice" a presentation.
- A little more expensive to prepare and mail.

- Use only one font throughout the resume and cover letter.
- Use a font that is easy to read, like Times Roman, Arial, or Hiroshige.
- Use no more than two font sizes, and use the larger size very sparingly.
- Use an 11-point font for general copy and an optional 14-point font for titles.
- Bold, italicize, underline, and space in a consistent way throughout your resume.
- Leave plenty of white space throughout your resume.
- Center or align text on the page so it is balanced and uses the whole page evenly.
- Use the whole page on every page. Don't submit a half-full second or third page.
- Don't use a photo, graphics, or logos unless you are sure they are appropriate.
- Choose a high-grade resume paper in a conservative color (gray, beige, light blue).
- Adjust the length of your resume to your particular situation and job search.

■ **TABLE 7.1**
General Resume-Design Guidelines

Control What the Reader Sees First

When you design your resume, think about what you want readers to see first. Given only a few seconds to sell yourself, how can you best grab their attention? What do you want someone to learn about you in that brief moment that truly reflects the heart and soul of your being? After you've decided what to say, you'll want to position it on your resume so that it stands out from the rest of the copy. As we previously mentioned, this is usually best done at the top of the first page of your resume. Be careful not to distract the reader's eye by including large, cumbersome, or unnecessary text or titles on your resume. To help in your design, we have included some of our guidelines (Table 7.1). These aren't rules, so feel free to adjust them to meet your own individual circumstances.

HEART & SOUL TIP

Make sure the reader sees whatever you feel is most important during that first glance at your resume.

What Do You Think About My Resume?

"Wow! I really like this resume, but I want to let my Uncle Jim review it. He's a manager for the telephone company. Also, I want to let my best friend, Marsha, look at it. She's been a secretary for several years." That's what a client told us one day after picking up a proof of her resume.

There is nothing wrong with seeking advice from friends and associates, but when you ask ten different people what they think about your resume, you'll get ten completely different answers. No matter how many people you ask, you will get just as many answers. Our resume-writing and resume-design guidelines in this book are based on many years of concrete results. With resumes, there is no absolute right or wrong, but people will try to tell you there is, all day long! Everyone is a critic. Remember that. Trust your own inner instincts. Listen to your inner voice! You are the one who has put your whole heart and soul into your resume—not your best friend or your Uncle Jim! Your individual circumstances are personal and unique, and you are the best judge of your situation!

HEART & SOUL TIP

You are the one who has put your whole heart and soul into your resume, so be careful about asking a friend or family member to critique it for you! They will most assuredly tell you that it needs this or that. Just be true to yourself and listen to your own inner guide!

If you ask employment or job-search professionals for an opinion on your resume, the answer will be based on what they like to use personally. Employment agencies often like one-page resumes because they are easy to fax to their clients. Headhunters or recruiters don't even necessarily like resumes but will often choose a simple one-page resume if given a choice. They would rather get you an interview based on their referral alone. This helps them control what the company knows about you.

Just the Fax, Ma'm

If you are asked to fax your resume, always fax the white master copy from the printer, instead of the finished resume on colored resume paper. It is much easier to read. The brochure resume will have to be faxed in three separate pages. Also, after you fax your resume, mail the employer a nice presentation copy as a follow-up courtesy (he or she will remember you). And, of course, you should always bring your complete resume to your interviews. Again, this will make you stand out among other candidates.

Surfing the Internet

Before Carl left our office, he told us he had just gotten on the Internet and would like to do some job searching electronically. That's easy, we told him. Using the Internet is really nothing more than another way to distribute your resume and search for employment leads. But, we cautioned him, the Internet is totally uncensored, and anybody can publish anything, so it is important to be skeptical about what you find and where you distribute your resume.

Carl asked us if the Internet would eventually do away with the need for a physical resume. We told him no—*not at all!* The Internet will definitely revolutionize the way some employers find candidates to interview, but it won't change the need for an attractively designed and well-written physical presentation! You will always need that for your face-to-face meetings as well as for important referrals and mailings.

Look at Table 7.2 if you are interested in how to do a job search on the Internet or with other computer technology. This field is expanding widely and rapidly—we would recommend further study on the subject. Check our Resources list at the back of this book for books that we highly recommend.

Before Carl left, we converted his executive summary resume to a version that could be scanned (see Figure 7.9). The process was simple. First we took out all the bold, italics, and underlining. Then we changed the font to Times Roman and the font size to 10 points (stay between 10 and 12 points).

■ **Scanning Resumes**
Some employers keep all their incoming resumes in a large database. They do this by scanning each physical resume they receive into their system. Whenever someone needs a new hire, they search this database by the key words you included in your resume (marketing manager, industrial engineer, etc.).

The only difference between a scannable resume and your main resume is that the scanned resume is printed in a basic Times Roman or Courier font without the use of any bolding, underlines, or italics. Without the clutter of text enhancements, the computer can read the resume more clearly. If you know the employer is using this scanning technology, you might consider sending both versions of your resume—a nice presentation copy for viewing, and a plain copy for scanning.

■ **Private Resume Banks/Job Postings**
There are companies that have and maintain a number of active resumes in a database. You may pay these companies to have your resume included, and employers may have to pay to access this pool of available candidates. Most major resume banks have a Web page or access through the Internet. Many of them also allow employers to post job openings that you can scroll through. Two good examples are The Monster Board (www.monster.com) and the On-Line Career Center (www.occ.com). Check these out or just enter a search for "careers" and see what comes up.

■ **Sending an Electronic Version of Your Resume**
Throughout your job search, you may have the option of sending your resume by *attaching* it to an e-mail message. The receiver then prints it out at his or her location. This is a very inexpensive way to send your resume, but, unfortunately, you have no control over what the reader actually sees. Depending on his or her system, your resume may lose some of its text enhancements and spacing. We suggest saving your resume in a file that is in a universal format (like a text file) before sending it. Or you may consider writing your resume as an original e-mail message (instead of attaching an on-file resume to an e-mail message).

■ **Internet Holdouts**
For those of you who don't want to or never plan to use the Internet but still enjoy some type of technology, don't worry! The fax machine still works pretty darn well!

■ **TABLE 7.2**
Conducting a Job Search Electronically

■ **FIGURE 7.9**
Carl Snyder's Executive One-Page Summary for Scanning

CARL P. SNYDER, CTC
145 Anywhere Street
City, State 10000
Phone Number

Here is Carl's Executive One-Page Summary, converted for employers with scanning technology.

PROFESSIONAL OBJECTIVE

To obtain a position as a corporate travel manager utilizing experience in hotel, car rental, and travel agency negotiations.

SUMMARY OF ACCOMPLISHMENTS

• ADMINISTRATION: Revised corporate travel policy to better monitor travelers' flights without changing travelers' routines. New policy is credited with saving the company over $75,000 per year.
• OPERATIONAL IMPROVEMENTS: Initiated a plan to install a satellite computer and ticket printer to expedite service from the travel agency.
• COMPUTER/SYSTEMS ADMINISTRATION: During employment at travel agency, planned, initiated, and executed a complete overhaul to a new computer system, SABRE. This was done with virtually no downtime for our customers.
• LEADERSHIP: Recognized as most valuable employee in 1989, mostly as a result of organizing and negotiating a meeting in Las Vegas that drew nearly 3,500 attendants.

PROFESSIONAL EXPERIENCE

CORPORATE TRAVEL MANAGER

July 1986 to
Present

NORTEL, Nashville, TN

Fully responsible for a $2.4 million travel budget to include four regional meetings per year and one nationwide annual meeting. Supervise a support staff of two people. Revamped the corporate travel policy to better monitor travel. Consolidated travel to two airlines, three hotel chains, and two auto rental companies. Increased volume to travel vendors, which improved negotiating power and cost savings. Review and consolidate all weekly, monthly, quarterly, and annual travel reports submitted from all vendors. Monitor travel patterns to make sure they are in line with all policies. Help regional offices design and implement their corporate travel strategies.

TRAVEL COORDINATOR

June 1979 to
July 1986

NORTEL, Nashville, TN

Assisted travel manager in all aspects of the travel department. Followed up on administrative problems with vendors. Headed up regional conventions, with the supervision of the travel manager.

EDUCATION

TRAINING, WORKSHOPS, & ONGOING EDUCATION

• Managing a telephone service center, Nashville, TN, 1990
• SABRE Advanced Booking, Dallas, TX, 1986

CERTIFIED TRAVEL CONSULTANT, Atlanta, GA
Licensed August 1979

BACHELOR OF SCIENCE DEGREE IN FINANCE, May 1975
University of Tennessee, Knoxville
Graduated with Honors

All Good Things Must Come to an End—Maybe

This is not really the end, friends, but just the beginning—of a new career, a new life, a new you! A new, confident, self-assured you who knows how to set goals, make life changes, and incorporate these seven never-before-published secrets to creating a successful resume.

In this book you have learned how to incorporate your heart and soul into resume writing and learned why these techniques are more successful than others. The seven secrets we've explored work together as a cohesive, synergistic whole to make your resume a true Heart & Soul resume—a higher, more evolved resume. In fact, it's more than just a resume. It's a psychological reflection of your inner self—your heart and soul in relation to careers and work experience. It is your vision as well as your past.

HEART & SOUL TIP

Our seven never-before-published secrets to creating a successful resume work together as a cohesive, synergistic whole to make your resume a true Heart & Soul resume!

You have learned how to use *creative visualization* to imagine and manifest what you want in life. You have quietly *contemplated* and listened to that inner voice guiding you and directing you in your life. You have practiced daily *affirmations* and understand how they can change the course of your life. You are what you think, and this is reflected in every step toward your career goals and in every daily thought and action.

You have learned that being *proactive* rather than reactive in your job search will benefit you many times over. You have studied how to differentiate between illusions and reality, and how to *set high but realistic goals.* You have learned how to be *objective* and how to determine whether your goals are in line with your qualifications.

You have come face to face with the responsibility of *"attending to attention"* and understand the importance of *attending to details.* You know the value of *being aware of the moment* and *listening* to your heart's messages as well as to the external world of newspaper ads, networking, and the Internet. You know how to listen and target your resume to meet the requirements for specific jobs.

You have courageously faced your pen and paper alone, when no words would come, and have practiced valuable, fun writing exercises to get past writer's block. You have learned how to *doodle,* tapping into that inner creative flow and getting your career information down on paper!

You have explored the *attitude of gratitude* and discovered how this is an important step in opening up so that your writing comes *from the heart.* You have learned how to *highlight accomplishments without boasting* and how to change your attitude from negative to positive.

Finally, you have incorporated all these synergistic parts into a cohesive whole—the complete writing and design of your resume—and the end result is a beautiful, attractive, Heart & Soul, sure-to-get-you-an-interview resume!

You can use these seven secrets not only to help you write a more successful, higher-echelon Heart & Soul resume but also to help you become a better you—to become the best that you can be. Use these seven never-before-published secrets to creating a successful resume to streamline your life in many and/or all areas.

Au Revoir!

We leave you only briefly, for we are just an e-mail message or letter away, to help you if you need any career assistance. And right this very minute we're writing other books to help you in your career. Remember, each of us has the ability to choose what we want to do with our life, so dream and build your goals. Choose wisely and, above all, choose a career that reflects the heart and soul of your being—choose a career that you love!

PART TWO

"BEFORE AND AFTER" RESUMES

Far away there in the sunshine are my highest aspirations. I can look up and see their beauty, believe in them, and try to follow where they lead.

LOUISA MAY ALCOTT

THIS SECTION PRESENTS TWENTY samples of "before and after" resumes. We show how we've taken unfocused, unsuccessful resumes and transformed them into Heart & Soul resumes, implementing the seven never-before-published secrets to creating a successful resume. Naturally, we have changed all names, addresses, and phone numbers to protect the privacy of the individuals involved, and any similarities to actual persons, living or dead, are purely coincidental.

We have included a variety of professions and personalities to give you a comprehensive look at our approach. We work with clients from all over the United States and abroad, and have written resumes for nearly every known profession! You'll notice that the usual quality of the old resumes isn't that good; we included them "as is" because they are authentic and we wanted to convey what they were really like when we first got them!

You'll notice that many of the "before" resumes don't have a "Professional Objective & Profile" section. Many of them are very sketchy in highlighting their goals and objectives. Most of them have no proactive career objective, do not "attend to attention," and are lacking the attitude of gratitude. Notice as well how many of the resumes aren't very appealing in their presentation. Not only are they written poorly, but they have no immediate eye appeal. We have pointed out on each resume specific areas that needed help, and we describe how we turned it into a Heart & Soul resume.

For ease of reading and presentation, the "after" resumes are all formatted in one consistent style. Note, however, that your Heart & Soul resume can be formatted in any of a variety of ways (see examples in Part One of this book). Just follow the resume-design guidelines in Table 7.1 on page 113 and let your own creativity do the rest!

We hope that you, after reading this book and reviewing these samples, are now prepared to write a true-to-self Heart & Soul resume of your own.

■ **RESUME 1**
Victoria Boyd's "Before" Resume

HEART & SOUL TIP

The Objective doesn't relate enough information about her career goals or experience. This is the first thing an employer will read! It needs to be more detailed.

Victoria Boyd
4420 Anywhere Street
City, State 10000
Phone Number

Objective: Position in the broadcast industry. -

Qualifications:
Production experience, writing experience, producer experience and travel experience.
Experienced working with government officials and executives.

Education:

       UNIVERSITY OF CAPETOWN, Capetown, South Africa
       Degree in Broadcast Production

Work History:

1995 to 1996   Independent Broadcast Company, Production Manager, "People
                 of South Africa." Johannesburg, South Africa.
                 Produced a television show, "People of South Africa." Responsible for show's
                 format and getting audience for shows. Hired musicians and involved in live
                 recordings. Wrote scripts for shows, as well as formats and outlines. Took care of
                 getting clients and sponsors for shows. Worked with government officials and all
                 types of people.

1994 to 1995   U. S. Network Television Affiliate—Satellite Uplink, "Live Coverage of the Election
                 of Nelson Mandela," Johannesburg, South Africa. Worked with South Africa and
                 television networks in the United States during Nelson Mandela's election. Was
                 responsible for raising money.

1993 to 1994   Good Ideas Company, South African Broadcast Company,
                 Assistant Producer & Director, "Lost Treasure Hunt Show," Johannesburg, South
    Africa. Handled all duties for this television show.

1990 to 1993   Communications Unlimited, Inc., Independent Producer,
                 Johannesburg, South Africa.
                 Wrote and produced stories in South Africa. Had to raise money for films. Did
                 programs on medical issues and environmental topics.

■ **RESUME 1**
Victoria Boyd's "After" Resume (Cover Sheet)

HEART & SOUL TIP

Notice how we developed Victoria's resume from the brief, sketchy one she brought us.

A PRESENTATION OF EXECUTIVE CREDENTIALS
IN BROADCAST PRODUCTION

VICTORIA BOYD

4420 Anywhere Street
City, State 10000
Phone Number

■ **RESUME 1 CONTINUED**
Victoria Boyd's "After" Resume (Page 1)

HEART & SOUL TIP

In the Heart & Soul version we have expanded on her "Objective" section and added depth.

PROFESSIONAL OBJECTIVE & PROFILE - - - - - - - - - - -

A dynamic, multitalented and experienced broadcast professional is seeking a position that will fully utilize an in-depth background as a television producer, production manager, independent producer, scriptwriter, and executive liaison to ABC, CNN, and BET networks in Johannesburg, South Africa. Experienced in working with foreign cultures and governments; open-minded, with a global, comprehensive understanding of international politics and their effects on the media.

Highly skilled in researching and identifying pertinent topics and in writing and producing television entertainment shows. Strong management skills. Self-directed and self-motivated. Seeking a challenging position that will provide an avenue for significantly contributing numerous talents and skills to the broadcast industry.

SUMMARY OF QUALIFICATIONS

TRACK RECORD OF SUCCESS
Background exemplifies a successful track record of career accomplishments in broadcast production, which includes more than 8 years of experience as broadcast producer, production manager, scriptwriter, and executive broadcast liaison to U.S. network affiliates.

TELEVISION/BROADCAST PRODUCTION
Multitalented and experienced in all facets of broadcast production for television. Production manager for *People of South Africa*, a one-hour magazine-format television program in Johannesburg, South Africa. Also assistant director for *Lost Treasure Hunt*, a one-hour entertainment program produced by Good Ideas Company for the South African Broadcast Company (SABC). Coordinated helicopters, fixed-wing plane, two-way radio links to base station and studio and live recordings to studio. Traveled extensively over South Africa and neighboring countries.

INTERNATIONAL & DOMESTIC RELATIONS— SATELLITE UPLINK
Experienced in communicating with foreign businesses, governments, and organizations to organize and produce television segments. Liaison between ABC, CNN, and BET networks to coordinate the satellite uplink during the live coverage of election of Nelson Mandela. Worked extensively with John Parr, movie and BET producer, to solicit and obtain $18 million in funds to support a joint venture between South Africa and BET International.

SCRIPTWRITING— TELEVISION & MOTION PICTURES
Wrote two scripts for motion pictures that were produced in South Africa. In-depth background in writing scripts, formats, and outlines for television shows.

EDUCATION

BACHELOR OF ARTS DEGREE IN BROADCAST PRODUCTION
University of Capetown, Capetown, South Africa

■ **RESUME 1 CONTINUED**
Victoria Boyd's "After" Resume (Page 2)

HEART & SOUL TIP

Notice how we described pertinent facts that will make her more marketable in the broadcast industry.

PROFESSIONAL EXPERIENCE

PRODUCTION MANAGER

INDEPENDENT BROADCAST COMPANY
People of South Africa Television Program
Johannesburg, South Africa, 1995 to 1996

- *Production Management:* Responsible for all facets of producing a one-hour magazine-format television program, *People of South Africa.* Work included coordinating production remotes as well as in-studio production. Arranged for a live audience during each taping. Created and developed format for the program and was in charge of producing each segment.
- *Studio Music Recordings:* Auditioned and hired musicians, selected music, and supervised live recordings.
- *Research:* Investigated, researched, and identified pertinent, timely topics for show.
- *Writing:* Wrote outlines, formats, and scripts for show.
- *Management & Supervision:* Delegated work responsibilities to production crew and monitored overall job performance to ensure accuracy and adherence to policies and procedures.
- *Sales & Account Management:* In charge of soliciting and obtaining clients to sponsor this television show. Major clientele included Avis, Cellular Phone Company, Apple Computers, ComAir Airlines, Pepsi, and Foodgro.
- *Business & Client Relations:* Established and maintained an excellent network of business associates as a result of in-depth contact and interaction with business owners, community, and government officials, artists/talent, and managers.

U.S. NETWORK TELEVISION AFFILIATE— SATELLITE UPLINK

LIVE COVERAGE OF THE ELECTION OF NELSON MANDELA
Johannesburg, South Africa

- *International Communications Liaison:* Liaison between South Africa and ABC, CNN, and BET networks in the United States to coordinate live coverage of the election of Nelson Mandela. Worked with networks before and after the elections to coordinate satellite uplink. Work involved extensive communication between U. S. network affiliates.
- *Fundraising:* Solicited and obtained $18 million in Johannesburg to support a joint television venture between BET network and Johannesburg.

ASSISTANT DIRECTOR & PRODUCER

GOOD IDEAS COMPANY
AFFILIATE OF SOUTH AFRICAN BROADCAST COMPANY (SABC)
Lost Treasure Hunt television show, Johannesburg, South Africa

- *Company Track Record of Success:* Hired initially as a production assistant and quickly promoted to floor manager and assistant director. Responsible for producing a weekly one-hour entertainment show.

INDEPENDENT PRODUCER

COMMUNICATIONS UNLIMITED INC.
Johannesburg, South Africa

- *Producer:* Independently wrote, developed, and produced stories as an independent producer. Responsible for obtaining operating funds, equipment, and staff to produce shows, which were aired on South African Broadcast Company (SABC) and M-Net. Programs included coverage of medical issues and environmental topics.

■ **RESUME 2**
Hans Dutton's "Before" Resume

HEART & SOUL TIP

This resume desperately needs more attention to detail and an expansion of qualifications.

Hans Dutton

MBA, University of Mississippi, 1996
GPA: 3.33/4.0
BBA with a focus on Managerial Finance at the University of Mississippi in 1995
Business Diploma at the Norwegian School of Management in Oslo, Norway

Financial Classes in College
Monetary/Banking Policies, Marketing Principles, Investments, Managerial Economics
Financial Statements, Inventory & Cost Control, Advanced Organizational Behavior
Microeconomics, Managing Financial Institution, Risk & Insurance
Portfolio Management, Statistics, Business Finance, Organizational Behavior
Operations Management, Policy Form & Administration
Business Career Planning, International Business Management
Financial Management, Strategic Management
Materials Administration, Business Logistics

Computers
QuattroPro, WordPerfect, Excel, Word, PowerPoint, Windows 3.1, Windows 95, DOS, Internet, E-Mail, and HTML Documents.

Professional Experience

Bjarne M. Due A/S Distribution Center, Oslo, Norway, 1989 to 1992
Materials Analyst & Inventory & Cost Control Supervisor
Responsible for material acquisition, control, and receiving. Wrote purchase orders and responsible for incoming material. Supervisor of employees. Also responsible for inventory.

SYNERGI-GROSSISTENE A/S BROKERAGE SERVICE, Oslo, Norway, 1990 to 1991
Accounting & Customer Service Assistant
Accounting, accounts receivable and data entry, billing, and collections.

VIDEOGALLERIETT A/S VIDEO COMPANY, Oslo, Norway, 1987 to 1988
Customer Service Representative
Rented video tapes to customers.

MEDICAL UNIT—NORWEGIAN CAVALRY, Norway, 1989 to 1990
Supervisor & Medical Assistant
Trained employees in warehouse. Supervised platoon of 12 enlisted personnel.

HEART & SOUL TIP

There needs to be more description regarding his jobs. There is nothing in the resume that will sell this candidate.

■ **RESUME 2**
Hans Dutton's "After" Resume (Cover Sheet)

HEART & SOUL TIP

This version has a proactive career focus on the first page. It has been developed and describes pertinent skills.

A PRESENTATION OF PROFESSIONAL CREDENTIALS

HANS DUTTON

Permanent Address	**Temporary Address**
P. O. Box 44	445 Anywhere Street
City, Country	City, State 10000
Phone Number	Phone Number

■ **RESUME 2 CONTINUED**
Hans Dutton's "After" Resume (Page 1)

PROFESSIONAL OBJECTIVE & PROFILE

Highly motivated professional is seeking a position that will fully utilize advanced education in managerial finance and experience in all areas of accounting, accounts payable, accounts receivable, customer service, inventory, cost control, and collections. Ability to manage highly complex financial system and data. Proven ability to define issues, propose solutions, and implement changes. Willing to relocate to any geographic location.

Excellent analytical, planning, organizational, and negotiation skills. Knowledge of P&L statements, investments, money and banking, advanced managerial finance, balance sheets, public finance and computerized accounting systems. Skills in research, analysis, decision making, and follow-through.

EDUCATION

MASTER'S DEGREE IN BUSINESS ADMINISTRATION
University of Mississippi, Oxford

BACHELOR'S DEGREE IN BUSINESS ADMINISTRATION—MANAGERIAL FINANCE
University of Mississippi, Oxford

BUSINESS DIPLOMA
Norwegian School of Management, Oslo

SUMMARY OF QUALIFICATIONS

AREAS OF KNOWLEDGE & EXPERTISE IN FINANCE & BUSINESS		
Monetary/Banking Policies	Marketing Principles
Investments	Managerial Economics
Financial Statements	Inventory & Cost Control
Advanced Organizational Behavior	Microeconomics
Financial Institution Management	Risk & Insurance
Portfolio Management	Statistics
Business Finance	Organizational Behavior
Operations Management	Policy Form & Administration
Business Career Planning	International Business Management
Financial Management	Strategic Management
Materials Administration	Business Logistics

COMPUTERS QuattroPro, WordPerfect, Excel, Word, PowerPoint, Windows 3.1, Windows 95, DOS, Internet, E-Mail, and HTML documents.

LANGUAGES Fluent in English, Norwegian, and German.

INTERNATIONAL EXPERTISE Have gained valuable experience in interacting with foreign cultures as a result of being born in Oslo, Norway, living in Tanzania, Kenya, and being educated in the United States. Ability to effectively communicate with all types of individuals and levels of personnel in the U.S. and abroad.

■ RESUME 2 CONTINUED
Hans Dutton's "After" Resume (Page 2)

PROFESSIONAL EXPERIENCE

MATERIALS ANALYST
INVENTORY & COST
CONTROL SUPERVISOR

BJARNE M. DUE A/S DISTRIBUTION CENTER, OSLO, NORWAY, 1989 TO 1992
- *Purchasing—Materials Analyst:* Coordinated materials acquisition, control, receiving, and operations for this distribution center. Prepared purchase orders, processed incoming materials, and coordinated distribution. Worked closely with field, warehouse, and management personnel to facilitate materials acquisition and distribution.
- *Vendor Relations:* Communicated effectively with vendors to expedite orders, material returns, reorders, and credits.
- *Supervision:* Delegated work responsibilities and monitored overall job performance to ensure accuracy and adherence to standards, specifications, rules, and regulations.
- *Employee Relations:* Planned and organized jobs for precise and timely execution. Encouraged and supported a teamlike work environment, which increased employee morale, productivity, and efficiency.
- *Cost Control:* Effectively utilized inventory in order to minimize and maintain inventory costs.

ACCOUNTING &
CUSTOMER SERVICE
ASSISTANT

SYNERGI-GROSSISTENE A/S BROKERAGE SERVICE, OSLO, NORWAY, 1990 TO 1991
- *Accounting:* Responsible for accounting procedures, including accounts receivable, accounts payable, general ledger, and data entry.
- *Invoicing/Collections:* Responsible for preparing invoices for billing and for collection. Contacted accounts and arranged payment schedules and plans.
- *Customer Service:* Effectively responded to customers' inquiries, suggestions, requests, and/or concerns.

CUSTOMER SERVICE
REPRESENTATIVE

VIDEOGALLERIETT A/S VIDEO COMPANY, OSLO, NORWAY, 1987 TO 1988
- *Sales & Marketing:* Sold and rented video products to customers in this video store. Responsible for integrating company's advertising and marketing strategies into everyday store operations.
- *Customer Service:* Assisted customers with purchases and was always willing to take the extra steps to ensure customer satisfaction.

MEDICAL ASSISTANT
& SUPERVISOR

MEDICAL UNIT—NORWEGIAN CAVALRY, NORWAY, 1989 TO 1990
- *Program Development:* Launched a series of internal realignment and reorganization initiatives to train and motivate medical staff members. In charge of developing and implementing training programs.
- *Personnel Training:* Trained up to 50 staff members in all areas of shipping and receiving.
- *Management & Supervision:* Directed and managed a platoon of 12 staff members, 2 armored personnel carriers, 2 ambulances, and 2 field hospitals, which provided medical support to the cavalry division.

References Available upon Request

■ **RESUME 3**
Ahmed Girgis's "Before" Resume

Ahmed Girgis
2988 Anywhere Street
City, State 10000
Phone Number

Objective	Technical position in the production or treatment of chemicals and related products.
Education	Zagazig University, Egypt. Degree with major in Chemistry.
Industrial Work:	Hosni Company for knitted products. Training courses in dyeing and production control. Put in charge of dyeing, finishing and softening. Responsible for prescribing chemical mixes and quantities for best quality and least cost of production. Interacted with clients for quality control.
7/92-3/4	International Company for Plastic Industries, Egypt Worked in the painting and electroplating department. Designed the test for adding phosphate and supervised the containers during the chemicals and powders. Quality control. Investigated alternatives to find the best effective chemical treatment.
Other experience:	Opryland Hotel Worked in the Hospitality and Attractions department.
Additional Information:	Permanent resident of the U.S. Proficient in the treatment of wallpapers, paints, and drawing and inscription.
References:	Available upon request.

HEART & SOUL TIP

This "before" resume has no "Summary of Skills" section and does not explain his citizenship. It needs more Heart & Soul depth and a more pleasing, aesthetic design. Also, the information about working in a hotel isn't relevant to his goals.

■ **RESUME 3**
Ahmed Girgis's "After" Resume

HEART & SOUL TIP

The Heart & Soul version is concise and succinctly highlights skills and experience relevant to career goals.

AHMED GIRGIS
2988 Anywhere Street
City, State 10000
Phone Number

PROFESSIONAL OBJECTIVE

Seeking a technical/laboratory position that will fully utilize my education and experience in chemistry, research, and production. Born in Egypt. Have obtained U.S. citizenship.

EDUCATION

BACHELOR OF SCIENCE DEGREE IN CHEMISTRY
Zagazig University, Egypt (Recognized by the World Education Services, Inc., in the U.S.)

SUMMARY OF QUALIFICATIONS

- Fluent in English and Arabic
- In-depth background in physics, chemistry, and biology
- Proficient in treatments and chemical procedures to produce wallpapers, paints, and drawings and inscriptions on glass and mirrors.

PROFESSIONAL EXPERIENCE

CHEMISTRY LAB RESEARCHER & LAB SUPERVISOR

HOSNI COMPANY FOR KNITTED PRODUCTS, EGYPT, 1994 TO 1995
Responsibilities were comprehensive and included the following areas:
- *Chemistry Analysis & Production:* Responsible for researching and determining appropriate mixtures needed for materials. In charge of mixing the chemicals in order to dye, finish, and soften fabrics/materials in this clothing manufacturing company.
- *Supervision:* Scheduled work shifts for laboratory personnel. Monitored and supervised employees to ensure accuracy and efficient job performance.
- *Quality Control:* Monitored and reviewed facilities and production techniques to ensure adherence to standards, specifications, rules, and regulations.
- *Cost Control:* Efficiently restructured production methods in order to streamline production operations and minimize and maintain labor costs.
- *Client Relations:* Established and maintained an excellent network of business relationships as a result of interacting extensively with clients and providing superior service.

PRODUCTION SUPERVISOR

INTERNATIONAL COMPANY FOR PLASTIC INDUSTRIES, EGYPT, 1992 TO 1994
- *Supervision:* Managed and supervised overall production operations in the painting and electroplating department. Delegated responsibilities and monitored overall job performance to ensure accuracy and adherence to policies and procedures.
- *Chemistry & Laboratory Production:* Researched, compiled, and administered the chemicals and powders needed for production.
- *Quality Control:* Monitored facilities and job performance to ensure accuracy and adherence to standards and specifications.

■ **RESUME 4**
Stewart Graves's "Before" Resume

HEART & SOUL TIP

This "before" resume is incomplete. Not enough information to get anyone's attention! It needs to be developed and completely rewritten!

STEWART GRAVES
225 Anywhere Street
City, State 10000
Phone Number

EDUCATION   **BA, UNIVERSITY OF PHOENIX**

ADVANCED TRAINING
          State of Tennessee Industrial Training
          NECA-IBEW
          Kawasaki Unimate Robots

PROFESSIONAL MANAGEMENT EXPERIENCE

<u>Area Manager,</u> NISSAN MOTOR MANUFACTURING CORPORATION, U.S.A.
Smyrna, Tennessee—1982 to Present
In charge of body assembly plant. Manage several teams in operations. Traveled to Japan to train on the IBAS system. Lead technician and quality control.

<u>Journeyman Electrician,</u> INTERNATIONAL BROTHERHOOD OF ELECTRICAL WORKERS
Nashville, Tennessee—1977 to 1982
Install wiring and repair equipment.

■ **RESUME 4**
Stewart Graves's "After" Resume (Cover Sheet)

HEART & SOUL TIP

Notice in our Heart & Soul version how we developed a proactive career focus in the "Professional Objective & Profile" section. Also pay attention to how we detailed his advanced training and honors.

A PRESENTATION OF PROFESSIONAL CREDENTIALS

STEWART GRAVES

225 Anywhere Street
City, State 10000
Phone Number

■ **RESUME 4 CONTINUED**
Stewart Graves's "After" Resume (Page 1)

HEART & SOUL TIP

It is important to be aware of the details of your backgrouond and emphasize these throughout the "Objective" section and body of the resume.

PROFESSIONAL OBJECTIVE & PROFILE

Professional automobile manufacturing manager with more than 15 years of experience building and leading integrated operations for Nissan Motor Manufacturing plant. Top-rated area manager in a company survey that included 500 management personnel. Consistently successful in troubleshooting and reengineering highly automated production methods that streamline operations, decrease downtime and labor costs, and increase profitability. Strong interpersonal skills and ability to communicate with diverse individuals and foreign cultures. Dynamic leader and mentor with strong general management qualifications in strategic planning and process/productivity/quality improvement. Excellent background in employee training & development, safety, and leadership.

Desire a management position in a manufacturing company that's progressive, open-minded, and that will provide a challenging opportunity to significantly contribute to a company's efficiency, productivity, and profitability.

SUMMARY OF PROFESSIONAL HONORS

Certificate of recognition for outstanding attendance
Nissan Motor Manufacturing Corporation U.S.A. (2 certificates)

Top-rated area manager in survey of 500 management personnel

One of 6 managers selected to go to Japan for training on Intelligent Body Assembly System (IBAS), which incorporates 51 robots in one work cell to set dimensionally and marry the car body together.

Recipient of the Eagle Club's recognition for achieving the first million-dollar United Way campaign for Nissan Motor Manufacturing Corporation U.S.A.

EDUCATION

BACHELOR OF ARTS DEGREE IN MANAGEMENT
University of Phoenix (Long-Distance Program), Nashville, Tennessee

ADVANCED TRAINING

STATE OF TENNESSEE INDUSTRIAL TRAINING SERVICE
Electronics —140 hours   Welding—60 Hours

NECA-IBEW ELECTRICAL/ELECTRONIC APPRENTICESHIP SCHOOL
800 Hours of Electrical & Electronic Theory

Kawasaki Unimate Robots
GMF Robotics—ARC MATE Operations & Programming
GMF Robotics —S-108 Maintenance
Electrician—Nashville Electrical Joint Apprenticeship Committee
Reliance Electronic DC/DDS Drives In-Plant Training Program
GM FANUC Robotics
Spottool Electrical
S-420 RG Operations, Programming & Maintenance
GM FANUC Automation—Series O Maintenance
Yaskawa Electric Corporation, Kitakyushu, Japan

■ **RESUME 4 CONTINUED**
Stewart Graves's "After" Resume (Page 2)

PROFESSIONAL MANAGEMENT EXPERIENCE

AREA MANAGER—
MAINTENANCE

NISSAN MOTOR MANUFACTURING CORPORATION U.S.A. BODY ASSEMBLY PLANT SMYRNA, TENNESSEE, 1982 TO PRESENT

- *Company Track Record of Success:* Began in 1982 as a maintenance technician, then was promoted to lead maintenance technician, and then to area manager/maintenance. Continuously advanced throughout tenure to positions of higher levels of responsibility and authority. Positions and responsibilities are highlighted below.

- *Management, 1989 to Present:* Manage and direct overall operations and administration of the maintenance for the Body Assembly Plant at Nissan Motor Manufacturing. Have been responsible for managing the manufacturing teams that launched the new Sentra, the new Nissan truck, and the Altima. Worked for 4 years in the Sentra Truck & Assembly Plant and 3 years in the Altima Plant. Conduct ongoing analyses to evaluate the efficiency and quality of operations.

- *International Relations:* One of 6 managers selected to go to Japan for 6 months to train on IBAS. After training, was responsible for returning to U.S. to train employees in the IBAS System. Gained valuable experience in interacting with a foreign culture in a business environment. Established and maintained an excellent network of business relationships as a result of strong communication skills.

- *Company Reengineering:* Continuously reengineer production procedures to streamline operations, reduce downtime and labor costs, and increase overall profitability for company.

- *Business Planning:* Responsible for designing long-range planning and strategic goals for plant.

- *Personnel, Training, & Supervision:* Interview, hire, train, and supervise maintenance technicians. Delegate work responsibilities and monitor overall job performance to ensure accuracy and adherence to specifications. Coordinate all training for maintenance technicians.

- *Employee Relations:* Interact extensively with engineering, production, and outside vendors to manufacture body parts for vehicles. Encourage and support a teamlike work environment that increases employee efficiency and productivity.

- *Troubleshooter:* Investigate and identify problems with production, equipment, and/or employees. Implement creative problem-solving techniques to resolve issues.

- *Quality Control:* Monitor facilities and job procedures to ensure accuracy and adherence to OSHA and other federal, state, and local laws, rules, and regulations.

- *Equipment & Maintenance:* Responsible for investigating and monitoring production to detect faulty equipment. Perform preventive maintenance and repairs on all process equipment.

- *Lead Maintenance Technician, 1985 to 1989:* As lead maintenance technician, was responsible for assisting area manager and leading other maintenance technicians in troubleshooting and repairing equipment.

- *Maintenance Technician, 1982 to 1985:* As a maintenance technician, was responsible for general maintenance tasks, which included programming and troubleshooting robots, PLCs, and various drive systems.

JOURNEYMAN ELECTRICIAN

INTERNATIONAL BROTHERHOOD OF ELECTRICAL WORKERS, NASHVILLE, TENNESSEE, 1977 TO 1982

- *Electrician:* Responsible for installing, wiring, and maintaining various equipment for the Ford Glass Plant, Arnold Engineering & Development Center, and Detroit Aluminum & Brass.

■ **RESUME 5**
Crystal Griffin's "Before" Resume (Page 1)

HEART & SOUL TIP

Crystal's resume is far too bunched and crowded and isn't written well. Details need to be highlighted clearly and placed in a more pleasing format.

PROFESSIONAL RESUME

OF

CRYSTAL GRIFFIN

879 ANYWHERE STREET

CITY, STATE 10000 PHONE NUMBER

JOB OBJECTIVE

STAGEHAND

—THEATRICAL PROFESSIONAL WITH STAGEHAND BACKGROUND—
—EXPERIENCED WITH THEME PARKS, MUSICALS, COMEDIES & DRAMAS, INCLUDING SHOW
& JAZZ CHOIRS—EXPERIENCED WITH VARIOUS TYPES OF MICROPHONES—WORKS AS A TEAM
PLAYER—ABILITY TO ENDURE REPETITION—ABLE TO RECOGNIZE PROBLEMATIC SITUA-
TIONS ON STAGE AND PLAN AHEAD FOR RESOLUTION—ABILITY TO KEEP CALM IN EVEN
THE MOST TENSE SITUATIONS—EXPERIENCED WITH PNEUMATIC PLATFORMS—PAYS KEEN
ATTENTION TO DETAIL—

Bright and talented professional stage technician, one with a B.S. degree
in communications from Western Michigan University with a minor in
Technical Theatre. Enjoyed broad experience in theatrical productions,
serving a number of times as stagehand, but also as: ASSISTANT DIRECTOR,
STAGE MANAGER, ASSISTANT STAGE MANAGER, AUDIO TECHNICIAN, FOLLOW SPOT OPER-
ATOR AND LIGHT BOARD OPERATOR. Worked efficiently with well-respected
Opryland U.S.A, as well as with show and jazz choirs, involving sound
equipment. Experienced with the use of live microphones during a production
and show property responsibility, in addition to being the type of STAGE-
HAND who projects a non-aggressive but nonetheless respected aura of professional etiquette. Able to keep cool even in the most critical of situations. Dedicated to the art, giving 100% of self to each and every project.

EQUPIMENT I HAVE USED:

    Microphones: SM48, SM58, SM81, Sony wireless (handheld and bodypack)
    Light Board: Two Scene Pre-set
    Audio Sound Board: Yamaha 24 Channel with portable Snake
    Follow Spots: Super-Trooper, Satellite HMI, 75 watts
    Pneumatic Interchangeable Platforms: Utilizing Pneumatic/Hydrogenoxide
    Rosco Fog Machines: Utilizing fog machine liquid
    Dry Ice Machines: Utilizing dry ice.

EDUCATIONAL   B.S. DEGREE IN COMMUNICATIONS, December 1985
CREDENTIALS   Western Michigan University, Kalamazoo, MI
             Majored in communications and minored in theater/technical,
             earning a "B" average overall.
             A.S. DEGREE IN GENERAL STUDIES

■ **RESUME 5 CONTINUED**
Crystal Griffin's "Before" Resume (Page 2)

PROFESSIONAL RESUME OF CRYSTAL GRIFFIN   page 2

CAREER   OPRYLAND U.S.A.   Summers 1983–November 1989
EXPERIENCES   and May–August 1992

1983 "I Hear America Singing," FOLLOW SPOT OPERATOR
1984 "I Hear America Singing," STAGEHAND
1985 "The Evening is Yours," on General Jackson Showboat,
FOLLOW SPOT OPERATOR.
1985 "Tennessee River Boys," LIGHT BOARD OPERATOR
1986 "The Evening is Yours," on General Jackson Showboat,
STAGEHAND
1987 "Showboat Follies of '22," on General Jackson Showboat,
STAGEHAND
1988 "Showboat Follies of '22," on General Jackson Showboat,
STAGEHAND
1989 "Our Land, Our Song," on General Jackson Showboat,
STAGEHAND
1992 "And the Winner is . . . ," STAGEHAND

OPRYLAND SPECIAL EVENTS July 1985-August 1987
Worked with various acts and industrials as STAGEHAND and
FOLLOW SPOT OPERATOR.

TENNESSEE REPERTORY THEATER, Nashville, TN, October-December
1992 "Grease" STAGEHAND, "TWELFTH NIGHT" STAGEHAND, "IT'S A
WONDERFUL LIFE," (United States Premier) STAGEHAND, Union
affiliated.

NASHVILLE SHAKESPEARE FESTIVAL, Nashville, TN August 1991
"Othello" ASSISTANT STAGE MANAGER

A.C.T.I., Nashville, TN—May 1991
"An Evening with Albee and Wiliams: The Zoo Story and 27
Wagons of Cotton—Two 1 act plays," STAGE MANAGER

ACTORS PLAYHOUSE, Nashvlle, TN December 1991
Titus Andronicus, ASSISTANT DIRECTOR

CIRCLE PLAYERS, Nashville, TN 1989-1991
1989, Brigadoon, STAGEHAND
1990, Joseph and the Amazing Technicolor Dreamcoat, LOFT
TECHNICIAN
1990, Kiss Me Kate, STAGEHAND
1990, Camelot, ASSISTANT STAGE MANAGER
1991, The Dining Room, STAGE MANAGER

HEART & SOUL TIP

Again , in this version, details are too crowded together and need a more pleasing format.

PROFESSIONAL RESUME OF CRYSTAL GRIFFIN   page 3

TRUE GRIST DINNER THEATER, Homer, MI September-December 1981
Grease, Tribute, On Golden Pond, and Deathtrap. Served as
STAGEHAND, Union affiliated/NETC associated.

JACKSON CIVIC PLAYERS February 1981
Love Rides the Rails, STAGE MANAGER

CLARK LAKE PLAYERS, Jackson, MI July 1981-August 1982
1981, Gigi, FOLLOW SPOT OPERATOR
1982, Cole, STAGE MANAGER
1982, The Sound of Music, ASSISTANT STAGE MANAGER

ETC… COMPANY, Jackson, MI September - December 1982
Jackson Community College
When You Coming Back, Red Ryder?, ASSISTANT STAGE MANAGER
A shot in the Dark, STAGE MANAGER

STARFLEET AMBASSADORS SHOW CHOIR September 1980-1982
Jackson Community College, Jackson, MI
Served as STAGE MANAGER/AUDIO ENGINEER (handling both responsibilities simultaneously), averaging 25 local performances
per semester and 2 annual concerts per year.

JACKSON ROSE QUEEN PAGEANT, Jackson, MI May 1983
Served as STAGEHAND
Rated high among local Miss America affiliate pageants across
the United States.

GOLD COMPANY I & II VOCAL JAZZ CHOIR September 1983-Dec. 1984
Western Michigan University, Kalamazoo, MI
Served as ASSISTANT AUDIO ENGINEER. Assisted head engineer in
all aspects of sound reinforcement. Averaged 70 shows per
semester and 2 annual concerts per year.

WESTERN MICHIGAN UNIVERSITY THEATER DEPARTMENT, Sept. 1983
Western Michigan University, Kalamazoo, MI
Gypsy, FOLLOW SPOT OPERATOR

GOLD COMPANY VOCAL JAZZ CLINICS March of 1983 & 1984
Western Michigan University, Kalamazoo, MI
Served as ASSISTANT AUDIO ENGINEER for state renowned jazz
artists and attended classes as well.

■ **RESUME 5**
Crystal Griffin's "After" Resume (Cover Sheet)

HEART & SOUL TIP

This version is pleasing to the eye and easy to read! .

A PRESENTATION OF EXECUTIVE CREDENTIALS
IN BROADCAST PRODUCTION

CRYSTAL GRIFFIN

879 Anywhere Street
City, State 10000
Phone Number

■ **RESUME 5 CONTINUED**
Crystal Griffin's "After" Resume (Page 1)

HEART & SOUL TIP

We have attended to the details in this Heart & Soul version and organized the resume to be easier to read. We simplied her Objective, which was too cluttered on the "before" resume.

PROFESSIONAL OBJECTIVE & PROFILE

Multitalented and experienced stage and theater production professional is seeking a position that will fully utilize more than 18 years of experience in all facets of production operations. Self-motivated and self-directed, with ability to work independently or as a team player. Detail-oriented, strong leader and motivator of others.

Skilled in problem resolution and committed to maintaining the highest standards of professionalism and work ethics. Desire a position that will provide a challenging opportunity to significantly contribute to a full-scale production.

EDUCATION

BACHELOR OF SCIENCE DEGREE IN COMMUNICATIONS
Minor: Theater/Technical
Western Michigan University, Kalamazoo

SUMMARY OF QUALIFICATIONS

MANAGEMENT

Have worked as stage manager for numerous productions and was responsible for directing overall operations of production. Trained and supervised staff members. Delegated work responsibilities and monitored overall job performance to ensure accuracy and adherence to specifications.

PRODUCTION ACCOMPLISHMENTS

In-depth background in positions such as stage manager, director, assistant stage manager, production assistant, stagehand, audio technician, follow spot operator, and light board operator. Provided services for all genres of production, including theater, music concerts, musicals, comedies, dramas, theme parks, show and jazz choirs.

TECHNICAL AREAS OF EXPERTISE

Microphones:	SM 48, SM 58, SM 81, Sony wireless (handheld & bodypack)
Lighting:	Light boards—Two-scene pre-set
	Follow spots—Super-Trooper, Satellite HMI, 75 watts
Audio Engineering:	Audio sound board—Yamaha 24-channel with portable snake
Stage:	Pneumatic interchangeable platforms, utilizing pneumatic/hydrogen oxide
Machines:	Rosco fog machines, utilizing fog-machine liquid Dry-ice machines

EMPLOYEE RELATIONS

Encourage and support a teamlike work environment, which increases employee morale, efficiency, and productivity. Strong interpersonal and communication skills.

■ **RESUME 5 CONTINUED**
Crystal Griffin's "After" Resume (Page 2)

HEART & SOUL TIP

We designed the details of her jobs to make them easier to read.

PROFESSIONAL PRODUCTION EXPERIENCE

PRODUCTION & STAGE ASSISTANT	**TENNESSEE REPERTORY THEATER—UNION AFFILIATION** **NASHVILLE, TENNESSEE**

West Side Story *Grease*
Twelfth Night *It's a Wonderful Life*
To Kill a Mockingbird *Hamlet*

PRODUCTION & STAGE ASSISTANT
FOLLOW SPOT OPERATOR
LIGHT BOARD OPERATOR

OPRYLAND SPECIAL EVENTS & OPRYLAND U.S.A.
NASHVILLE, TENNESSEE
And the Winner Is
Our Land, Our Song, General Jackson Showboat
The General Jackson All-Star Revue, General Jackson Showboat
Showboat Follies of '22, General Jackson Showboat (2 years running)
The Evening Is Yours, General Jackson Showboat (2 years running)
Tennessee River Boys
I Hear America Singing

STAGE MANAGER

A.C.T.I.
NASHVILLE, TENNESSEE
An Evening with Albee & Williams
The Zoo Story & 27 Wagons of Cotton—two one-act plays

ASSISTANT DIRECTOR

ACTORS PLAYHOUSE
NASHVILLE, TENNESSEE
Titus Andronicus

STAGE MANAGER & ASSISTANT STAGE MANAGER & STAGE HAND

CIRCLE PLAYERS
NASHVILLE, TENNESSEE
Little Shop of Horrors (SH) *Brigadoon* (SH)
Cabaret (SH) *The Dining Room* (SM)
Camelot (ASM) *Kiss Me Kate* (SH)
Joseph and the Amazing Technicolor Dreamcoat (SH)

■ **RESUME 5 CONTINUED**
Crystal Griffin's "After" Resume (Page 3)

PROFESSIONAL PRODUCTION EXPERIENCE

PRODUCTION ASSISTANT   TRUE GRIST DINER THEATER, UNION AFFILIATION
HOMER, MICHIGAN

Grease	*Tribute*
On Golden Pond	*Deathtrap*

STAGE MANAGER   JACKSON CIVIC PLAYERS
JACKSON, MICHIGAN
Love Rides the Rails

STAGE MANAGER,   CLARK LAKE PLAYERS
ASSISTANT   JACKSON, MICHIGAN
STAGE MANAGER &   *Gigi*
FOLLOW SPOT OPERATOR   *The Sound of Music*
Cole

STAGE MANAGER &   STARFLEET AMBASSADORS SHOW CHOIR
AUDIO ENGINEER   JACKSON COMMUNITY COLLEGE
JACKSON, MICHIGAN
Provided services for 25 local performances and 2 annual concerts. Set up and
performed sound check for rehearsals and performances.

PRODUCTION ASSISTANT   JACKSON ROSE QUEEN PAGEANT, JACKSON, MICHIGAN

ASSISTANT   GOLD COMPANY I & II VOCAL JAZZ CHOIR
AUDIO ENGINEER   WESTERN MICHIGAN UNIVERSITY
KALAMAZOO, MICHIGAN
Provided services for 70 shows and 2 annual concerts, handling both simultaneously.

ASSISTANT   GOLD COMPANY VOCAL JAZZ CLINICS
AUDIO ENGINEER   KALAMAZOO, MICHIGAN
Worked as engineer for state-renowned jazz clinics and jazz artists.

FOLLOW SPOT OPERATOR   WESTERN MICHIGAN UNIVERSITY THEATER DEPARTMENT
KALAMAZOO, MICHIGAN
Gypsy

■ **RESUME 6**
James Hamby's "Before" Resume

HEART & SOUL TIP

This has no career focus. There is little attention to the details, and the aesthetic quality of the resume is poor.

JAMES HAMBY, M.D., F.A.C.S.
Urological Surgery and Psychiatry
212 Anywhere Street, City, State 10000
Phone Number

Board Certification
National Board Certified and American Board Certified—Urological Surgery

Licensure: Tennessee, Mississippi

Education
MD
TUFTS UNIVERSITY SCHOOL OF MEDICINE, Boston, Massachusetts, 1953

BA
BROWN UNIVERSITY, Providence, Rhode Island, 1949

Residency
Surgical Resident and Urology Resident, ORANGE MEMORIAL HOSPITAL, Orlando, Florida, 7/54
to 6/59
Internal Medicine, U.S. NAVAL HOSPITAL, Bethesda, Maryland, 7/53 to 6/54

Assistant Medical Director, 1990–1996
TENNESSEE DEPARTMENT OF HEALTH BUREAU OF TENNCARE, Nashville, Tennessee

Psychiatry, 1989–1996
CLINICAL SERVICES, INC., Memphis, Tennessee

Chief of Urology, 1987–1989
VETERANS ADMINISTRATION HOSPITAL, Montgomery, Alabama

Chief of Urology, 1984–1987
VETERANS ADMINISTRATION HOSPITAL, Biloxi, Mississippi

MURFREESBORO MEDICAL CLINIC, P.A., Murfreesboro, Tennessee, 1970 to 1984

HERTZLER CLINIC, Halstead, Kansas, 1959 to 1969

United States Navy, 1945 to 1946 and 1953 to 1954
Desert Storm, 98 GENERAL HOSPITAL, Nuremburg, Germany—1990 to 1991

■ **RESUME 6**
James Hamby's "After" Resume

HEART & SOUL TIP

In the Heart & Soul version, we listed a simple Career Profile that described this physician and his goals. It is a very specialized resume and doesn't need elaborate explanations.

JAMES HAMBY, M.D. F.A.C.S.
212 Anywhere Street
City, State 10000
Phone Number

CAREER PROFILE

Physician with more than 30 years of experience is seeking a part-time position in health care administration. Areas of specialty include urological surgery and psychiatry.

BOARD CERTIFICATION

National Board Certified and American Board Certified—Urological Surgery

PROFESSIONAL AFFILIATIONS

Primary Care Advisory Board, Present to 1999
Tennessee State Veteran's Home Board (TSVH), Present to 1999
American Medical Association   Stones River Medical Society
American College of Surgeons   Tennessee Medical Association

LICENSURE
Tennessee, Mississippi

EDUCATION

DOCTOR OF MEDICINE
Tufts University School of Medicine, Boston

BACHELOR OF SCIENCE DEGREE
Brown University, Providence, Rhode Island

RESIDENCY

SURGICAL RESIDENT   **ORANGE MEMORIAL HOSPITAL, ORLANDO, FLORIDA, MAY 1954 TO JUNE 1959**
& UROLOGY RESIDENT

INTERNAL MEDICINE   **U.S. NAVAL HOSPITAL, BETHESDA, MARYLAND, JULY 1953 TO JUNE 1959**

MEDICAL & ADMINISTRATIVE EXPERIENCE

1990 to 1996   **ASSISTANT MEDICAL DIRECTOR**
TENNESSEE DEPARTMENT OF HEALTH, BUREAU OF TENNCARE, Nashville
1989 to 1990   **PSYCHIATRY**
CLINICAL SERVICES, INC., Memphis, Tennessee
1987 to 1989   **CHIEF OF UROLOGY**
VETERANS ADMINISTRATION HOSPITAL, Montgomery, Alabama
1984 to 1987   **CHIEF OF UROLOGY**
VETERANS ADMINISTRATION HOSPITAL, Biloxi, Mississippi
1970 to 1984   MURFREESBORO MEDICAL CLINIC, Murfreesboro, Tennessee
1959 to 1969   HERTZLER CLINIC, Halstead, Kansas

MILITARY

United States Navy, 1945 to 1946 and 1953 to 1954
Desert Storm, 98 GENERAL HOSPITAL, Nuremburg, Germany, 1990 to 1991

Latania Kelly's "Before" Resume

HEART & SOUL TIP

This resume needs a Career Objective & Profile, as well as extensive writing about her jobs and qualifications. It is incomplete.

Latania Kelly

113 Anywhere Street
City, State 10000
Phone Number

Education

BS
Major in Accounting
WILBERFORCE UNIVERSITY, Wilberforce, Ohio

Military—UNITED STATES ARMY, 1983 to 1989

Professional Experience

Dispatcher & Load Planner
MOTOR FREIGHT COMPANY
Fremont, Ohio—1994 to Present
Schedule pickup of freight. Dispatch orders to drivers.
Work with customers and help them with problems.

Shipping Administrator & Traffic Clerk
CROWN BATTERY MANUFACTURING COMPANY
Fremont, Ohio—1991 to 1994
Schedule pickup of freight. Dispatch orders to drivers.
Work with customers and help them with problems. Also, prepare invoices.

UNITED STATES ARMY, 1983 to 1989
Worked in material planning for a military facility in Europe. Supervised enlisted soldiers. Trained solders in supplies. Also, worked with budget and quality control, and inventory and purchasing.

■ **RESUME 7**
Latania Kelly's "After" Resume (Page 1)

HEART & SOUL TIP

In the Heart & Soul version, we have focused on her goals and highlighted qualifications to support these goals.

LATANIA KELLY
113 Anywhere Street
City, State 10000
Phone Number

PROFESSIONAL OBJECTIVE & PROFILE

Highly qualified manager and business administrator with over 13 years of experience building and leading integrated operations in inventory, purchasing, customer service, traffic, and budget management. Consistently successful in managing and directing multidisciplinary operations. Strong general management qualifications in strategic planning, capital equipment acquisition, and process/productivity/quality improvement. Excellent experience in customer service, personnel training & development, office administration, and leadership.

Seeking a management position that will provide a challenging opportunity for significantly contributing to a company's efficiency, organization, growth, and profitability.

SUMMARY OF QUALIFICATIONS

TRACK RECORD OF SUCCESS
Background exemplifies a successful track record of career accomplishments, which include more than 13 years of professional experience, encompassing positions such as dispatcher and load planner, shipping administrator and traffic clerk, and materials analyst and supervisor. Continuously advanced to positions of higher levels of authority and responsibility throughout career.

MANAGEMENT & PERSONNEL
Skilled in managing and directing multidisciplinary operations within companies. Experienced in training and supervising personnel staff members.

TIME MANAGEMENT
Ability to prioritize responsibilities and manage multiple projects simultaneously. Detail-oriented and extremely organized. Skilled in working in fast-paced, hectic environments.

LEADERSHIP & EMPLOYEE RELATIONS
Strong leader and motivator of others. Ability to effectively guide and direct associates to achieve their highest potential. Encourage and support a teamlike work environment, which results in increased efficiency and productivity.

ACCOUNTING
Experience as an accounting trainee for National Aeronautics and Space Administration (NASA) while in college. This trainee position provided valuable experience in accounts payable, general ledger, and bookkeeping.

COMPUTER OPERATIONS
Experienced in all types of computerized systems and specialized computer software.

EDUCATION & ADVANCED TRAINING

BACHELOR OF SCIENCE DEGREE IN ACCOUNTING
Wilberforce University, Wilberforce, Ohio

Leadership & Development, United States Army
Material Control & Accounting, United States Army

MILITARY

United States Army, 1983 to 1989

■ **RESUME 7 CONTINUED**
Latania Kelly's "After" Resume (Page 2)

LATANIA KELLY   Page 2

PROFESSIONAL EXPERIENCE

DISPATCHER
& LOAD PLANNER

MOTOR FREIGHT COMPANY
FREMONT, OHIO, 1994 TO PRESENT
- *Dispatcher:* Responsible for coordinating and scheduling pickup of freight, which involves researching and determining which carriers to use based on rates, reliability, and service. Responsible for dispatching changes in orders to drivers when necessary.
- *Customer Service:* Provide superior service to customers by effectively responding to requests, inquiries, suggestions, and/or concerns regarding shipping of freight.
- *Troubleshooter:* Investigate and research freight to identify and determine problematic areas. Utilize creative problem-solving techniques to resolve issues.

SHIPPING
ADMINISTRATOR
& TRAFFIC CLERK

CROWN BATTERY MANUFACTURING COMPANY
FREMONT, OHIO, 1991 TO 1994
- *Traffic:* Responsibilities were basically the same as those described above and included all areas of dispatching, invoicing, customer service, and troubleshooting.
- *Shipping:* Guided and directed overall operations for shipping and distribution. Prepared shipping reports, bills of lading, packing and load lists as needed.
- *Invoices:* Responsible for preparing invoices for customers regarding freight, including preparing Canadian customs invoices.

MATERIALS ANALYST
& SUPERVISOR

UNITED STATES ARMY
CALIFORNIA AND EUROPE, 1983 TO 1989
Began as a supply technician in California in 1983 and advanced to management position in 1986. Responsibilities were comprehensive and included the following areas of expertise.
- *Management—Materials Analyst:* Directed and managed all materials planning, capital equipment acquisition, and procurement and supply operations for more than 650 separate communication system parts for military facility in Europe.
- *Personnel Supervision:* Managed and supervised employees. Delegated work responsibilities and monitored overall job performance to ensure accuracy and adherence to standards, rules, and regulations.
- *Training:* Trained and oriented staff members in all areas of procurement and supply operations.
- *Budget Analysis & Management:* Administered funds allocated for operations and general expenditures. Analyzed budget variances and initiated appropriate strategies to more aggressively control expenditures.
- *Quality Control—Inspections:* Oversaw inspections of customer supply operations and procedures to ensure accuracy and adherence to rules, regulations, and standards.
- *Inventory & Purchasing:* Monitored inventory levels by analyzing computerized reports and determined needs for purchasing. Researched all inventory discrepancies and updated and maintained inventory system as needed.

References Available Upon Request

■ **RESUME 8**
Steven Menendez's "Before" Resume

HEART & SOUL TIP

In this version there is no strong career focus, and the design of the resume is poor.

Stephen Menendez
334 Anywhere Street, City, State 10000 Phone Number

Education

Embry Riddle	Aeronautical Science
California State University	Communications
United Parcel Service	Executive Management
Flight Safety	Lear Jet

Experience

Aviation/California West Airlines
Responsibilities: Vice President of Operations
Responsible for ramp personnel, maintenance team, pilots, entire marketing operations and traffic management program. Arranged and hosted corporate functions and special events: Hunt Oil, Fruit of the Loom, Seattle Seahawks, Kenny Rogers, etc.
Accomplishments: Negotiated contracts with numerous companies American Airlines, Fruit of the Loom, Federal Express, Continental, UPS, World Airways and numerous operators. Assumed control of FBO with no money, employees, fuel or customers.
Generated $100,000 per month income within 6 months. Grew charter department from $65,000 to $700,000 per month within 3 years.
Developed inventory system for $2,000,000 in parts.
Developed distribution system that saved over $600,000.
Fuel/defuel 727, 737, MD-80, DC 10, MD-11, ATP with type rating SA-227. SIC Lear 20 & 30 series aircraft.

US ARMY
Operations Officer/PIC/Safety Officer/Desert Storm 1985—1991
Responsibilities: Company Operations Officer of 15 Black Hawks
All mission control, logistics and maintenance support.
Entire flying program of 3800 total hours at $1700 per hour.
Conduct aviation classes for ground support units.
Accomplishments: 1 of 8 pilots (selected from a pool of 158) to fly covert Cyprus and Beirut operations.
Selected to fly numerous dignitaries (US Ambassador to Germany)
Combat Experience
Selected to fly for the Drug Enforcement Agency, as company s safety officer & executive officer during Desert Shield, to fly commanding general and all support missions, to fly flight lead for reconnaissance missions into Iraq. To fill post as aviation liaison officer to the commanding staff.

Continental Award, Night Shift Manager, 1984—1985

■ **RESUME 8**
Stephen Menendez's "After" Resume (Cover Sheet)

HEART & SOUL TIP

In this version we highlighted special quali-fications in the descriptions of Stephen's jobs and focused on the details to make his skills more marketable.

A PRESENTATION OF EXECUTIVE CREDENTIALS

STEPHEN MENENDEZ

334 Anywhere Street
City, State 10000
Phone Number

■ **RESUME 8 CONTINUED**
Stephen Menendez's "After" Resume (Page 1)

HEART & SOUL TIP

This profile has a strong, proactive career focus.

EXECUTIVE PROFILE

High-caliber, aggressive air charter operations executive, with more than 7 years of experience building and leading integrated operations for Aviation/California West Airlines. An experienced pilot with more than 20 years of comprehensive experience encompassing positions in management, safety, logistics, maintenance, and business operations.

Skilled executive liaison who is extremely talented and successful in developing, building, and expanding business operations through client development, contract negotiations and networking. Successful in leading business opportunities and marketing strategies to maximize growth and profitability and in accomplishing mission of integrated operations. Experienced in employee training, supervision, development, and leadership.

Desire a management and leadership position in aircraft operations that will provide a challenging opportunity for significantly contributing to a company's efficiency, organization, growth, and profitability.

EDUCATION

MASTER'S DEGREE IN AERONAUTICAL SCIENCE
Area of Concentration: Management
Embry Riddle University, Sacramento, California

BACHELOR OF ARTS DEGREE IN COMMUNICATIONS
California State University, Hayward

HEART & SOUL TIP

Observe in this version how we have fine-tuned the details in the "Advanced Training" section.

ADVANCED TRAINING

Executive management, United Parcel Service, Oakland, California
Lear Jet, flight safety, Tucson, Arizona
Metro Turbo Prop, flight safety, San Antonio, Texas
Dunker Qualification, United States Army, Jacksonville, Florida
Officer Candidate School

PROFESSIONAL AWARDS

Recipient of numerous awards while in the U.S. Army, including the Army Commendation Medal (3), Air Medal, and Defense Medal.

EXECUTIVE EXPERIENCE

VICE PRESIDENT OF OPERATIONS
**AVIATION/CALIFORNIA WEST AIRLINES ,
CALIFORNIA, 1992 TO 1997 AND 1982 TO 1984**
- *Company Track Record of Success:* Recruited to work for Aviation/California West Airlines as a vice president and general manager after completion of tour in U.S. Army. Advanced to executive position of vice president of operations and assumed higher levels of responsibility and authority.
- *Charter Department Development:* Initially recruited to direct an aggressive development and staffing of company fixed base operations, which included developing a complete charter department. (FBO had no assets, employees, or customers). Totally in charge of building business from ground up through sales, networking, and successfully negotiated contracts. Responsible for obtaining federal agreements for fueling customs and border patrol aircraft.
- *Profitability:* Grew charter from $65,000 to $700,000 per month within 3 years and generated $100,000 per month in income within 6 months, which significantly increased profitability for company.

■ **RESUME 8 CONTINUED**
Stephen Menendez's "After" Resume (Page 2)

HEART & SOUL TIP

Attention to detail is implemented in describing his jobs, areas of expertise, and qualifications.

EXECUTIVE EXPERIENCE

VICE PRESIDENT OF OPERATIONS

- *Executive Management:* Manage and direct overall operations for this company which includes administration, marketing, traffic operations, personnel, and maintenance. Held full decision-making authority for developing financial objectives and preparing long-range strategic business plans. Conducted ongoing analyses to evaluate the efficiency, productivity and quality of multidisciplinary operations.
- *Account Management:* Managed new business development and strategic planning to maximize growth and profitability. Established growth plans for individual accounts and personally managed account calls, presentations, and negotiations.
- *Marketing:* Launched a series of companywide marketing strategies to reposition company in marketplace and to achieve revenue growth and profitability.
- *Inventory & Distribution Systems Development:* Reengineered, designed, and implemented an inventory system that included more than $2 million in equipment and parts, and developed a distribution system that yielded savings of more than $600,000 for company.
- *Public Relations—Special Events:* Held high-visibility public relations position as the direct liaison to major corporate clients, community leaders, government officials, and national association members. Organized and hosted special events for celebrities and notable public officials.
- *Budget Management:* Managed, analyzed and projected budget for operating expenditures. Analyzed budget variances and initiated appropriate guidelines to more aggressively control expenditures. Established budget guidelines and operated within budgets.
- *Materials Analyst—Purchasing:* Negotiated, controlled, and maintained capital equipment, materials, and supplies. Analyzed and established strategic plans regarding equipment.
- *General Manager:* While employed with company, served as general manager of several areas, including Texas FBO, Hayward FBO, and Stockton FBO, in conjunction with managing entire traffic operations.

OPERATIONS OFFICER & SAFETY OFFICER

DESERT STORM, UNITED STATES ARMY, 1985 TO 1991
- *Aviation Management:* Managed and supervised aviation activities in Desert Storm. Responsible for all mission control, logistics, and maintenance of aircraft.
- *Education/Instruction:* Taught aviation classes for ground-support units.
- *Pilot:* One of 8 pilots selected to fly in the Cyprus and Beirut operations.

MANAGER

CONTINENTAL AWARD, CALIFORNIA, 1984 TO 1985
- *Management:* Responsible for managing overall operations and administration of business during the night shift for this company, which was the second-largest food distributor in the U.S.
- *Cost & Inventory Control:* After taking over management, decreased overall labor costs and increased productivity from 57% to 90%.
- *Personnel & Supervision:* Delegated work responsibilities and supervised overall job performance.

■ **RESUME 9**
Allison Meyers's "Before" Resume

HEART & SOUL TIP

Here, the parents wrote a resume for their baby to get modeling jobs. It is written more like a letter and doesn't have much eye appeal.

Paula and John Meyers
4300 Anywhere Street
City, State 10000
Phone Number

To whom it may concern:

We would like to have our daughter, Allison, model for your television commercial and/or print advertisement, or anything that might be available. We believe she has a lot of talents and is a very beautiful baby. She has been in a number of commercials and is a very friendly baby. We have listed her skills below.

* She can crawl and stand up.
* Her day care teacher said that she's her star pupil and giggles all the time.
* She's very easy to get along with.
* She was born 2/29/96, has blond hair and blue eyes. She weighs 20 lbs., and wears a size 9-months in dress. She's 2 ½ feet tall.
* She smiles all the time.
* Electric commercial, Nashville, Tennessee
* Baby food commercial, Chicago, Illinois
* On-air talent, actress, baby diaper commercial, Nashville, Tennessee

■ **RESUME 9**
Allison Meyers's "After" Resume

HEART & SOUL TIP

In the Heart & Soul version, we have written an Objective & Profile and added lots of career focus and detail.

ALLISON "ALLIE" MEYERS

Paula & John Meyers, Parents
4300 Anywhere Street
City, State 10000
Phone Number

PROFESSIONAL OBJECTIVE & PROFILE

Extremely vivacious and talented, I am above my age group in all areas of performing and basic lifeskills. Already crawling and standing up, I adore the camera and know how to really ham it up. My day care teacher recently said, "She's my star pupil. She giggles all the time." That's because I'm happy, very cooperative, nondemanding, and easy to work with.

My goals are to model for print and broadcast, including television commercials, promotional public service announcements, and/or corporate industrial films. I am open to discussing any professional job with potential for career growth and professional advancement.

PERSONAL

Date of Birth: 2/29/96   Weight: 20 lbs.
Hair: Blonde   Height: 30"
Eyes: Sparkling blue   Dress size: 9 months
Shoe size: 3

SUMMARY OF SPECIAL TALENTS

Smiles on cue when you say "cheese."
Adorable, with very outgoing, friendly personality.
Expert in giggling and flashing "baby blues" at camera.
Runway experience includes crawling around the floor. Can stand alone.
Excellent public speaking skills with ability to say "Mama" and "Da-Da."
Very team-oriented. Loves to work with other models.
Poised and professional. Can eat meals with only a few messes on face, clothes, and floor.
Prefers applesauce and bananas.
Can look confused and disoriented upon request.

PROFESSIONAL EXPERIENCE

Actress, NES TV commercial, Nashville, TN
Actress, Baby food TV commercial, Chicago, IL
Actress, Baby diaper TV commercial, Nashville, TN

■ **RESUME 10**
April Morningstar's "Before" Resume

HEART & SOUL TIP

In this version, April needs a proactive career objective. She has much more experience than she put on her resume. She had always been told to "keep it to one page" and as a result left off very important information. Also, this font is too "artsy" and hard to read and inappropriate for a non-creative type of job.

April Morningstar
1203 Anywhere Street
City, State 10000

Objective:
A position in Environmental Resource Management -

Education:
MS in Environmental Resource Management & Administration
New England Graduate School, Keene, NH
BS in Education, University of Connecticut, Stores, CT

Highlight of Qualifications
--Motivated, creative, willing to assume responsibility and take pride in achieving goals.
--Communicate and work well with all types of people.
--Talent for seeing the whole picture with sharp eye for details to narrow and define project.
--Equally effective working as enthusiastic team member or independently.
--Quick learner and proven ability to work in challenging conditions.

Relevant Work Experience
Economic & Environmental Planning, Dove Lake Paiute Tribe, Dove Lake, Nevada
--Researched and facilitated program planning, funding and analysis.
--Establishment of long and short term community development while ensuring preservation of historic sites and federally listed threatened trout within fragile high plains desert ecosystem.
--Presented to and represented a sovereign council government with interagency relations, bid and contractual negotiation.
--Researched CPR laws sovereign government to state and federal authority relations.
--Drafted and facilitated passage of multiple resolutions and the first water pollution prevention ordinance for reservation.
--Initiated and negotiated a multifaceted community and infrastructure building constraints sensisitivity analysis scope for EIS evaluation.
--Grant writing, narrative reports and modification requests.

Environmental Auditor, 1995–1996 -
--Conducted multi-media EPA and OSHA regulatory audits.
--Wrote and presented audit reports.
--Assisted in annual emergency response operations training.
--Consulted water purification plant on hazardous materials handling and emergency response including update of unwritten plan.

Engineering Assistant, 1994-1996
--Responsible for creation of ISO 14000 Manual, Policy and Procedures for registration services.
--Selected in-house inspectors for ISO 9000 auditor traiing.
--Negotiated bids and hiring of accredited training company.

HEART & SOUL TIP

No name or address of company: incomplete and evasive.

■ **RESUME 10**
April Morningstar's "After" Resume (Cover Sheet)

HEART & SOUL TIP

In this version we designed a more focused Objective & Profile, and highlighted specific job titles within the job descriptions, making it easier to read.

A PRESENTATION OF ECONOMIC
AND ENVIRONMENTAL PLANNING CREDENTIALS

APRIL MORNINGSTAR

1203 Anywhere Street
City, State 10000
Phone Number

■ **RESUME 10 CONTINUED**
April Morningstar's "After" Resume (Page 1)

PROFESSIONAL OBJECTIVE & PROFILE

Talented environmental resource manager and administrator is seeking a position that will fully utilize more than 5 years of comprehensive experience building and leading integrated operations in environmental consulting, auditing, waste engineering, nuclear operations security, program development, and training. Strong focus on the International Organization of Standardization (ISO 14000) environmental management system. Especially talented in long- and short-term analysis of economic and environmental development plans in relation to federal, state, and local laws and regulations.

Seeking a position in a progressive organization that will provide a challenging opportunity for significantly contributing to its environmental resource program through effective planning, analysis, and teamwork.

EDUCATION

MASTER OF SCIENCE DEGREE IN ENVIRONMENTAL RESOURCE MANAGEMENT
Antioch New England Graduate School, Keene, New Hampshire

BACHELOR OF SCIENCE DEGREE IN SCIENCE & BIOLOGY
University of Connecticut, Storrs

Advanced ISO 14000 & BS 7750 Auditor Certification Course

PROFESSIONAL EXPERIENCE

ECONOMIC &
ENVIRONMENTAL
PLANNING MANAGER

DOVE LAKE PAIUTE TRIBE, DOVE LAKE, NEVADA, 1996 TO PRESENT
- *Management:* Guide and direct overall economic and environmental planning operations for a reservation encompassing 10,000 sq. ft. and 80 tribe members. Conduct ongoing analyses to evaluate the efficiency, quality, and productivity of economic and environmental program planning.
- *Community Relations:* Establish and continuously maintain an exemplary network of business associates, using extensive interaction and strong communication skills.
- *Environmental Legislation:* Responsible for drafting and implementing the first water-pollution prevention ordinance for the reservation, which incorporated multiple resolutions.
- *Public Speaking:* Interagency Liaison: Public spokesperson and representative of the tribe's Council regarding interagency relations and contract negotiations.
- *Program Development:* Research, develop, and facilitate community programs that focus on economic and environmental planning, funding, and analysis.
- *Community & Public Affairs:* Responsible for establishing mandates, policies, and procedures for long- and short-term community development and preservation of historical sites and federally listed threatened trout within high-plains desert ecosystem.
- *Writing & Editing:* Write and edit newsletters for reservation to provide information regarding economic and environmental development in the community. Also write and submit grants, reports, and modification requests.

HEART & SOUL TIP

Notice how highlighting job titles within job descriptions make them easier to read.

■ **RESUME 10 CONTINUED**
April Morningstar's "After" Resume (Page 2)

PROFESSIONAL EXPERIENCE

ENVIRONMENTAL
AUDITOR—INTERN

ENVIRONMENTAL COMPANIES, INC., LAS VEGAS, NEVADA - 1995 TO 1996
- *Quality Control:* Responsible for reviewing and monitoring facilities to ensure adherence to EPA and OSHA regulations, standards, and rules. Conducted multimedia EPA and OSHA audits and wrote and presented assessment reports. Provided information to the Providence Water Purification Plant regarding hazardous materials handling and emergency response. Wrote and revised emergency response plan.
- *Training:* Assisted in training staff members in emergency response operations.

ENGINEERING ASSISTANT

HARTFORD STEAM BOILER INSPECTION & INSURANCE COMPANY
HARTFORD, CONNECTICUT, 1994 TO 1996
- *Policy Development—Writing & Editing:* Responsible for developing, co-writing, and implementing an ISO 9000 manual in everyday operations. Also created and developed policies and procedures for the ISO 14000 manual for registration services.
- *Contract Negotiations:* Negotiated contract for hiring an accredited training company.
- *Event Planning:* Organized training seminar and coordinated travel itineraries for company employees. Selected in-house inspectors to receive ISO 9000 auditor training.
- *Marketing:* Assisted in creating and developing innovative marketing materials for engineering services.

ASSISTANT IN WASTE
ENGINEERING &
ENFORCEMENT DIVISION—
INTERN

STATE OF CONNECTICUT STATE DEPARTMENT OF ENVIRONMENTAL PROTECTION (DEP)
HARTFORD, CONNECTICUT, 1995 TO 1996
- *Environmental Equity Program:* Responsible for researching and assessing the Environmental Equity Program. Created and implemented a tracking spreadsheet that more efficiently and accurately tracked system.
- *ISO 14000:* Introduced the ISO 14000 to DEP personnel.
- *Environmental Analysis:* Analyzed and evaluated proposed HWIR RCRA exit-level criteria with comparative analysis to existing water-quality exit data.

NUCLEAR OPERATIONS
ASSISTANT, SECURITY &
AUDITING

NORTHEAST UTILITIES, BERLIN, CONNECTICUT, 1992 TO 1994
- *Auditing:* Responsible for auditing contractor files and tracking company audits to determine progress on implementation of corrective action.
- *National Liaison:* Communications liaison responsible for communicating critical information regarding nuclear-operations systems on a national scale.
- *Computer Program Development:* Assisted in developing a cost-effective, nationwide computer access authorization index system, which streamlined operations and increased efficiency. Also developed a Lotus expense-tracking system.
- *Research:* Conducted research and analysis of CFR and NRC rules and regulations.
- *Supervision:* Supervised the microfilming of sensitive historical records.

■ **RESUME 11**
Danielle Olson's "Before" Resume

HEART & SOUL TIP

There is no career objective, the type is way too small to read, and this resume is incomplete—more recent experience is not included.

Danielle Olson
443 Anywhere Street
City, State 10000
Phone Number

Experience:
1982–1984

FAMILY ADVOCACY COORDINATOR (Army Community Services) Ft. McClellan, AL
Implemented Family Advocacy Pilot Program for the United States Army. Developed a postwide education program for the prevention of abuse to include writing scripts, developing slides and visual aids for presentations.
Spokesperson for FAP program to media, colleges, post and general public.
Provided crisis counseling and referrals.
Trained and supervised volunteers.
Performed administration duties associated with the FAP program.
Managed office records, statistics and information.
Additional responsibilities included operating victim's safe house, food basket for needy families, gathering statistical information on community resources, certifying child care homes.

Volunteer

FUNDRAISING DIRECTOR (Chemical Corps Museum) Ft. McClellan, AL
Experience: Launched initial fund raisers for museum, recruited broad base of groups to raise funds for museum, organized dinners, silent auctions, alumni mailouts, car washes and runs.
VOLUNTEER COORDINATOR (Chemical Corps Museum) Ft. McClellan, AL
Recruited original 35 charter volunteers, organized volunteer training, planned awards and recognition luncheons for volunteers, spokesperson to various groups to explain reorganization of museum and volunteer program.
VICE PRESIDENT, PARENT-TEACHER ORGANIZATION (Ft. McClellan Elementary)
Primary duty was to plan monthly programs and secure guest speakers. In addition, VP assisted in organizing two yearly fund raisers.
SECRETARY FOR PARENTS ASSOCIATION (Ft. McClellan Child Care Center)
Primary purpose to publish minutes, newsletter and publicize organization.
FUNDRAISING CHAIRPERSON
Responsible for organizing seasonal fundraising events.

EXPERIENCE
1979–1980

RESIDENT ADVISOR (Knoxville Job Corps Center), Knoxville, TN
Counseled large groups of disadvantaged youths.
Taught after school educational information program.
Provided appropriate referrals to youths with special needs.
Administrative duties included daily casework file updates and maintaining log book.

EXPERIENCE
1974–1977

HIGH SCHOOL COUNSELOR (Vicenza American High School), Vicenza, Italy
Counseled high school students in resident setting.
Advised on education, health, and multi-variable problems.
Referred students to other professionals in commuity for assistance.
Planned informational meetings with parents and students.
Organized student activities in Italian and military community.
Administrative duties included maintaining log book student files and performed clerical duties.

VOLUNTEER
EXPERIENCE

HIGH SCHOOL SPONSOR (Vicenza American High School), Vicenza, Italy
Chaperone to Senior Prom
Advisor to Senior Play

GUEST SPEAKER (Central Texas College), Vicenza, Italy
Spoke bimonthly to students attending "Careers of the 70's"

GIRL SCOUT ADVISOR (Girl Scouts of America) Vicenza, Italy
Events coordinator for all posts events.

EDUCATION

BA Liberal Arts (University of Tennessee), Knoxville, TN
Human Services in 1973

REFERENCES

Available on request.

■ **RESUME 11**
Danielle Olson's "After" Resume (Cover Sheet)

HEART & SOUL TIP

In this version we wrote a proactive Objective & Profile and then paid close attention to detail to describe Danielle's job functions.

A PRESENTATION OF PROFESSIONAL CREDENTIALS

DANIELLE OLSON

443 Anywhere Street
City, State 10000
Phone Number

■ **RESUME 11 CONTINUED**
Danielle Olson's "After" Resume (Page 1)

PROFESSIONAL OBJECTIVE & PROFILE

Highly motivated, goal-oriented business professional is seeking a position in human services that will fully utilize more than 20 years of experience building and leading integrated operations for residential facilities. Consistently successful in managing and directing multidisciplinary operations, which includes all facets of community affairs, public relations, marketing, personnel, budget, and client services. Extremely community service–oriented, with in-depth background in community services and teamwork.

Excellent experience in counseling, client relations, personnel training, development, and leadership. Seeking a position that will provide a challenging opportunity for significantly contributing to a company's efficiency, organization, growth, and profitability.

EDUCATION

BACHELOR OF ARTS DEGREE IN HUMAN SERVICES
University of Tennessee, Knoxville

HUMAN SERVICES EXPERIENCE

EXECUTIVE DIRECTOR **T.R.A.C. (TEMPORARY RESIDENCE FOR ADOLESCENTS IN CRISIS)**
NASHVILLE, TENNESSEE, 1990 TO 1995
- *Company Track Record of Success:* Began with T.R.A.C. as a primary adolescent counselor and after one year was promoted to executive director. Responsibilities were comprehensive and included the following areas of expertise.
- *Management:* Directed and managed overall operations and administration of this residential facility for teenagers in crisis. This involved creating and incorporating administrative policies and procedures for facility. As executive director, was on call 24 hours per day to advise staff in crisis situations. Facility was initially housed in two old houses, but after taking over management, I was able to work with board of directors to build and develop a state-of-the-art 11,000 sq. ft. facility.
- *Program Director:* As interim program director, developed and implemented program to meet to meet the residential, social, and recreational needs of residents. Ensured that program met state regulatory guidelines. Monitored facility and program performance to ensure compliance with state regulating agency.
- *Seminars & Public Speaking:* Facilitated seminars to educate the public on child abuse and for fundraising purposes, to promote new facility. Also spoke at meetings to promote the United Way of Tennessee.
- *Community Affairs:* Established and maintained an exemplary network of business associates, interacting extensively with community organizations, businesses, state and local officials, and individuals.
- *Family Relations:* Liaison between state and local officials, family members, residents, and residential facility. Strong interpersonal skills utilized in counseling, with ability to effectively communicate with diverse individuals. Worked closely with residents to reintegrate them into the family.
- *Personnel & Supervision:* Interviewed, hired, trained, and supervised 25 staff members, including primary and residential counselors, program director, and administrative staff.

■ **RESUME 11 CONTINUED**
Danielle Olson's "After" Resume (Page 2)

HUMAN RESOURCES EXPERIENCE

- *Budget Management:* Managed, analyzed, and administered budget for operating expenditures and capital asset projects. Responsible for financial performance analysis and business planning/development functions. Analyzed budget variances and initiated appropriate guidelines to more aggressively control expenditures. Established budget guidelines.
- *Counseling:* As a primary adolescent counselor, was responsible for providing individual, group, and family counseling for teenagers on a variety of topics, including drug and sexual abuse, behavior modification, and basic lifeskills. Responsible for needs assessment, which involved interviewing residents and determining specific needs for each individual.
- *Case Management:* Managed overall cases, which involved coordinating and scheduling activities and health care for individual residents.

FAMILY ADVOCACY
PROGRAM COORDINATOR
A.C.S. (ARMY COMMUNITY SERVICES), FT. MCCLELLAN, ALABAMA, 1982 TO 1985
- *Program Development:* Created and established educational program for military families and the public concerning the prevention of child and spousal abuse. Wrote and prepared audiovisual presentations.
- *Counseling:* Provided crisis counseling to victims of child and spousal abuse and neglect, both on site at Ft. McClellan and at area hospitals.
- *Educator & Training Coordinator:* Taught classes to teachers, child care workers, and hospital staff to train them how to recognize abuse.
- *Resource Management:* After assessing clients' needs, referred them to a variety of resources in human services, including clergy, community agencies, and health care professionals.
- *Case Management Team:* Member of the case management team, chaired by hospital commander, psychiatrist, police chief, and state protective services; responsible for reviewing critical cases.

GUIDANCE COUNSELOR
UNITED STATES DEPARTMENT OF DEFENSE
VICENZA AMERICAN HIGH SCHOOL, VICENZA, ITALY, 1974 TO 1977
- *Counselor:* Provided guidance counseling to teenagers in a residential/dormitory setting. Counseled students on education, health, and basic life issues.
- *Community Affairs:* Organized and supervised numerous community and travel activities and special events to integrate teenagers into new European cultural and social environments.
- *Resource Management:* After assessing students' needs, referred them to a variety of resources in human services, including clergy, community agencies, and health care professionals.
- *Family Relations:* Coordinated meetings with families to provide information regarding students' activities and academic status.

OTHER CAREER EXPERIENCE

RESIDENTIAL
COUNSELOR/ADVISOR
MINORITIES IN ACTION, KNOXVILLE, TENNESSEE, 1979 TO 1980

EXECUTIVE REPRESENTATIVE
DELTA AIRLINES, NASHVILLE, TENNESSEE, 1995 TO PRESENT

■ **RESUME 12**
Rebecca Patterson's "Before" Resume

HEART & SOUL TIP

This version has no career objective or focus. The words are crowded and hard to read.

Rebecca Patterson, 211 Anywhere Street, City, Country

EXPERIENCE:

INTERNATIONAL CRIMINAL TRIBUNAL FOR RWANDA, Kigali, Rwanda—May 1996 to Present
Assistant Trial Attorney: In charge of coordinating and directing the investigation of suspected war criminals responsible for the 1994 genocide, during which one million civilians were killed in Rwanda, Africa. Work involves interaction with over 40 different nationalities within the Tribunal on a daily basis. Prepare, draft and present legal indictments and other legal documents in Arusha, Tanzania. Develop overall strategy of genocide prosecutions. Responsible for conducting the trials of charged war criminals before the International Criminal Tribunal. Interact extensively with governments worldwide to coordinate investigations and apprehend Tribunal fugitives.

UNITED STATES ATTORNEY'S OFFICE, Santa Fe, New Mexico—August 1990 to May 1996
Assistant United States Attorney: Prosecuted federal crimes including narcotics conspiracies, wire and mail fraud, extortion, gun offenses and crimes committed on federal land, with substantial focus on violent crimes such as murder, aggravated assault and sex crimes. Involved in many long-term investigations with multi-agency task forces using various investigative methods such as wiretaps. Prepared numerous search warrants and also responsible for conducting extensive Federal Grand Jury proceedings. Prepared and argued federal criminal appeals before the Ninth Circuit Federal Court of Appeals in San Francisco, California. Responsible for prosecuting major federal crimes such as large narcotics conspiracies, bank robberies, kidnappings, extortion, wire & mail fraud, and other federal offenses. Substantial focus on violent crimes such as murder, aggravated assault and sex crimes.
OTHER EXPERIENCE: Attorney General's Advocacy Institute/Child Sex Abuse & Exploitation Seminar, Washington, D.C., June 1993, Criminal Trial Advocacy Course, Washington, D.C., June 1992, National Center for Missing & Exploited Children Training Center, Alexandria, Virginia, July 1992, Marana Law Enforcement Training Center/Investigation of Sex Crimes, Marana, New Mexico, October 1991, 8th National Symposium on Child Sexual Abuse, Huntsville, Alabama, February 1992
Conducted numerous informal trainings with various state, local and federal law enforcement agencies.

WOMBLE, CARLYLE, SANDRIDGE & RICE, Winston-Salem, North Carolina—1988 to 1990
Litigation Associate: Performed all activities involved with a general practice law firm, such as preparing, and arguing pre-trial motions; preparing and conducting discovery, analyzing and preparing defense strategy and conducting settlement conferences. Was 100% successful in litigation. Performed extensive research in support of major litigation.

Education

Doctor of Jurisprudence, 1988—With Honors, UNIVERSITY OF NEW YORK COLLEGE OF LAW, New York, New York, Top 11% of Class, McClung Medal for Excellence in Trial & Appellate Advocacy, Order of the Barristers, American Jurisprudence Award in Constitutional Law
Contributing Editor of Tennessee Judicial Newsletter
Bachelor of Arts in Political Science & French, 1985—With High Honors, UNIVERSITY OF KENTUCKY, Lexington, Kentucky, Scholarship: McClure Fellowship for the Study of International Law, Scholarship: Ruth Stephens Award in International Relations & International Law
INSTITUT EUROPEEN DES HAUTES ETUDES INTERNATIONALES, University of Nice, 1984–1985—Diploma With Honors, Area of Concentration: Law of the European Union, Nice, France

Licensure   Admitted to practice in North Carolina, Washington, D.C., Kentucky, and New Mexico.

Memberships   Member of several professional organizations.

Personal   Willing to travel and/or relocate. Ability to speak French fluently.

■ **RESUME 12**
Rebecca Patterson's "After" Resume (Page 1)

HEART & SOUL TIP

In this Heart & Soul version, we have written an Objective and have redesigned the entire resume to make it more pleasing to the eye and easier to read.

REBECCA PATTERSON

211 Anywhere Street
City, Country

PROFESSIONAL OBJECTIVE & PROFILE

A multitalented, trilingual (English, French, and German) assistant trial attorney is seeking a position in Europe that will fully utilize an extensive background in prosecuting federal crimes. In-depth experience in conducting trials of suspected war criminals before the International Criminal Tribunal. Set protocol for peers by establishing and maintaining the highest standards of professionalism and work ethics. Available to relocate immediately and travel if needed.

PROFESSIONAL EXPERIENCE

ASSISTANT TRIAL ATTORNEY

INTERNATIONAL CRIMINAL TRIBUNAL FOR RWANDA
KIGALI, RWANDA, MAY 1996 TO PRESENT

- *Genocide Investigation:* In charge of coordinating and directing the investigation of suspected war criminals charged in the 1994 genocide, during which one million civilians were killed in Rwanda. Work involves interaction with over 40 different nationalities within the tribunal on a daily basis.
- *Legal Duties:* Prepare, draft, and present legal indictments and other legal documents in Arusha, Tanzania. Develop overall strategy of genocide prosecutions.
- *Prosecution:* Responsible for conducting the trials of suspected war criminals before the International Criminal Tribunal.
- *International Relations:* Interact extensively with governments worldwide to coordinate investigations and apprehend fugitives.
- *Foreign Language:* Work conducted primarily in French. Extensive foreign travel.

ASSISTANT UNITED STATES ATTORNEY

UNITED STATES ATTORNEY'S OFFICE
SANTA FE, NEW MEXICO, AUGUST 1990 TO MAY 1996

- *Federal Investigations:* Conducted long-term investigations with multiagency task forces using various investigative methods such as wiretaps. Prepared numerous search warrants and conducted extensive federal grand jury proceedings. Prepared and argued federal criminal appeals before the Ninth Circuit Federal Court of Appeals in San Francisco, California.
- *Prosecution:* Responsible for prosecuting major federal crimes such as large narcotics conspiracies, bank robberies, kidnappings, extortion, wire and mail fraud, and other federal offenses. Substantial focus on violent crimes such as murder, aggravated assault, and sex crimes.

INSTRUCTOR/SPEAKER

- Attorney General's Advocacy Institute/Child Sex Abuse and Exploitation Seminar, Washington, D.C., June 1993
- Criminal Trial Advocacy Course, Washington, D.C., June 1992
- National Center for Missing and Exploited Children Training Center, Alexandria, Virginia, July 1992
- Marana Law Enforcement Training Center/Investigation of Sex Crimes, Santa Fe, New Mexico, October 1991
- 8th National Symposium on Child Sexual Abuse, Huntsville, Alabama, February 1992
- Numerous informal trainings with various state, local, and federal law enforcement agencies

Continued

■ **RESUME 12 CONTINUED**
Rebecca Patterson's "After" Resume (Page 2)

REBECCA PATTERSON   Page 2

PROFESSIONAL EXPERIENCE

LITIGATION ASSOCIATE
WOMBLE, CARLYLE, SANDRIDGE & RICE
WINSTON-SALEM, NORTH CAROLINA, 1988 TO 1990
- *Litigation:* Performed all activities involved with a general practice law firm, such as preparing and arguing pre-trial motions, preparing and conducting discovery, analyzing and preparing defense strategy, and conducting settlement conferences. Was 100% successful in litigation.
- *Research:* Performed extensive research in support of major litigation.

LICENSURE

Admitted to practice in North Carolina, Washington, D.C., Tennessee, and Arizona

EDUCATION

DOCTOR OF JURISPRUDENCE DEGREE
University of New York College of Law, New York, New York
Graduated with honors

BACHELOR OF ARTS DEGREE IN POLITICAL SCIENCE, GERMAN & FRENCH
University of Kentucky, Lexington
Graduated with honors

DIPLOMA WITH HONORS, 1984 TO 1985
Area of Concentration: Law of the European Union
Institut Européen des Hautes Etudes Internationales
University of Nice, France

ACADEMIC HONORS

McClung Medal for Excellence in Trial & Appellate Advocacy
Order of the Barristers
American Jurisprudence Award in Constitutional Law
Contributing Editor of *Tennessee Judicial Newsletter*
McClure Fellowship for the Study of International Law
Ruth Stephens Award in International Relations & International Law

■ **RESUME 13**
Helmut von Schultz's "Before" Resume

HELMUT VON SCHULTZ

321 Anywhere Street
City, State 10000 - Home Address
Phone Number - Home Telephone

OBJECTIVE
A position in Marketing.

Education   <u>**MBA**</u>
GEORGIA STATE UNIVERSITY, Atlanta, Georgia, 1993

BS
UNIVERSITY OF GEORGIA, Athens, Georgia, 1988

Professional Affiliations
American Marketing Association, American Management Association, Member of Project Management Institute

Professional Experience

Project Manager, EURAM INTERNATIONAL, INC., Roswell, Georgia—1997 to Present
Report directly to the Vice-President for this consulting company. Provide market research activities to bulid containerized modular homes all over the world. Work with developers, attorneys, architects, engineers and city officials.

Department Head—Product Management
Sales Support Manager, IMS GERMANY, Frankfurt, Germany—1995 to 1996
Responsible for pharmaceutical database products. Full P&L responsibility. Developed a CD-ROM version of the monthly German pharmaceutical sales report. Managed 2 Junior Product Managers. Assisted in sales and marketing. Reported directly to the Sales Director.

Business Development Manager, AMGEN, Munich, Germany—1993 to 1995
Reported directly to Germany's Country Manager and responsible for managing business development. Created an in-house Qualitative Analysis & Market Research Division.

International Product Manager—Sales Executive, G.I.B. CHEMICALS, Roswell, Georgia—1989 to 1993
Reported directly to the President of this importer/distributor of chemicals and specialty tiles. Reported directly to the Sales Manager.

HEART & SOUL TIP

In this version there is no career focus or objective. There is no attention to detail and no pleasing, aesthetic quality.

■ **RESUME 13**
Helmut von Schultz's "After" Resume (Cover Sheet)

HEART & SOUL TIP

In this version we have written an Objective & Profile to describe the candidate. This information adds insight into the person's character and is very important in a Heart & Soul resume.

A PRESENTATION OF MANAGEMENT CREDENTIALS

HELMUT VON SCHULTZ

321 Anywhere Street
City, State 10000
Phone Number

■ **RESUME 13 CONTINUED**
Helmut von Schultz's "After" Resume (Page 1)

PROFESSIONAL OBJECTIVE & PROFILE

International and executive marketing manager with more than 8 years of experience developing and managing international products and projects. Talented in leading and developing business opportunities and marketing strategies to maximize growth and profitability and accomplish mission of integrated, multifunctional operations.

Fluent in German and English with special talents in managing cross-cultural and foreign teams of engineering and survey consultants, architects, development consultants, attorneys, and builders to coordinate and develop projects. Strong general management qualifications in strategic planning, research and feasibility analysis, cost estimating, and financial planning. Skilled executive liaison with international and domestic business leaders. Exceptional skills in process/productivity and quality improvement.

Desire a career opportunity in project management that will provide a challenging avenue for significantly contributing to a company's efficiency, organization, growth, and profitability.

EDUCATION

MASTER'S DEGREE IN BUSINESS ADMINISTRATION
Georgia State University, Atlanta

BACHELOR OF SCIENCE DEGREE IN BIOLOGY
University of Georgia, Athens

PROFESSIONAL AFFILIATIONS

American Marketing Association
American Management Association
Project Management Institute

PROFESSIONAL EXPERIENCE

PROJECT MANAGER

HEART & SOUL TIP

Here we've added lots of attention to detail in describing Helmut's jobs. This provides more insight into his work and capabilities.

EURAM INTERNATIONAL, INC., ROSWELL, GEORGIA, 1997 TO PRESENT

■ *Operations Management:* Responsible for managing and directing overall operations and administration of major high-tech projects conducted throughout the world for this consulting company. Report directly to the vice-president. Conduct ongoing analyses to evaluate the efficiency, quality, and productivity of integrated operations.

■ *Consultant:* Serve as a consultant to European and Australian manufacturers and provide product management, brand management, and market research activities.

■ *Project Management:* Plan, develop, and coordinate the building of containerized modular homes for export to the Philippines. Also currently planning and developing strategies to export these homes to Greece, Germany, and Poland.

■ *International & Domestic Management:* Manage and direct an international team of engineers and manufacturers who develop and produce multimillion-dollar projects throughout the world. Interact closely with developers, attorneys, architects, engineers, and city officials. Negotiate contracts with vendors, suppliers, and subcontractors. Institute analytical tools and methods to evaluate performance, supplier/contractor quality, and capabilities. Hold full decision-making authority for preparing long-range strategic business plans and evaluating technological and manpower requirements.

■ *Marketing & Research:* Prepare feasibility studies for European and Australian manufacturers, and research and investigate demographic areas to determine profitability ratios.

■ **RESUME 13 CONTINUED**
Helmut von Schultz's "After" Resume (Page 2)

MANAGEMENT EXPERIENCE

DEPARTMENT HEAD—
PRODUCT MANAGEMENT
SALES SUPPORT MANAGER

IMS GERMANY—HEALTHCARE SOFTWARE
FRANKFURT, GERMANY, 1995 TO 1996

■ *Company Track Record of Success:* Began with this company as a department head in product management and in 1996 was transferred to sales division as sales support manager.
■ *Product Management:* Held full P & L responsibility for pharmaceutical database products. Responsible for developing and nurturing client relationships, core prospect marketing, financial analysis and affairs, competitive bidding, and entire project management.
■ *Product Development:* Conceptualized, developed, and launched a CD-ROM version of the monthly German pharmaceutical sales report.
■ *Cost Control & Profitability:* As a result of the new CD-ROM version, reduced production costs by 50% and increased overall profitability for company.
■ *Employee Management & Supervision:* Managed two junior product managers and delegated work responsibilities. Monitored and evaluated overall job performance to ensure accuracy and adherence to policies and procedures.
■ *Sales Support Management:* Responsible for providing sales and marketing support to sales staff. Reported directly to the sales director and provided pharmaceutical database and information technology services to global pharmaceutical companies. Created and implemented innovative decision-support solutions to increase business and revenue.
■ *Sales Product Development:* Spearheaded a project to customize individual, cost-effective sales reports for pharmaceutical companies undergoing mergers and acquisitions. Directed a multidisciplinary team to develop and produce these reports for clients.

BUSINESS
DEVELOPMENT MANAGER

AMGEN PHARMACEUTICAL COMPANY, MUNICH, GERMANY, 1993 TO 1995

■ *Management:* Reported directly to country manager of this leading biopharmaceutical company. Responsible for managing business development. Held direct responsibility for developing and nurturing clients, core prospect marketing, financial analysis, contract negotiations, and entire business planning/development functions. Used excellent analytical, planning, organizational, and negotiation skills.
■ *Division Development:* Created, developed, and initiated an in-house qualitative analysis and market research division, which eliminated the need for outside consultants. This decreased costs and increased overall company profitability.

INTERNATIONAL
PRODUCT MANAGER—
SALES EXECUTIVE

G.I.B. CHEMICALS, ROSWELL, GEORGIA, 1989 TO 1993

■ *Company Track Record of Success:* Began with this company as a sales executive in 1989, and in 1991 was promoted to international product manager.
■ *Management:* Reported directly to the president of this importer/distributor of chemicals and specialty tiles. Responsible for managing and directing brand development and product life cycles and introducing new products into the marketplace.
■ *Profitability:* Consistently exceeded sales goal by 15% annually for three consecutive years.

■ **RESUME 14**
Anna Sepulveda's "Before" Resume

HEART & SOUL TIP

This resume is unprofessional in its appearance and writing. It is lacking in the attitude of gratitude and does not incorporate attention to detail.

Anna Sepulveda, 41 Anywhere Street, City, State

Objective To attain a position in Physical Therapy that will provide an avenue for growth and career advancement.

Education *Bachelor of Science in Physical Therapy*
UNIVERSITY OF LA FRONTERA
TEMUCO REGIONAL TEACHING HOSPITAL, Temuco, Chile,
1989   to 1992
1 Year at the Temuco Regional Teaching Hospital, doing clinical rotations.

MCKENZIE INSTITUTE, U.S.A., Chicago, Illinois 1996
FORT SANDERS REGIONAL MEDICAL CENTER, Chicago, Illinois, 1996

Internship McMASTER UNIVERSITY, Hamilton, Ontario, Canada—3 Months
Observed physical therapy.

Licensure *Illinois Physical Therapy License*

Certification CPR Certified

Professional Affiliation, American Physical Therapy Association

Professional Experience

Chicago Medical Center & Hospital
Physical Therapist, Chicago, Illinois
Treated patients in orthopedics and neurology. Cases included CVA, fractures, peripheral vascular diseases, peripheral nerve injuries, low back pain, arthritis, knee replacement and wound care. Teach patients how to take care of themselves by using special equipment.

Chicago Nursing Homes
Physical Therapist, Chicago, Illinois
Worked with a team of physical therapists and supervised therapists during routines. Taught physical therapists and physical therapy technicians. Worked with a variety of health care professionals. Examined patients, made assessments and formulated procedures. Assisted patients in all areas of physical therapy.

Outpatient Clinic, Mutual de Seguridad
Physical Therapist, Temuco, Chile
Responsibilities were the same as those above.

■ **RESUME 14**
Anna Sepulveda's "After" Resume (Cover Sheet)

HEART & SOUL TIP

Notice in this version how we have incorporated the attitude of gratitude into the Objective & Profile section, which implies a sense of service to humanity. This will make her stand out over other candidates with similar backgrounds.

A PRESENTATION OF PROFESSIONAL CREDENTIALS
IN PHYSICAL THERAPY

ANNA SEPULVEDA

41 Anywhere Street
City, State 10000
Phone Number

■ **RESUME 14 CONTINUED**
Anna Sepulveda's "After" Resume (Page 1)

PROFESSIONAL OBJECTIVE & PROFILE

As a multitalented, achievement-oriented and experienced physical therapist, I am seeking a position that will fully utilize my advanced skills and education in all areas of physical therapy.

Dedicated and committed to the advancement and progress of medicine, I am seeking a position that will provide a challenging opportunity for significantly contributing to the enlightenment and education of individuals and society through my endeavors and achievements in health care. People-oriented with strong interpersonal skills. Documented resident alien. Seeking a position in a team environment where I can provide leadership and specialized skills in physical therapy.

EDUCATION

BACHELOR OF SCIENCE DEGREE IN PHYSICAL THERAPY
University of La Frontera
Temuco Regional Teaching Hospital, Temuco, Chile
1 year of clinical rotations at the Temuco Regional Teaching Hospital, supervised by physical therapists.

Seminar Presentation: Prepared and facilitated a special seminar for staff that focused on psychomotricity, which involved all facets of motor development in deaf children compared to normal children.

INTERNSHIP

McMaster University, Hamilton, Ontario, Canada
3- month internship that involved observing all areas of Physical Therapy

LICENSURE

Illinois Physical Therapy License

CERTIFICATION

CPR Certified

PROFESSIONAL AFFILIATION

American Physical Therapy Association

CONTINUING EDUCATION

Mechanical Diagnosis and Therapy of the Lumbar Spine
McKenzie Institute, Chicago, 1996

Maitland/Australian Spinal Workshop
Fort Sanders Regional Medical Center, Chicago, 1996

Wound Care Seminar
Chicago, 1995

Upper Quadrant Soft Tissue Dysfunction: Total Body Treatment Strategies
Charlotte, North Carolina, 1995

Ultrasound and Electrical Stimulation
Physiotherapy Associates, Ft. Lauderdale, Florida, 1995

■ **RESUME 14 CONTINUED**
Anna Sepulveda's "After" Resume (Page 2)

HEART & SOUL TIP

We have expanded on her job descriptions and incorporated more in-depth attention to detail concerning her experience.

PROFESSIONAL EXPERIENCE

PHYSICAL THERAPIST | **CHICAGO MEDICAL CENTER & HOSPITAL**
CHICAGO, ILLINOIS
- *Physical Therapy:* Provide physical therapy to patients of all ages including all facets of treatment, patient exercises, and wound care. Care for patients with various medical problems, such as orthopedics and neurological cases including CVA, fractures, peripheral vascular disease, peripheral nerve injuries, low back pain, arthritis, total hip/total knee replacement, and wound care.
- *Medical Units:* Work in a variety of medical units at this hospital including neurology, orthopedics, geriatrics, and in any area as needed.
- *Teaching/Instruction:* Teach patients how to use special medical equipment and how to utilize different exercise methods and procedures involved in treatments.
- *Patient Relations:* Establish and maintain an excellent rapport with patients, and provide information to them and their families concerning treatments and procedures.

PHYSICAL THERAPIST | **CHICAGO NURSING HOMES**
CHICAGO, ILLINOIS
- *Team Supervision:* Lead and direct team of physical therapists throughout facility by delegating responsibilities and monitoring overall job performance to ensure adherence to standards and regulations. Assist in teaching new physical therapists and physical therapy technicians.
- *Staff Relations:* Encourage a teamlike work environment, which increases staff morale and productivity.
- *Physical Therapy & Patient Relations:* Do initial evaluations for patients, assessing their present level of function and dysfunction. Organize and analyze assessment data to identify all current problems in order to determine appropriate treatment goals. Formulate short- and long-term goals and provide appropriate therapeutic procedures to achieve these goals.
- *Patient Care:* Help patients gain functional restoration, and identify appropriate physical therapy treatment procedures such as range-of-motion exercises, muscle-strengthening activities, and endurance and coordination training for specific muscle groups. Assist patients with sitting, standing, balance transfers, and ambulation, including wheelchair and bipedal. Assess patients' wheelchair needs and assist with individualized wheelchair prescriptions.

PHYSICAL THERAPIST | **OUTPATIENT CLINIC, MUTUAL DE SEGURIDAD**
TEMUCO, CHILE, 1993
- *Physical Therapy:* Responsibilities were basically the same as those described above.

SUMMARY OF QUALIFICATIONS

TRACK RECORD OF SUCCESS | Background exemplifies a successful track record of career accomplishments, which include more than 4 years of professional experience as a physical therapist in diverse environments, including outpatient clinics, medical centers/hospitals, home health care settings, and nursing homes.

INTERNATIONAL EXPERTISE | In-depth background in working with foreign cultures and in communicating with all types of individuals.

FOREIGN LANGUAGES | Completed the TSE & TOEFL Exams. Fluent in Spanish.

PATIENT SERVICES | Committed and dedicated to providing superior physical therapy services to patients.

■ **RESUME 15**
Melody Tartington's "Before" Resume

> **HEART & SOUL TIP**
>
> *Melody's resume does not have a career focus or objective (like so many of the resumes we see). The type is too small and it's hard to read.*

Melody Tartington
3533 Anywhere Street
City, State 10000
Phone Number

Education: **MASTER OF SCIENCE IN BIOLOGY**
MOLECULAR CELL BIOLOGY
UNION UNIVERSITY, National Dean's List

> **HEART & SOUL TIP**
>
> *It is good to be detailed, but the details here are too hard to read. The technical words all run together in a blur!*

BACHELOR OF SCIENCE IN BIOLOGY
AREAS OF EMPHASIS: MOLECULAR CELL BIOLOGY
VANDERBILT UNIVERSITY, National Dean's List
Areas of Study: Immunology, Cell Biology, Molecular Biology, Biochemistry, Physiology, Zoology, Botany, Organic Chemistry, Physical Chemistry & Physics
Centrifugation, Light & Oil Immersion, Gas, HPLC Chromatography, Cell Culture
Isoelectric Focusing, Restriction Mapping, Subcloning, HPLC, Gas Electrophoresis
Enzyme Purification, Octherlony Plating, Ion Exchange, DNA Extraction, DNA Sequencing
Monoclonal Antibodies, Protein Purification, Radioisotopic Labeling, Nuclear Magnetic
Spectroscopy, Assays, Mass Spectrometer, Resonance Imaging

Awards Tennessee Academy of Science Award for Best Biology Research Presentation, 1995.
Tennessee Academy of Sciences Honorary Member, 1995.
Union University's Chapter Founding Member of American Chemical Society, 1993.
Honor Student Association President, 1988.
Alpha Chi Honor Fraternity, 1987.

Computers: IBM/IBM Compatibles: 80868 to Pentium, Hyperchem, Extended Huckel, Mathematica, WordPerfect 6.0, 5.0, Excel, Lotus 1-2-3, Cricketgraph.

> **HEART & SOUL TIP**
>
> *In this version, we don't even know what position Melody held at each job.*

Experience

DEPARTMENT OF RADIOLOGY
VANDERBILT UNIVERSITY MEDICAL CENTER
Nashville, Tennessee—May 1995 to Present
Generated tests on rat models through controlled diet and daily injections of thiamine inhibitor for choline study of rat cerebrum. Gave anesthesia for routine nuclear magnetic resonance spectroscopy scans. Determined and administered thiamine replacement dosages. Excised and preserved tissue for histopathological study.

DEPARTMENT OF RADIOLOGY
VANDERBILT UNIVERSITY MEDICAL CENTER
Nashville, Tennessee—July 1995 to September 1995
Responsible for data for the development of an experimental magnetic resonance imaging contrast agent which was awaiting Food and Drug Administration testing.

VANDERBILT CLINIC
VANDERBILT UNIVERSITY MEDICAL CENTER
Nashville, Tennessee—1994 to1995
Worked at the Cardiology Heart Station and assisted as needed in all testing and procedures as related to Cardiology. Responsible for ECG traces and observed Holter monitor attach.

VANDERBILT UNIVERSITY HOSPITAL INPATIENT PHARMACY
Nashville, Tennessee—1992 to 1993
Carried medicines to floors and returned prescriptions to pharmacy. Also responsible for data entry of customer information into computer system.

■ **RESUME 15**
Melody Tartington's "After" Resume (Cover Sheet)

HEART & SOUL TIP

In this version we have written an "Objective" section and provided job titles and detailed descriptions of experience, which were absent from the "before" version.

CURRICULUM VITAE FOR

MELODY TARTINGTON

3533 Anywhere Street
City, State 10000
Phone Number

■ **RESUME 15 CONTINUED**
Melody Tartington's "After" Resume (Page 1)

PROFESSIONAL OBJECTIVE

An experienced and talented professional is seeking a position as research assistant that will fully utilize her skills and experience in molecular cell biology and cellular biochemistry. Technically and analytically inclined. Self-starter who is very success-oriented.

EDUCATION

MASTER OF SCIENCE DEGREE IN BIOLOGY
Area of emphasis: Molecular cell biology
Union University, Jackson, Tennessee

BACHELOR OF SCIENCE DEGREE IN BIOLOGY
Area of emphasis: Molecular cell biology
Vanderbilt University, Nashville, Tennessee

AREAS OF STUDY

Immunology	Cell biology	Molecular biology
Biochemistry	Physiology	Zoology
Botany	Organic chemistry	Physical chemistry and physics

TECHNICAL SKILLS

Centrifugation	Light and oil immersion	Gas, HPLC chromatography
Cell culture	Isoelectric focusing	Restriction mapping
Subcloning	HPLC, gas	Electrophoresis
Enzyme purification	Octherlony plating	Ion exchange
DNA extraction	DNA sequencing	Monoclonal antibodies
Protein purification	Radioisotopic labeling	Nuclear magnetic spectroscopy
Assays	Mass spectrometry	Resonance imaging

HONORS/AWARDS

- Tennessee Academy of Science Award for Best Biology Research Presentation, 1995
- Tennessee Academy of Sciences Honorary Member, 1995

COMPUTER EXPERTISE

- Hardware IBM/IBM compatibles (80868 to Pentium)
- Software: Hyperchem, Extended Huckel, Mathematica, WordPerfect 5.0, 6.0, Excel, Lotus 1-2-3, Cricketgraph

■ **RESUME 15 CONTINUED**
Melody Tartington's "After" Resume (Page 2)

PROFESSIONAL MEDICAL/SCIENTIFIC EXPERIENCE

RESEARCH ASSISTANT

DEPARTMENT OF RADIOLOGY
VANDERBILT UNIVERSITY MEDICAL CENTER
NASHVILLE, TENNESSEE, MAY 1995 TO PRESENT
As an undergraduate research assistant, was responsible for researching a variety of technical and scientific areas that included the following:

- Generated thiamine-deficient, Wernicke's encephalopathy rat models through controlled diet and daily injections of thiamine inhibitor for choline study of rat cerebrum.
- Administered and quanitified animal behavior.
- Administered anesthesia for routine nuclear magnetic resonance spectroscopy scans.
- Determined and administered thiamine replacement dosages.
- Conducted righting reflex tests.
- Excised and preserved tissue for histopathological study.
- Statistically analyzed body weight and animal behavior.

SCIENTIFIC PROJECT—
DEVELOPMENT
ASSISTANT

DEPARTMENT OF RADIOLOGY
VANDERBILT UNIVERSITY MEDICAL CENTER
NASHVILLE, TENNESSEE, JULY 1995 TO SEPTEMBER 1995

- Recorded and organized data for the development of an experimental magnetic resonance imaging contrast agent that was awaiting Food and Drug Administration testing.
- Catheterized rabbit and administered anethesia for operational procedure.
- Created cranial lesions using *Staphylococcus* bacteria for surgical procedure.
- Monitored intravenous fluids, administered analgesics, and conducted sternal recumbency test for postoperative care.

CARDIOLOGY—HEART
STATION ASSISTANT

VANDERBILT CLINIC
VANDERBILT UNIVERSITY MEDICAL CENTER
NASHVILLE, TENNESSEE, 1994 TO 1995

- Volunteered services at the heart station and assisted as needed in all testing and procedures related to cardiology. Performed ECG traces and observed Holter monitor attach.

INPATIENT PHARMACY
TECHNICIAN

VANDERBILT UNIVERSITY HOSPITAL INPATIENT PHARMACY
NASHVILLE, TENNESSEE, 1992 TO 1993

- Responsible for filling out prescriptions and I.V. preps. Transported medicines to hospital units and returned prescriptions to pharmacy. Also responsible for entry of customer information into computer system.

■ **RESUME 16**
Maurice Thomas's "Before" Resume

HEART & SOUL TIP

Maurice has no Objective or Profile. There is no personality in this "before" version.

**Maurice Thomas, Ph.d., 212 Anywhere Street, City, State 10000
Psychological Examiner & Counselor**

EDUCATION

Doctorate in Clinical Psychology, **FOREST INSTITUTE OF PROFESSIONAL PSYCHOLOGY**
Springfield, Missouri

Master of Arts in Clinical Psychology, **FOREST INSTITUTE OF PROFESSIONAL PSYCHOLOGY**
Springfield, Missouri

Master's in Divinity, **ANDREWS UNIVERSITY**, Berrien Springs, Michigan

Bachelor of Arts in Religion & Practical Theology, **SOUTHERN COLLEGE**, Collegedale, Tennessee

Practical Nursing Diploma, **ORANGE COUNTY VOCATIONAL SCHOOL,** Orlando, Florida

Licensed Psychological Examiner, State of Tennessee

American Psychological Association (Division 51)
Tennessee Psychological Association, Psi Chi National Honor Society, Who's Who Among College Students in America,
American Cancer Society, American Heart & American Lung Certified Instructor for Stop Smoking Seminars
Family Therapy Techniques
Rational Emotive Therapy
Borderline Personality Disorder: Assessment & Treatment
Counseling the Family
Hypnosis

PROFESSIONAL EXPERIENCE

Licensed Psychological Examiner
DEPARTMENT OF CORRECTIONS—SPECIAL NEEDS PSYCHIATRIC FACILITY, Nashville, Tennessee—1995 to 1996

Licensed Psychological Examiner
PRIVATE PRACTICE, Murfreesboro, Tennessee—1995

Licensed Psychological Examiner
FOREST FAMILY CLINIC, Springfield, Missouri—1993 to 1995

Licensed Psychological Examiner
PERSONAL GROWTH RESOURCE, Shelbyville, Tennessee—1993 to 1994

Business & Community Affairs Director
KENTUCKY-TENNESSEE CONFERENCE ADVENTIST CHURCH
Nashville and Murfreesboro, Tennessee—1982 to 1993

■ **RESUME 16**
Maurice Thomas's "After" Resume (Cover Sheet)

HEART & SOUL TIP

In this version, we have written an "Objective & Profile" section that provides insight into the candidate's character and career goals.

MAURICE THOMAS, PH.D.

212 Anywhere Street
City, State 10000
Phone Number

■ **RESUME 16 CONTINUED**
Maurice Thomas's "After" Resume (Page 1)

HEART & SOUL TIP

We fine-tuned the details and were able to condense the resume to 2 pages of text. A lot of the information on the "before" resume was not needed on this "after" resume.

PROFESSIONAL OBJECTIVE & PROFILE

High-caliber psychological examiner and counselor with more than 15 years of experience guiding and leading integrated human services operations for clinics, psychiatric facilities, and a worldwide organization. Consistently successful in managing and directing multidisciplinary operations, which include counseling, public relations, community affairs, and client services.

Excellent background in individual, group, and family counseling. Proven abilities in effecting changes in individuals and in guiding them to achieve their maximum potential. Skilled in establishing and maintaining an exemplary network of business associates as a result of extensive interaction with community organizations, businesses, and leaders.

A strong advocate of personal education, with an unlimited vision for the advancement and enlightenment of individuals and society through effective guidance and education. Seeking a leadership and/or counseling position that will provide a challenging opportunity for significantly contributing to a company's efficiency, organization, growth, and profitability.

EDUCATION

DOCTORATE IN CLINICAL PSYCHOLOGY
Forest Institute of Professional Psychology, Springfield, Missouri

MASTER OF ARTS DEGREE IN CLINICAL PYCHOLOGY
Forest Institute of Professional Psychology, Springfield, Missouri

MASTER'S DEGREE IN DIVINITY
Andrews University, Berrien Springs, Michigan

BACHELOR OF ARTS DEGREE IN RELIGION & PRACTICAL THEOLOGY
Southern College, Collegedale, Tennessee

PRACTICAL NURSING DIPLOMA
Orange County Vocational School, Orlando, Florida

LICENSURE

Licensed Psychological Examiner, State of Tennessee

PROFESSIONAL AFFILIATIONS & HONORS

American Psychological Association (Division 51)
Tennessee Psychological Association
American Heart & American Lung Certified Instructor for Stop Smoking Seminars

ADVANCED TRAINING

Family therapy techniques
Rational-emotive therapy
Borderline personality disorder: Assessment and treatment
Counseling the family
Hypnosis

■ **RESUME 16 CONTINUED**
Maurice Thomas's "After" Resume (Page 2)

PROFESSIONAL EXPERIENCE

LICENSED PSYCHOLOGICAL
EXAMINER

DEPARTMENT OF CORRECTIONS—SPECIAL NEEDS PSYCHIATRIC FACILITY
Nashville, Tennessee, 1995 to 1996
- *Psychology Internship:* This internship provided extensive hands-on experience as a psychologist intern and counselor for inmates (inpatients and outpatients) of the Department of Corrections.
- *Counseling:* Interviewed and counseled patients and determined specific needs through forensic, parole, and neuropsychological evaluations. Provided individual and group counseling for adults on a variety of topics including behavior modification, drug and alcohol abuse, anger management, self-esteem, and basic life issues.

LICENSED PSYCHOLOGICAL
EXAMINER

PRIVATE PRACTICE—MURFREESBORO FAMILY CENTER
Murfreesboro, Tennessee, 1995
- *Psychological Examiner:* Provided individual and group counseling for adults and children on a variety of topics. Therapy included group and marital therapy and psychological evaluations.
- *Needs Assessment:* Interviewed patients and assessed patients' condition.

LICENSED PSYCHOLOGICAL
EXAMINER

FOREST FAMILY CLINIC
Springfield, Missouri, 1993 to 1995
- *Psychological Examiner:* As an intern, was responsible for individual and group counseling. Services included gerontological group therapy as well as therapy for young adults and children.
- *Program Development:* Developed and implemented a program that focused on family relations, self-esteem, and stress management.

LICENSED PSYCHOLOGICAL
EXAMINER

PERSONAL GROWTH RESOURCE
Shelbyville, Tennessee, 1993 to 1994
- *Psychological Examiner:* Conducted interviews with patients and provided individual and group psychotherapy. Utilized a variety of psychological approaches to treat patients including behavioral, cognitive, and psychodynamic interventions, hypnosis, and guided imagery.
- *Resource Management:* After assessing patients' needs, referred them to a variety of resources in human services, including community agencies and health care professionals, to get them the care they needed.

BUSINESS & COMMUNITY
AFFAIRS DIRECTOR

KENTUCKY-TENNESSEE CONFERENCE ADVENTIST CHURCH
Nashville and Murfreesboro, Tennessee, 1982 to 1993
- *Management:* Responsible for overall operations of organization, which included all facets of communication and community services.
- *Budget Management:* Held full decision-making responsibility for developing annual financial objectives and prepared long-range strategic business and budgetary plans. Designed and projected annual operating budget.
- *Client/Family Relations Counseling:* Counseled individuals and groups in many areas of family relations, which included marital, family, divorce, and grief issues, and provided career and child guidance.

■ **RESUME 17**
Jared Watkins's "Before" Resume

HEART & SOUL TIP

This "before" version needs lots of attending to attention and attention to detail! It also needs a career objective and job descriptions!

Jared Watkins
134 Anywhere Street, City, Street 10000 Phone Number

Educational Background
        1971 M. ED University of Virginia, Charlottesville, VA
        1967 AB in Physical Education, College of William & Mary, Williamsburg VA

Employment History
        1988–94—Assistant Track Coach at the University of Alabama, in charge of men's and women's field events and multi-events. In charge of equipment and facilities.
        1985—Assistant Track Coach at the University of Virginia
        1975–84—Men's Head Cross Country and Track Coach, James Madison University, Harrisonburg, VA
        1967–75—Head Cross Country coach and track coach, Nelson County High School, Lovingston, VA

Personal Achievements
        Cocaptain William & Mary Track Team
        Nationally ranked in long jump
        Virginia and William & Mary records in long jump and spring relays.

Professional Achievements
        3 Olympic finalists in 1992 Olympic games.
        14 Olympians since 1988
        Recruited athletes who earned 37 all-American positions at Alabama
        Assisted Univ. of Alabama Men's & Women's teams to several top 3 team finishes and in SEC and top 5 in NCAA including 1994 indoor & outdoor women's SEC championships and an indoor finish of 2nd at the NCAA.
        Advisor/Coach to 8 world ranked athletes.
        Assisted the Univ. of Virginia track program where the 1985 women's team won the Atlantic Coast Conference Championship by a 100 point margin.
        Bought James Madison's men's track program from its beginning as a non-scholarship program to a div. 1 program with numerous national level competitors although only 5 scholarships became available.
        Served as TAC representative for the southern region in the long jump from 1988 to 1993.
        Have published several articles in major journals on cross country, distance running, horizontal jumps, team organization, meet strategy, and strength and power development.
        Spoke at 3 national level clinics on jumping events, meet strategy, and team organization.

High School
        Coaching record of 183 wins and 18 losses (13 losses were to schools in higher classifications)
        9 state championships
        Won every regional championship contested
        Over 75 individual state champions.
        First and only school in Virginia to win AA state championships in cross country, indoor and outdoor track in the same year.
        Established the first cross country program in the district in 1968 and established one of the first women's track programs in Virginia.
        Received the Walt Cormack award in 1974 for outstanding contributions to track and field.

■ **RESUME 17**
Jared Watkins's "After" Resume (Cover Sheet)

HEART & SOUL TIP

We have highlighted areas of expertise and special qualifications that make this candidate shine above the others.

CREDENTIALS IN TRACK & FIELD AND CROSS-COUNTRY

JARED WATKINS

134 Anywhere Street
City, State 10000
Phone Number

■ **RESUME 17 CONTINUED**
Jared Watkins's "After" Resume (Page 1)

HEART & SOUL TIP

In this version, we have provided an "Objective & Profile" section. In one quick read, an employer will know Jared's career background and career goals.

PROFESSIONAL OBJECTIVE & PROFILE

Experienced track & field and cross-country coach is seeking a position as head coach that will fully utilize 27 years of experience building and leading multidimensional athletic programs at universities and high schools. Comprehensive knowledge of and experience in all areas of track & field and cross-country. In-depth understanding of entire athletic program with ability to develop and build championship athletes. Strong leader and powerful motivator with excellent recruiting skills. Have continuously established and maintained an exemplary network of associates as a result of strong interaction and communication skills.

EDUCATION

MASTER'S DEGREE IN EDUCATION
University of Virginia, Charlottesville

BACHELOR OF ARTS DEGREE IN PHYSICAL EDUCATION
College of William and Mary, Williamsburg, Virginia

SUMMARY OF PROFESSIONAL ACCOMPLISHMENTS

TRACK RECORD OF SUCCESS—RECRUITMENT & DEVELOPMENT

In-depth background in recruitment and development of country's top athletes. Special coaching accomplishments include the following:
- Developed and trained 3 Olympic finalists in the 1992 summer Olympic games.
- Responsible for developing and training 14 Olympians since 1988.
- Advisor and coach to 8 world-ranked athletes.
- Won high school and university cross-country and track Coach of the Year awards.
- As assistant track coach at the University of Alabama, recruited athletes who earned 37 All-American awards.
- Coached men's and women's teams to achieve high ranking in the NCAA and SEC championships. Teams finished in the top 3 in the SEC and in the top 5 in the NCAA, including the 1994 Indoor & Outdoor Women's SEC championships and an Indoor finish of 2nd at the NCAA championship.
- Assisted in leading women's team to win the Atlantic Coast Conference Championship by a 100-point margin in 1985 while at the University of Virginia.

ATHLETIC PROGRAM DEVELOPMENT

- Developed and advanced James Madison University men's track program from a Division II program with no scholarships to a Division I program with numerous national-level competitors.
- Established the first cross-country program in the district and was responsible for its development as a sport in the district. Helped organize and develop women's track at the state level in Virginia. Along with two other coaches, developed indoor track into a recognized sport at the state level. (Worked in cooperation with the Virginia High School League on all three of these projects.)

PUBLIC RELATIONS & COMMUNITY AFFAIRS

- Served as TAC Representative for the Southern Region in the long jump, 1988 to 1993.
- Facilitated 3 national-level clinics involving jumping events, meet strategy, and team organization.

■ **RESUME 17 CONTINUED**
Jared Watkins's "After" Resume (Page 2)

PROFESSIONAL COACHING EXPERIENCE

ASSISTANT TRACK COACH　　**UNIVERSITY OF ALABAMA, TUSCALOOSA**
- *Athletic Program—Management:* Assisted the track coach in managing overall operations and administration of the track & field athletic program. In charge of specific projects, field events, multievents, facilities, and equipment.
- *Athletic Achievements:* Assisted in coaching the men's and women's teams to rank in the top 3 in the SEC tournaments and in the top 5 in the NCAA Championships.
- *Recruitment & Development:* Recruited, signed, and developed outstanding athletes. Worked one-on-one and in groups to train and counsel athletes in all areas of team-building, motivation, and goal-setting. Developed nutritional and physical training programs to build top-notch performers.
- *Team-Building:* Encouraged and supported a teamlike environment among athletes, which produced high levels of performance.

ASSISTANT TRACK COACH　　**UNIVERSITY OF VIRGINIA, CHARLOTTESVILLE**
- *Athletic Program—Management:* Assisted in directing and guiding all facets of the athletic program at the University of Virginia.
- *Athletic Achievements:* Assisted in coaching the women's team to win the Atlantic Coast Conference championship by a 100-point margin.

MEN'S HEAD
CROSS-COUNTRY
& TRACK COACH　　**JAMES MADISON UNIVERSITY, HARRISONBURG, VIRGINIA**
- *Management:* Managed cross-country and track athletic program at James Madison University.
- *Athletic Achievements:* Developed the men's track program to a Division 1 program with numerous national-level competitors.

HEAD CROSS-COUNTRY
& TRACK COACH　　**NELSON COUNTY HIGH SCHOOL, LOVINGSTON, VIRGINIA**
- *Management:* Directed and managed the high school's cross-country and track athletic program.
- *Athletic Achievements:* Achieved a coaching record of 183 wins and 18 losses. Won 9 state championships and won every regional championship contested. Developed over 75 individual state champions at the first and only school in Virginia to win the AA state championships in cross-country, indoor, and outdoor track in same year.

PROFESSIONAL BUSINESS EXPERIENCE

OWNER & MANAGER　　**SPORTS NUTRITION CENTER, TUSCALOOSA, ALABAMA**
- *Management:* Founded, built, and manage this sports nutrition center. Hold full decision-making responsibility for developing annual financial objectives and preparing long-range strategic business plans, which include sales/marketing, client/owner relationships, finance/accounting, cost estimating, and personnel.
- *Clientele:* Provide sports nutrition counseling and training to numerous professional athletes and prospective professional athletes. Work one-on-one with individuals to provide specialized physical training and nutritional support. Align objectives of individuals within program and design customized sports programs to accommodate specific needs. Provide nutritional support, supplementation, and success-building methods. Develop unique and original software programs in training and nutrition and market these to gyms.
- *Marketing & Advertising:* Research potential markets and create and implement innovative marketing strategies to advertise and promote services.

■ **RESUME 18**

Demetrius Xixis's "Before" Resume

HEART & SOUL TIP

This "before" resume needs lots of attention to detail. It is inappropriate to list one's personal information. There needs to be a proactive career objective, job descriptions need to be developed, and special areas of qualification need to be highlighted.

Demetrius Xixis
220 Anywhere Street
City, Country
Phone Number

PERSONAL DATA
Age: 34
Birthdate: 18th of April 1961
Race: White
Sex: Male
Marital Status: Married, 2 children
Nationality: Greek
Religion: Greek Orthodox

EDUCATIONAL BACKGROUND

BS, Middle Tennessee University, Murfreesboro, Tennessee
MBA, Henley/Brunel Management College, London, England

Learning Program with the cooperation of EEDe.
Seminar 7 months in UNIX operating system and C language
Seminar 3 months in telecommunications, Networks Packet
Packet Switching Technologies (X25, X28, PADS, X400, etc.)
Seminar 3 months in Division Management in the 90's.
Seminars in Microsoft Office Programs
* Access 2
* Excel 5
* Word 6
* Power Point 3
Seminar in Principles of Management
Seminar in Employeeship
Seminar in Banking and Foreign Exchange Market
Seminar in Management of Human Resources
Seminar 3 months in Internet

LANGUAGES
Greek (Native)
English (Excellent)
French (Read only)

PROGRAMMING LANGUAGES:
COBOL, Basic, FORTRAN, RPGII, Pascal, PL/a, ALGOL, BAL, ABAL, C, Prologue, SQL, PL/SQL

OPERATING SYSTEMS
IBM 3000, PDPII, HONEYWELL 99, CDC CYBER 70-170, POINT 4 IRIS 8.2C, MS-DOS 3/4/5/6, UNIX, PRO-LOGUE, NOVELL 3.11, 3.12, R ORACLE 7.

EXPERIENCE

Position: Information Technology Services Manager
                       International Air Transport Association
                       Athens, Greece—1991 to 1996

■ **RESUME 18 CONTINUED**
Demetrius Xixis's "Before" Resume (Page 2)

Demetrius Xixis
Page 2

Position: Analyst—Programmer
                 Sofroniadis Group of Companies
Duties: Organized all their Information Systems in their three companies,
                 plus the applications I developed here are:
                 a) Spare auto parts, b) accounting and c) sales.

Position: Programmer
                 Datamedia S.A.
Duties: Datamedia is a software house and I worked there as a programmer in a small team
                 creating an on-line business application.

Position: Private Soldier—Programmer
                 Hellenic Armed Forces
Duties: During my obligatory military service, I worked as a programmer at the Army's
                 headquarters in Athens.

PERSONAL INTERESTS:

                 My work is my hobby, but besides that, I like tennis, basketball, soccer and spending time at
                 home with my family.

REFERENCES: Available upon request.

SALARY REQUIREMENTS: Negotiable.

■ **RESUME 18**
Demetrius Xixis's "After" Resume (Cover Sheet)

HEART & SOUL TIP

In this version, we have written an Objective with a direct focus on his goals and special qualifications, which will make him very marketable in his field.

A PRESENTATION OF
PROFESSIONAL MANAGEMENT CREDENTIALS

DEMETRIUS XIXIS

220 Anywhere Street
City, Country
Phone Number

U.S. Citizen

■ **RESUME 18 CONTINUED**
Demetrius Xixis's "After" Resume (Page 1)

PROFESSIONAL OBJECTIVE & PROFILE

I am a highly skilled, experienced, and multitalented business professional who is seeking a position in a company that will fully utilize my extensive background and education in the following areas:

■ Information Technology/Data Processing, and Computer Programming
■ Airline Industry
■ Business Administration & Operations

I desire a position that will provide a challenging opportunity for significantly contributing to a company's efficiency, organization, growth, and profitability.

EDUCATION

MASTER'S DEGREE IN BUSINESS ADMINISTRATION
Henley/Brunel Management College, London, England

BACHELOR OF SCIENCE DEGREE IN COMPUTER INFORMATION SYSTEMS
Middle Tennessee State University, Murfreesboro

SUMMARY OF ACCOMPLISHMENTS & QUALIFICATIONS

TRACK RECORD OF SUCCESS
Background exemplifies a successful track record of career accomplishments, which include 14 years of experience in such positions as information technology services manager, EDP manager, senior analyst, and computer programmer.

FINANCE, BUDGET, AND BUSINESS MANAGEMENT
Experienced in managing a $550-million operation for International Air Transport Association in Athens, Greece. Work involved extensive budget research and analysis. In charge of coordinating and managing all financial transactions in banking, company assets, and stocks.

INFORMATION SYSTEMS— COMPUTER PROGRAMMING
Created, developed, and implemented numerous computer software programs throughout career, including accounting and sales software for communications, airline, hotel, and accounting.

HUMAN RESOURCES— PERSONNEL
Experienced in recruiting, interviewing, hiring, training, and supervising staff employees.

INTERNATIONAL BUSINESS EXPERTISE
Experienced in working with companies all over the world. Project leader who guided and directed the establishment of new information technology offices in Russia, Poland, Saudi Arabia, Malta, Cyprus, the Eastern Caribbean, Ireland, and Malaysia.

FOREIGN LANGUAGES
Fluent in English, Greek, and French.

PROGRAMMING & OPERATING LANGUAGES
Extensive background in COBOL, Basic, FORTRAN, RPGII, Pascal, PL/1, ALGOL, BAL, and ABAL. Operating systems include IBM 3000, Honeywell 99, Novel 3.11, 3.12, 4, Oracle 7, and more.

■ **RESUME 18 CONTINUED**
Demetrius Xixis's "After" Resume (Page 2)

PROFESSIONAL EXPERIENCE

INFORMATION TECHNOLOGY SERVICES MANAGER	**INTERNATIONAL AIR TRANSPORT ASSOCIATION (IATA)** **ATHENS, GREECE, 1991 TO 1996** ■ *Management:* Responsible for the overall management of operations and administration of the International Air Transport Association's information technology services division in Greece. ■ *International Relations—Project Leader & Business Development:* As project leader, spearheaded, guided, and directed the establishment of new information technology offices in Russia, Poland, Saudi Arabia, Malta, Cyprus, the Eastern Caribbean, Ireland, and Malaysia. ■ *Accounting, Finance, and Budget Management:* Manage, direct and control all accounting procedures and financial transactions, including banking, stocks, and company assets. ■ *Computer Software:* In charge of developing, updating, and maintaining everyday operations of software applications in the Data Processing Center for this company. ■ *Client Relations:* Communications liaison between airlines, travel agents, cargo, and corporate headquarters. Communicate changes in policies, procedures, and regulations. ■ *Marketing:* Create, develop, and implement innovative marketing and advertising campaigns for all products and services in the airline industry. ■ *Personnel & Supervision:* Recruit, interview, hire, train, and supervise 15 full-time staff employees and 8 part-time employees in all areas of data processing. ■ *Human Resources—Employee Relations:* Encourage and support a teamlike work environment, which increases employee efficiency and productivity. Responsible for coordinating employees' benefit packages and retirement plans.
EDP MANAGER	**INTERSERVICE S.A., ATHENS, GREECE, 1989 TO 1991** ■ *Management:* Managed and directed the Electronic Data Processing Department. ■ *Computer Program Development:* Developed and implemented the information system of Interservice S.A. - I.D.L., which streamlined computer operations. Also developed and installed "On-Line Automatic Flight Invoicing," "Weight Balance," and "Traffic Rights" computer programs.
EDP MANAGER SENIOR ANALYST/ PROGRAMMER	**ATHENS, GREECE, 1987 TO 1989** ■ *Management:* Responsible for managing and supervising all software applications for this software company.
ANALYST/PROGRAMMER	**SOFRONIADIS GROUP, ATHENS, GREECE, 1985 TO 1987** ■ *Programmer:* In charge of compiling and organizing the information systems for 3 companies. Developed and installed "Spare Auto Parts," "Accounting," and "Sales" applications software.
COMPUTER PROGRAMMER	**DATAMEDIA S.A., ATHENS, GREECE, 1983 TO 1985** ■ *Programmer:* Responsible for programming. Created and implemented the "On-Line Business" application.
COMPUTER PROGRAMMER	**HELLENIC ARMED FORCES—ATHENS, GREECE, 1982 TO 1983** ■ *Programmer:* Served as a computer programmer while in the military.

Additional information regarding advanced training available upon request

■ **RESUME 19**
Philip Young's "Before" Resume

HEART & SOUL TIP

This resume needs everything—career objective and profile, descriptions of jobs, and in-depth attention to detail!

PHILIP YOUNG
225 Anywhere Street
City, State 10000
Phone Number

Desire a career opportunity in business.

Education

Bachelor of Arts in Spanish
Minor: Business Administration
Emphasis: International Business/Logistics & Transportation
UNIVERSITY OF TENNESSEE
Knoxville, Tennessee, 1994

FORRESTER INSTITUTO INTERNACIONAL
San José, Costa Rica, Summer 1993

Professional Experience

Distribution Center Manager
CH ROBINSON COMPANY
Nashville, Tennessee—1994 to Present
Supervise employees and manage distribution center. Work extensively with customers and prepare job rate proposals. Research markets and maintain data base information. Responsible for budget.

Supervisor
THE SPAGHETTI WAREHOUSE, INC
Knoxville, Tennessee—1992 to 1994
Supervised and trained employees. Managed budget.

Bartender
FROSTBITE'S, INC.
Knoxville, Tennessee—Summer 1992
Worked as a bartender and server.

References Available Upon Reques

■ **RESUME 19**
Philip Young's First "After" Resume (Cover Sheet)

HEART & SOUL TIP

For this client, we wrote two versions, each targeted at a different career goal. This one is for a position in business and management.

A PRESENTATION OF
PROFESSIONAL MANAGEMENT CREDENTIALS

PHILIP YOUNG

225 Anywhere Street
City, State 10000
Phone Number

■ **RESUME 19 CONTINUED**
Philip Young's "After" Resume (Page 1)

HEART & SOUL TIP

Using creative visualization, we visualized Philip in a management position. Notice how we wrote the Objective for this first version.

PROFESSIONAL OBJECTIVE & PROFILE

High-caliber business manager is seeking a position in business administration that will fully utilize more than 5 years of management and supervisory experience. Strong general management qualifications in strategic planning, inventory and purchasing, employee supervision and development, and leadership. Skilled in leading and in developing business opportunities and marketing strategies to maximize growth and profitability. Excellent analytical, planning, organizational, and negotiation skills.

Desire a career opportunity in leadership and management, with a progressive company that will provide a challenging avenue for significantly contributing to its efficiency, organization, growth, and profitability.

SUMMARY OF QUALIFICATIONS

TRACK RECORD OF SUCCESS
Background exemplifies a successful track record of career accomplishments as distribution center manager and logistics manager for CH Robinson Company. Consistently advanced throughout tenure to positions of higher levels of responsibility and authority.

BUSINESS MANAGEMENT
Skilled in managing all facets of logistics and transportation for major distribution center. Work includes organizational management, personnel training and development, inventory and purchasing, budget, client relations, research, and computer operations.

FUNDRAISING & SPECIAL EVENTS
Experienced in coordinating and organizing fundraising activities, sporting events, and special committees as a member of the Kappa Alpha fraternity. Gained valuable public relations experience working with community businesses, organizations, and agencies.

EMPLOYEE RELATIONS & LEADERSHIP
Strong motivator and leader of others. Encourage and support a teamlike work environment, which increases employee morale, efficiency, and productivity. Style exhibits maturity, high energy, teamwork, and the ability to relate to a wide variety of people and cultures.

EDUCATION

BACHELOR OF ARTS DEGREE IN SPANISH
Minor: Business Administration
Emphasis: International Business/Logistics & Transportation
University of Tennessee, Knoxville

Forrester Instituto Internacional
San José, Costa Rica, Summer 1993
Areas of Concentration: Spanish language and literature, Latin American culture and customs

■ **RESUME 19 CONTINUED**
Philip Young's First "After" Resume (Page 2)

HEART & SOUL TIP

*Page 2 of this resume
is the same for
both versions.*

PROFESSIONAL EXPERIENCE

DISTRIBUTION CENTER MANAGER LOGISTICS MANAGER	**CH ROBINSON COMPANY, NASHVILLE, TENNESSEE, 1994 TO PRESENT**

- *Company Track Record of Success:* Began as a broker/logistics manager, and advanced to position of distribution center manager. Responsible for opening and developing a major distribution center in Nashville.
- *Management:* Manage and direct overall operations and administration of distribution center for this 3rd-party transportation company. Work involves coordinating the distribution of printed materials for printing company as well as other major accounts.
- *Personnel & Supervision:* Interview, hire, train, and supervise clerical and warehouse employees. Schedule and delegate responsibilities. Monitor and supervise job performance to ensure accuracy and adherence to specifications, rules, and regulations.
- *Transportation Research:* Coordinate market research activities, investigate different rates and routes of carriers, maintain database and competitor information, and determine most economic and efficient transportation methods for distributing products.
- *Computer Operations:* Utilize customized software to enter data concerning carriers and distribution. Update and maintain information regarding inventory and routing in computer system.
- *Broker:* Served as the liaison between clients and carriers. Investigated and identified problems within service and implemented creative problem-solving techniques to resolve issues. Negotiated rates between customers and carriers to maximize profitability and service.
- *Budget:* Analyze budget variances and initiate appropriate guidelines to more aggressively control expenditures.

SUPERVISOR **THE SPAGHETTI WAREHOUSE, INC., KNOXVILLE, TENNESSEE, 1992 TO 1994**

- *Inventory & Purchasing:* Monitored inventory levels of beverages and supplies and purchased as needed.
- *Training:* Responsible for training new employees in all areas of bartending and customer service.
- *Budget:* Managed and analyzed budget for operating expenditures in bar area. Responsible for financial performance analysis and business planning/development functions. Operated within budget guidelines and efficiently controlled expenditures.

BARTENDER **FROSTBITE'S, INC., KNOXVILLE, TENNESSEE, SUMMER 1992**

- *Sales:* Sold food and beverages to customers in a bar and restaurant environment. Upsold items in order to increase sales and profitability.
- *Inventory:* Monitored inventory levels of supplies and stocked as needed.

References Available Upon Request

■ **RESUME 19**
Philip Young's Second "After" Resume (Cover Sheet)

HEART & SOUL TIP

This second version is targeted to international business. We changed the cover sheet to reflect this.

A PRESENTATION OF
PROFESSIONAL MANAGEMENT & INTERNATIONAL BUSINESS CREDENTIALS

PHILIP YOUNG

225 Anywhere Street
City, State 10000
Phone Number

■ **RESUME 19 CONTINUED**
Philip Young's Second "After" Resume (Page 1) (See page 194 for the second page of this "after" resume.)

PROFESSIONAL OBJECTIVE & PROFILE

High-caliber manager interested in international business is seeking a position that will fully utilize advanced study and experience of the Spanish language and Latin American culture and customs. Studying and living with a Spanish family in San José, Costa Rica, I gained valuable experience in multicultural and international relations.

With more than 5 years of management and supervisory experience, I possess strong general management qualifications in strategic planning, inventory and purchasing, employee supervision and development, and leadership. Skilled in leading and in developing business opportunities and marketing strategies to maximize growth and profitability.

Desire a career opportunity in leadership and management with a progressive international company that will provide a challenging avenue for significantly contributing to its efficiency, organization, growth, and profitability.

SUMMARY OF QUALIFICATIONS

TRACK RECORD OF SUCCESS
Background exemplifies a successful track record of career accomplishments as distribution center manager and logistics manager for CH Robinson Company. Consistently advanced throughout tenure to positions of higher levels of responsibility and authority.

INTERNATIONAL BUSINESS EXPERTISE
General knowledge of Spanish language and Latin American culture. Extensive study in international economics, international management, and international logistics and transportation. Gained valuable experience interacting with foreign culture while living with a local family in San José, Costa Rica.

BUSINESS MANAGEMENT
Skilled in managing all facets of logistics and transportation for major distribution center. Work includes organizational management, personnel training and development, inventory and purchasing, budget, client relations, research, and computer operations.

FUNDRAISING & SPECIAL EVENTS
Experienced in coordinating and organizing fundraising activities, sporting events and special committees as a member of the Kappa Alpha fraternity. Gained valuable public relations experience working with community businesses, organizations, and agencies.

EMPLOYEE RELATIONS & LEADERSHIP
Strong motivator and leader of others. Encourage and support a teamlike work environment, which increases employee morale, efficiency, and productivity. Style exhibits maturity, high energy, teamwork, and the ability to relate to a wide variety of people and cultures.

EDUCATION

BACHELOR OF ARTS DEGREE IN SPANISH
Emphasis: International Business/Logistics & Transportation
University of Tennessee, Knoxville

Forrester Instituto Internacional
San José, Costa Rica, Summer 1993
Areas of Concentration: Spanish language and literature, Latin American culture and customs

■ **RESUME 20**
Edward Yeltson's "Before" Resume

HEART & SOUL TIP

This resume is full of boasting statements in its Objective.

EDWARD YELTSON

577 Anywhere Street
City, Country

OBJECTIVE: I have been an outstanding student and attended numerous seminars. I was also honored to be in Epsilon Pi Tau Honorary Professional fraternity, which is only for special students like myself. In addition, because I tested so high on my achievement tests, I was asked to represent American University at a conference only for the most intelligent students. It was at this conference that I was able to find a job overseas in South Africa because they said I was an outstanding student with exceptional intelligence. I know how to lead people and would excel in a position as an Engineer.

EDUCATION
MBA, Heriot-Watt University, Scotland

B.S. Industrial Science, American University, Washington, D.C.

WORK HISTORY:
1992 to 1995   Industrial Engineer, Glacier Bearings, Pinetown, South Africa
                  This company produced bearings. Involved in researching and developing engineering products. Analyzed product conformance and quality. Involved in budget. Experienced in CAD.

1991 to 1992   Quality Engineer, supervisor, A.E. Bearings, Pinetown, South Africa
                  This company manufactured automotive parts. In charge of 25 employees. Responsible for quality, cost control and labor control. Resolved problems.

1987 to 1990   Statistical Process Engineer, Quality Control, Roberts Control Company, South Africa
                  Responsible for quality control and engineering. Worked with customers and helped them. Resolved problems. On several committees.

■ **RESUME 20**
Edward Yeltson's "After" Resume (Cover Sheet)

HEART & SOUL TIP

This Heart & Soul resume clearly highlights accomplishments and honors without boasting.

A PRESENTATION OF
ENGINEERING CREDENTIALS

EDWARD YELTSON

557 Anywhere Street
City, State 10000
Phone Number

■ **RESUME 20 CONTINUED**
Edward Yeltson's "After" Resume (Page 1)

PROFESSIONAL OBJECTIVE & PROFILE

An experienced engineer is seeking an executive position that will fully utilize a diversified background and education, provide a challenging opportunity to significantly contribute to a company's efficiency, organization, growth, and profitability. A self-starter who works well independently or as a team member.

EDUCATION

MASTER'S DEGREE IN BUSINESS ADMINISTRATION
Heriot-Watt University, Edinburgh, Scotland

BACHELOR OF SCIENCE DEGREE IN INDUSTRIAL TECHNOLOGY
American University, Washington, D.C.

PROFESSIONAL SEMINARS

Ford Motor Company Team Oriented Problem Solving seminar
Continuous Flow Manufacturing seminar

HONORS

Foundry Educational Foundation (FEF) quarterly scholarship recipient, 1986 and 1987

SUMMARY OF QUALIFICATIONS & SKILLS

TRACK RECORD OF SUCCESS
Eight years of experience as an engineer in such positions as statistical process engineer, quality engineer, and industrial engineer.

INTERNATIONAL EXPERTISE
Seven years of experience working as an industrial and quality engineer for a major manufacturer in South Africa. Gained valuable experience in establishing excellent business relationships with diverse cultures and all levels of management and personnel.

MANAGEMENT & SUPERVISION
Experienced in managing and supervising staff of 25, including foremen, inspectors, and auditors.

QUALITY CONTROL
Expertise in reviewing and monitoring engineering jobs and products to ensure the highest quality and adherence to all regulations.

LEADERSHIP & COMMUNICATIONS
Strong interpersonal skills with ability to lead and motivate others.

■ **RESUME 20 CONTINUED**
Edward Yeltson's "After" Resume (Page 2)

PROFESSIONAL EXPERIENCE

INDUSTRIAL ENGINEER
GLACIER BEARINGS
DIVISION OF T&N HOLDINGS, LTD., A SOUTH AFRICAN COMPANY
PART OF T&N PLC, A UNITED KINGDOM–BASED COMPANY
PINETOWN, SOUTH AFRICA, 1992 TO 1995
- *Engineer:* Responsible for all industrial engineering duties for this company, which produced bearings and various other products related to the industrial market.
- *Industrial Research & Development:* In charge of researching, developing, and producing a new hydraulic filtration unit, which included all phases of planning, development, cost evaluation, and production.
- *Product analysis:* Investigated and analyzed product conformance and quality requirements for numerous projects including the new hydraulic filtration unit.
- *Budget Analysis:* Reviewed spreadsheets and production cost data in order to analyze and predict costs and expenditures for projects.
- *Technical:* Experienced in basic CAD operation.

QUALITY ENGINEER—
SUPERVISOR
A.E. BEARINGS
DIVISION OF T&N HOLDINGS LTD., PINETOWN, SOUTH AFRICA, 1991 TO 1992
- *Supervision & Management:* Managed and supervised 25 staff members including foremen, inspectors, and auditors for this automotive products manufacturer. In charge of scheduling and delegating work assignments.
- *Operations & Administration:* Continuously reviewed and restructured company operations in order to increase production and profitability.
- *Client Relations:* Worked one-on-one with clients to review new products and ensure the highest quality.
- *Employee Relations:* Encouraged and supported a teamwork environment in order to strengthen employee morale and production.
- *Labor & Cost Control:* Efficiently scheduled employees in order to minimize labor costs and increase production.
- *Quality Control:* Reviewed and monitored all processes, from raw materials to customer dispatch, to ensure compliance with ISO 9001 rules and regulations.
- *Troubleshooting:* Researched and identified potential problems in production and implemented creative problem-solving techniques to ensure efficient operations.

STATISTICAL PROCESS—
QUALITY ENGINEER
ROBERTS CONTROL COMPANY
JOHANNESBURG, SOUTH AFRICA, 1987 TO 1990
- *Quality Control:* Responsible for incoming and outgoing quality control of 3 specific product lines and a parts-fabrication department.
- *Program Development:* Developed and implemented the Quality & SPC Charting Plans program, which was used to control the production of automotive and non-automotive products.
- *Customer & Supplier Representative:* Liaison between customers and company. Guided and advised suppliers on quality-related issues. Responded to requests, inquiries, suggestions, and/or problems and implemented creative problem-solving techniques to ensure customer satisfaction.
- *New Product Initiation:* In charge of submitting the company's new product Initial Sample Inspection Reports to clients.
- *Committee Chair:* Served as chair of the departmental Scrap Reduction Committee.

Using the Myers-Briggs Type Indicator *& the* Strong Interest Inventory *in Heart & Soul* Resume Writing

The *Myers-Briggs Type Indicator* (MBTI) and the *Strong Interest Inventory (Strong)* are invaluable tools in writing a resume and cover letter with "heart and soul." By combining your values, interests, and personality (as illustrated in the MBTI and the *Strong*) with your skills and experience developed over a lifetime, along with the seven never-before-published secrets to creating a successful resume, you can transform your old resume (or a new one) into a powerful resume with real heart and soul, one that reflects you from a higher, more in-depth perspective.

Both the MBTI and the *Strong* must be administered and interpreted by a counseling professional, who not only will interpret the results of the instruments but also will discuss with you and analyze other issues in your life that are pertinent to your career and life decisions. Call a career counselor for more information. For immediate purposes, if you haven't used the MBTI or the *Strong* instrument, following are a brief history of each and some basic concepts that may help you right away when preparing a Heart & Soul resume.

History of the Myers-Briggs Type Indicator *(MBTI)*

The MBTI personality inventory was developed by Isabel Myers and Katharine Briggs to make Carl Jung's theory of psychological types understandable and useful in people's lives. Jung believed that many of the apparently random differences in people's behavior were actually a result of their preferred modes of perception and judgment. Perception refers to how you gather information, while judgment refers to how you come to conclusions based on what you have perceived. There are two opposite ways of perceiving, through Sensing or Intuition, and likewise two opposite ways of forming judgments, through Thinking or Feeling. Jung referred to these two pairs of opposites as the *functions*. He also described differences in the ways people prefer to focus these functions and identified another pair of opposites, which he called Extroversion and Introversion. Myers and Briggs, when constructing the MBTI instrument, added a fourth dichotomy that they thought was implicit in Jung's theory. This was the Judging and Perceiving dichotomy, which relates to one's preferences for using either one of the judging functions (Thinking or Feeling) or one of the perceiving functions (Sensing or Intuition) as the primary means of dealing with the outer world.

All of us use all eight preferences at different times. Your MBTI results indicate which of each pair of opposites you most prefer. Together, these four preferences make up what is called your *type*. Your type can be identified by the letters that are associated with your preferences on each of the four dichotomies. For example, if your type is reported as ENFP, this means you indicated preferences for Extraversion, iNtuition, Feeling, and Perceiving when you answered the MBTI items.

Table A.1 summarizes the four MBTI dichotomies. Since there are two opposites for each dichotomy, there are a total of eight preferences.

The various combinations of each of the four dichotomies make up sixteen different personality types. If you don't already know your type, Table A.2, "Characteristics Associated with Each Type," may help you in analyzing yours.

Please note that while the names of the MBTI preferences are familiar, in everyday use they have meanings that are different from their MBTI meanings. Remember:

- *Extravert* does not mean "talkative."
- *Introvert* does not mean "shy" or "inhibited."
- *Feeling* does not mean "emotional."
- *Judging* does not mean "judgmental."
- *Perceiving* does not mean "perceptive."

Direction of Energy

Extraversion (E)

Focus on the people and things in the outer world

Introversion (I)

Focus on the thoughts, feelings, and impressions of the inner world

Gathering Information

Sensing (S)

Focus on facts and details that can be confirmed by experience

Intuition (N)

Focus on possibilities and relationships among ideas

Making Decisions

Thinking (T)

Use impersonal, objective, logical analysis to reach conclusions

Feeling (F)

Use person-centered, subjective analysis to reach conclusions

Dealing with the Outer World

Judging (J)

Plan and organize; make decisions and come to closure

Perceiving (P)

Be spontaneous and adaptable; collect information and stay open to new options

From Introduction to Type and Careers, *Allen L. Hammer. Copyright 1993 by Consulting Psychologists Press. Reproduced with permission.*

■ **TABLE A.1**
MBTI Preferences

Characteristics Associated with Each MBTI Preference

If you have not yet used the *Myers-Briggs Type Indicator* instrument, but have reviewed the above section, you may be able to identify some characteristics or preferences that apply to you. In Table A.3 we have compiled characteristics commonly associated with each MBTI preference. Read through each section and mark the characteristics that you believe strongly correlate with your personality and work ethic. Even if a particular characteristic is not in "your type," you still may have developed a certain skill or affinity for it and will want to incorporate it into your resume. Incorporate any relevant phrases into sentences that best describe you. Once you have identified a personal characteristic, think of examples and stories you may tell to illustrate it. Remember, when making a positive comment about yourself, you should always support your statement with real-life illustrations of your success. For example, don't just say, "Excellent communicator." Instead, write, "Excellent communication skills exemplified as a national workshop presenter for special industry trade shows."

	Sensing Types		Intuitive Types	
Introverts	**ISTJ** Serious, quiet, earn success by concentration and thoroughness. Practical, orderly, matter-of-fact, logical, realistic, and dependable. See to it that everything is well organized. Take responsibility. Make up their own minds as to what should be accomplished and work toward it steadily, regardless of protests or distractions.	**ISFJ** Quiet, friendly, responsible, and conscientious. Work devotedly to meet their obligations. Lend stability to any project or group. Thorough, painstaking, accurate. Their interests are usually not technical. Can be patient with necessary details. Loyal, considerate, perceptive, concerned with how other people feel.	**INFJ** Succeed by preseverance, originality, and desire to do whatever is needed or wanted. Put their best efforts into their work. Quietly forceful, conscientious, concerned for others. Respected for their firm principles. Likely to be honored and followed for their clear vision as to how to best serve the common good.	**INTJ** Have original minds and great drive for their own ideas and purposes. Have long-range vision and quickly find meaningful patterns in external events. In fields that appeal to them, they have a fine power to organize a job and carry it through. Skeptical, critical, independent, determined; have high standards of competence and performance.
	ISTP Cool onlookers—quiet, reserved, observing and analyzing life with detached curiosity and unexpected flashes of original humor. Usually interested in cause and effect, how and why mechanical things work, and organizing facts using logical principles. Excel at getting to the core of a practical problem and finding the solution.	**ISFP** Retiring, quietly friendly, sensitive, kind, modest about their abilities. Shun disagreements, do not force their opinions or values on others. Usually do not care to lead but are often loyal followers. Often relaxed about getting things done because they enjoy the present moment and do not want to spoil it by undue haste or exertion.	**INFP** Quiet observers, idealistic, loyal. Important that outer life be congruent with inner values. Curious, quick to see possibilities, often serve as catalysts to implement ideas. Adaptable, flexible, and accepting unless a value is threatened. Want to understand people and ways of fulfilling human potential. Little concern with possessions or surroundings.	**INTP** Quiet and reserved. Especially enjoy theoretical or scientific pursuits. Like solving problems with logic and analysis. Interested mainly in ideas, with little liking for parties or small talk. Tend to have sharply defined interests. Need careers where some strong interest can be used and useful.
Extraverts	**ESTP** Good at on-the-spot problem solving. Like action, enjoy whatever comes along. Tend to like mechanical things and sports, with friends on the side. Adaptable, tolerant, pragmatic; focused on getting results. Dislike long explanations. Are best with real things that can be worked, handled, taken apart, or put together.	**ESFP** Outgoing, accepting, friendly, enjoy everything and make things more fun for others by their enjoyment. Like action and making things happen. Know what's going on and join in eagerly. Find remembering facts easier than mastering theories. Are best in situations that need sound common sense and practical ability with people.	**ENFP** Warmly enthusiastic, high-spirited, ingenious, imaginative. Able to do almost anything that interests them. Quick with a solution or any difficulty and ready to help anyone with a problem. Often rely on their ability to improvise instead of preparing in advance. Can usually find compelling reasons for whatever they want.	**ENTP** Quick, ingenious, good at many things. Stimulating company, alert, and outspoken. May argue for fun on either side of a question. Resourceful in solving new and challenging problems, but may neglect routine assignments. Apt to turn to one new interest after another. Skillful in finding logical reasons for what they want.
	ESTJ Practical, realistic, matter-of-fact, with a natural head for business or mechanics. Not interested in abstract theories; want learning to have direct and immediate application. Like to organize and run activities. Often make good administrators; are decisive, quickly move to implement decisions; take care of routine details.	**ESFJ** Warm-hearted, talkative, popular, conscientious, born cooperators, active committee members. Need harmony and may be good at creating it. Always doing something nice for someone. Work best with encouragement and praise. Main interest is in things that directly and visibly affect people's lives.	**ENFJ** Responsive and responsible. Feel real concern for what others think or want, and try to handle things with due regard for the other's feelings. Can present a proposal or lead a group discussion with ease and tact. Sociable, popular, sympathetic. Responsive to praise and criticism. Like to facilitate others and enable people to achieve their potential.	**ENTJ** Frank, decisive. Leaders in activities. Develop and implement comprehensive systems to solve orgnizational problems. Good in anything that requires reasoning and intelligent talk, such as public speaking. Are usualy well informed and enjoy adding to their fund of knowledge.

From Introduction to Type *(5th ed.), Isabel Briggs Myers. Copyright 1993 by Consulting Psychologists Press, Inc. Reproduced with permission.*

■ **TABLE A.2**
Characteristics Frequently Associated with Each Type

Table A.3 lists just a small sampling of characteristics associated with each of the preferences. Look at the Resources at the back of this book for more detailed information on the MBTI and the *Strong* instruments or, as we mentioned earlier, call a career counselor.

Studying the MBTI and the *Strong* is an excellent aid to understanding who you are, a necessary component of writing a Heart & Soul resume.

Extraversion (E)
- Excellent verbal communicator
- Wide variety of skills and interests
- Strong public speaking skills
- Take initiative
- Networking skills

Introversion (I)
- Excellent written communicator
- Focused on and attentive to the problems at hand
- Highly skilled and adept within the industry
- Review alternatives thoroughly before making insightful recommendations
- Work quietly and efficiently

Sensing (S)
- Extremely resourceful
- Work well with details
- Readily identify and communicate pertinent facts of the problem at hand
- Address and manage the realities of the current situation or problem
- Build morale by appreciating and communicating the positives of the moment

Intuition (N)
- Long-term planner
- Recognize unseen business opportunities
- Vision for future possibilities
- Think of new and exciting ideas
- Apply insight to complex problem solving
- Objectively see how seemingly unrelated events and facts tie together
- Anticipate and prepare for future trends within the company and the industry
- Thrive in challenging, ever-changing environments

Thinking (T)
- Analytical, logical problem solver
- Objective, reasonable, and fair
- Strong negotiator
- Analyze consequences and implications of difficult decisions
- Identify and see flaws or problems before they happen
- Consistently maintain fair and objective policies and procedures
- Stand firm for principles that are important to the company
- Create and maintain rational, fair systems of operations

Feeling (F)
- Work well with a wide variety of people
- Excellent listener
- Create strong bonds with peers, clients, and supervisors
- Excel in a team-oriented environment
- Forecast how others will feel about new issues within the company
- Teach and coach others to be their best
- Stand firm for values that are important to the work force
- Organize people and tasks harmoniously

Judging (J)
- Organized and methodical
- Coordinate complex projects to successful closure
- Schedule and implement projects, labor hours, and systems
- Recognized for getting tasks done on time and under budget
- Maintain tight controls on operations

Perceiving (P)
- Thrive in fast-paced, competitive environments
- Adapt quickly to ever-changing environments
- Encourage feedback and new ideas from staff
- Review all options thoroughly before making decisions
- Remain flexible and open to the changes common in the workplace

■ **TABLE A.3**
Type Characteristics

Phrases from Combinations of Judgment and External Preferences

Thinking and Judging (TJ)
- Tough-minded, analytical, and instrumental leader
- Make sound decisions based on principles and systems, overall impacts and rational analysis of outcomes

Feeling and Judging (FJ)
- Lead by teaching and inspiring employees
- Observant within corporate culture to create a productive and vibrant work environment

Thinking and Perceiving (TP)
- Objective and critical analysis of operations and excessive expenditures
- Structure a fair and organized system for employees to work within

Feeling and Perceiving (FP)
- Build strong working relationships within teams and various work groups
- Lead and supervise through strong employee support, coaching, and encouragement

Phrases from Combinations of Judgment and Perception Preferences

Sensing and Thinking (ST)
- Results- and bottom-line–oriented

Intuition and Thinking (NT)
- Thrive on opportunities for problem solving, analysis, and design

Sensing and Feeling (SF)
- Drawn to opportunities for practical service to people

Intuition and Feeling (NF)
- Recognize and help people reach their full potential

Phrases from Combinations of Direction of Energy and External Orientation

Introversion and Judging (IJ)
- Persevere through challenging tasks and assignments
- Develop organized, well–thought-out systems

Extraversion and Judging (EJ)
- Lead and work quickly and confidently
- Recognized for getting things done!

Introversion and Perceiving (IP)
- Extremely flexible within daily operations
- Believe in and work toward sound principles set within the company

Extraversion and Perceiving (EP)
- Thrive in a fast-paced, ever-changing environment
- Readily accept and enjoy new challenges

Adapted from Introduction to Type *(5th ed.), Isabel Briggs Myers. Copyright 1993 by Consulting Psychologists Press. Reprinted with permission.*

■ **TABLE A.4**
Phrases from Combinations of Preferences

A Brief History of the Strong Interest Inventory (Strong)

The idea of measuring people's interests has been around since World War I, when military psychologists wrestled with the problem of how to determine which recruits should be cooks and which should be members of the cavalry. Most of us recognize that the type of person who likes the job of cooking is different from the type of person who likes the job of riding and tending horses, and the idea of classifying people by their interests has some intuitive appeal. After World War I, it became clear to some of those same psychologists that the idea had important implications for civilians as well. If it were possible to measure people's vocational interests and to use those data along with information about abilities and values, it might be possible to perform two important interrelated services. First, individuals could be helped in making educational and career plans. Second, the common interests of people working in various occupations could be described. These ideas led to the development of the *Strong Interest Inventory.*

The *Strong* compares a person's responses to various questions regarding career interests to the patterns of responses of people of different personality types and in different occupations. This combination of information allows assumptions to be made about whether an individual is likely to find satisfaction in the work typically done in a given occupation.

The *Strong* gives the respondent five main types of information: first, scores on 6 General Occupational Themes, which reflect the respondent's overall orientation to work; second, scores on 25 Basic Interest Scales, which report consistency of interests or aversions in 25 specific areas, such as art, science, and public speaking; third, scores on 211 Occupational Scales representing 109 different occupations, which indicate the degree of similarity between the respondent's interests and the characteristic interests of women and men working in those occupations; fourth, scores on 4 Personal Style Scales, which measure aspects of the style with which an individual likes to learn, work, assume leadership, and take risks; and fifth, 3 types of Administrative Indexes, which help identify invalid or unusual profiles for special attention.

Common Phrases Associated with Each General Occupational Theme

Table A.4 presents phrases commonly associated with the General Occupational Themes (GOTs) found in the *Strong Interest Inventory*. These descriptive phrases can help a person understand why he or she likes certain work environments more than others and responds better to certain types of work situations than others. The results of the *Strong Interest Inventory* can be extremely valuable in helping you get to the heart and soul of your career dreams. Look at the phrases we've listed. Which ones best describe you? What examples can you think of to support each phrase?

General Occupational Themes

The six General Occupational Themes describe vocational or career interests, as well as occupations and working environments. The following chart provides you with examples of interests, activities, skills, and values of people who fall into each of the six Themes. These examples, however, are generalizations; none will fit any one person exactly. In fact, most people's interests combine several Themes to some degree. Although some people do not indicate interests in any of the Themes, or in only one of them, most show an average or a high degree of interest in two or three of them. In career planning, try to identify occupations whose typical activities combine the interests suggested by your General Occupational Theme scores.

These six themes can be arranged around a hexagon with the types most similar to each other falling next to each other, and those

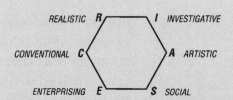

most dissimilar falling directly across the hexagon from one another. For example, as shown in the hexagon above, the Realistic and Investigative Themes are next to each other. People of these two types show some similarity—they generally like to solve technical problems and to work alone. On the other hand, the Realistic and Social Themes are opposite one another on the hexagon. Therefore, people of these two types usually have dissimilar interests. For example, unlike the Realistic types who like working through problems on their own, the Social types like to solve problems by discussing them with others in groups.

THEME	INTERESTS	WORK ACTIVITIES	POTENTIAL SKILLS	VALUES
Realistic (R)	Machines, tools, outdoors	Operating equipment, using tools, building, repairing	Mechanical ingenuity and dexterity, physical coordination	Tradition, practicality, common sense
Investigative (I)	Science, theories, ideas, data	Performing lab work, solving abstract problems, researching	Math, writing, analysis	Independence, curiosity, learning
Artistic (A)	Self-expression, art appreciation	Composing music, writing, creating visual art	Creativity, musical talent, artistic expression	Beauty, originality, independence, imagination
Social (S)	People, team work, human welfare, community service	Teaching, explaining, helping	People skills, verbal ability, listening, showing understanding	Cooperation, generosity, service to others
Enterprising (E)	Business, politics, leadership, influence	Selling, managing, persuading	Verbal ability, ability to motivate and direct others	Risk taking, status, competition
Conventional (C)	Organization, data, finance	Setting up procedures, organizing, operating computers	Math, data analysis, record keeping, attention to detail	Accuracy, stability, efficiency

From Strong Interest Inventory: Applications and Technical Guide, Lenore W. Harmon, Jo-Ida Hansen, Fred H. Borgen, Allen L. Hammer. Copyright 1993 by Consulting Psychologists Press. Reproduced with permission.

■ **FIGURE A.1**
General Occupational Themes (GOTs)

The Realistic Type
- Concrete problem solver
- Stable, dedicated, and hardworking employee
- Thrive in new, challenging environments
- Lead by example
- Work independently
- Take initiative with little or no supervision
- Set and achieve clear, measurable goals and deadlines
- Strong physical and motor skills
- Appreciate traditional systems and corporate cultures
- Excellent project manager

The Investigative Type
- Solve highly complex and intellectual problems
- Work well independently and autonomously
- Create and design solutions to problems
- Insightful and analytical problem solver
- Take initiative
- Strategic planner with strong analytical skills
- Develop and nurture an intellectually stimulating environment
- Constantly striving for a better way of doing things
- Motivate intellectual achievement
- Monitor progress on goals

The Artistic Type
- Develop inventive and creative projects
- Inspired by new, challenging projects
- Remain flexible in fast-paced, ever-changing environment
- Skilled at bringing new ideas to the table when called upon
- Encourage staff to work independently, with minimal supervision
- Excellent communicator
- Excited and enthusiastic about products and services
- Imaginative and observant
- Create new and exciting systems and designs

The Social Type
- Build motivated work environment
- Improve productivity by listening and helping employees work through problems
- Maintain the highest professional, ethical, and service standards
- Work extremely hard
- "Hands-on" leader, willing to work at all levels to get the job done
- Skilled at positioning staff where they will be most productive
- Strong team player
- Excellent at appeasing customers and employees in stressful or trying situations
- Maintain willingness and desire to help others
- Friendly, cheerful, and warm

■ **TABLE A.4**
Common Phrases Associated with Each General Occupational Theme

The Enterprising Type
- Proven marketing and sales skills
- Strong negotiator
- Thrive in a challenging, competitive environment
- Excellent leadership skills
- Sell and promote ideas
- Possess a dynamic, outgoing, and energetic style
- Work diligently to get the most out of others
- Provide direction and leadership to company
- Excel in competitive, highly visible positions
- Comfortably take charge when called upon

The Conventional Type
- Conscientious, responsible, and reliable
- Run operations and procedures according to plan
- Build and maintain consistent methodology and systems
- Proven ability to organize complex systems
- Excellent with details, providing clear, explicit instructions
- Lead and supervise with clear goals and work well in a team environment
- Utilize strong experience base to carefully and completely train staff
- Clearly write and implement policies and procedures
- Emphasize efficiency and accuracy within department
- Excellent numerical, computing, and organizational skills
- Work well with company leadership, follow and adhere to lines of authority

Adapted from Strong Interest Inventory: Applications and Technical Guide, *Lenore W. Harmon, Jo-Ida Hansen, Fred H. Borgen, Allen L. Hammer. Copyright 1993 by Consulting Psychologists Press. Reproduced with permission.*

■ **TABLE A.4 CONTINUED**
Common Phrases Associated with Each General Occupational Theme

Resources

Other Books to Help You in Your Career Planning and All "Heart & Soul" Endeavors

To Build the Life You Want, Create the Work You Love

Marsha Sinetar
St. Martin's Griffin, 1996

Chicken Soup for the Soul

Jack Canfield and Mark Victor Hansen
Health Communications, Inc., 1993

Daily Reflections for Highly Effective People

Stephen R. Covey
Simon & Schuster, 1994

Dare to Win

Jack Canfield and Mark Victor Hansen
Berkley Books, 1996

Do What You Are
Discover the Perfect Career for You Through the Secrets of Personality Type

Paul D. Tieger and Barbara Barron-Tieger
Little, Brown & Company, 1995

Do What You Love, the Money Will Follow
Discovering Your Right Livelihood

Marsha Sinetar
Dell Publishing Co., 1987

Electronic Job Search Revolution
Win with the New Technology That's Reshaping Today's Job Market

Joyce Lain Kennedy
John Wiley & Sons, Inc., 1900

The Healing Power of Love

Brad Steiger
Whitford Press, 1988

Heart at Work
Stories and Strategies for Building Self-Esteem and Reawakening the Soul at Work

Jack Canfield and Jacqueline Miller
McGraw-Hill Book Company, 1900

Hook Up, Get Hired!
The Internet Job Search Revolution

Joyce Lain Kennedy
John Wiley & Sons, Inc., 1900

Job Search Networking
Learn How More Than 68% of All Jobs Are Found . . .

Richard Beatty
Bob Adams, Inc., 1994

Real People, Real Jobs
Reflecting Your Interests in the World of Work

David H. Montross, Zandy B. Leibowitz, and Christopher J. Shinkman
Davies-Black Publishing, 1995

Starting Out, Starting Over
Finding the Work That's Waiting for You

Linda Peterson
Davies-Black Publishing, 1995

Synergetics
Your Whole Life Fitness Plan

Taylor and Joanna Hay
Simon & Schuster, 1990

Success Is a Choice

Rick Pitino
Broadway Books, 1997

The 1997 What Color Is Your Parachute?
A Practical Manual for Job-Hunters & Career-Changers

Richard Nelson Bolles
Ten Speed Press, 1997

About the Authors

CHUCK COCHRAN

Besides his slowly improving golf game, Chuck Cochran's greatest passions lie in writing, music, and running his business. Chuck graduated from the University of Tennessee with a degree in business management science. While his technical degree helped him manage the details of his work, he found his most gratifying work helping his clients turn their lives around.

He started his present business, ResumePLUS, Inc. (now The Heart & Soul Career Center, dba ResumePLUS, Inc.), in Nashville in 1991, where it grew by leaps and bounds within only a few years. Overwhelmed by the growth, in 1993 Chuck delegated the writing duties to Donna Peerce in order to allow him more time for in-depth career consulting and outplacement work incorporating the *Myers-Briggs Type Indicator* and the *Strong Interest Inventory*.

Chuck's first business out of college was a Corporate Travel Agency franchise that he purchased and built up from the ground floor. Touted as the youngest franchisee in the entire six-hundred-store chain, he achieved over $1 million in sales in the first year.

Singing, writing songs, and playing acoustic and electric guitar in his own band have kept Chuck invigorated and creative. His personal and professional goals are to break 80 on a top-rated golf course, travel with his wife whenever possible, and vigorously teach the Heart and Soul way to personal and professional satisfaction.

Currently Chuck consults with businesses and/or individuals on career planning, outplacement techniques, resume writing, professional development, organizational development, team building, and starting and building your own successful business. He lives in Nashville with his wife, Michelle, and their two dogs, Eddie (a mixed breed from the pound) and Emma (a dalmatian).

DONNA PEERCE

Donna Peerce began her professional writing career in elementary school when she published her first short story in a newspaper. This inspired her to continue in her writing endeavors and to combine these with art, broadcast production, and business communications. Throughout her life, she has always implemented a "heart and soul" approach to her writing and to her everyday experiences.

While attending Western Kentucky University in Bowling Green, Donna won several literary awards for short stories, essays, and poetry. After graduating with a bachelor of arts degree in radio, television and journalism, she worked for commercial and public television studios, honing her skills as a producer/director and scriptwriter. Combining her video production skills with writing was a natural for her, and she continues to freelance as a broadcast producer and writer. As an international workshop presenter, Donna travels throughout the United States and Canada to facilitate Heart & Soul writing workshops.

With more than fifteen years of experience as a professional writer, Donna has worked for national advertising agencies and is a ghostwriter of six published fiction books. An accomplished artist, her work has been published by Hallmark, American Greetings, and Gibson Greeting Cards. Donna's hobbies include aerobics, bike spinning, reading, art, writing songs for fun, singing, and travel.

Donna is a world traveler and has roamed the quaint villages of Europe in search of her true destiny. After numerous years of travel, dream study, and spiritual study, Donna firmly believes that all of life is a spiritual experience and that the real search for the meaning of life begins within yourself. Therein lie all answers. Her professional goal is to show people how to put heart and soul into their lives and discover their own inner answers.

Born in Kentucky, the eldest of eight siblings, Donna now resides in Nashville, Tennessee. She began writing resumes to supplement her income in 1988 and, in 1993 joined Chuck Cochran at The Heart & Soul Career Center, dba ResumePLUS, Inc., in Nashville, where she is vice president of writing services. Together, Chuck and Donna have built the company into one of the nation's most successful resume and career development centers. They are working on several more career books to be included in their "Heart & Soul" series, and they look forward to sharing more "heart and soul" experiences with their readers!

HOW TO REACH THE AUTHORS

We would love to hear your stories. Please write, e-mail, or call! If you are having trouble with your resume, we would be glad to critique it for you. Contact us for our availability on speaking and consulting.

OUR WEB PAGE	www.mindspring.com/~heartsoul
E-MAIL	Chuck Cochran: heartsoul@mindspring.com Donna Peerce: dpeerce@mindspring.com
OUR ADDRESS	The Heart & Soul Career Center Resume*PLUS,* Inc. 1808 West End, Suite 1012 Nashville, TN 37203 (615) 329-0300
OR CONTACT	Davies-Black Publishing An Imprint of Consulting Psychologists Press, Inc. 3803 East Bayshore Road Palo Alto, CA 94303 www.cpp-db.com

HEART & SOUL TIP

Check out our Web site for the latest information on our books, services, and company.

Acknowledgments

I would like to thank all of our clients who have allowed us to work for them. The experiences all of them have shared have allowed us to write this book from a very personal perspective. We know the resumes we write are just reflections of them and of their great talent and potential.

Also thanks to Donna for her great writing and hard work, to all my friends and family for their ongoing support, and to my wife, Michelle, for being such a good friend!

CHUCK COCHRAN

I wish to thank my parents for always sticking by me, no matter what path I have wandered down in life; my seven brothers and sisters, who have become very good friends and whom I enjoy very much; Jackie, my best friend, who continues to enrich my life with friendship, humor, and wisdom; Randy and Bryce, for giving me my first computer; Harold, my spiritual guide and mentor; and, of course, Chuck, my partner, for giving me the opportunity of a lifetime and totally turning my life around!

I thank all of you who have been a major part of my life (you know who you are) and have shared my pain, joy, hopes, and dreams. You have all contributed to this book in some way.

DONNA PEERCE

We would both like to extend our deepest gratitude to Melinda Adams Merino at Davies- Black Publishing for sharing our vision of this book.

DONNA & CHUCK

Index

Adams, Scott ("Dilbert" creator), 8
ads. *See* newspaper ads
affirmations, 8, 13
    See also creative visualization
appeal to the heart. *See* emotional appeal
"as if" principle, 12, 13
attention. *See* targeting the position
attitude of gratitude, 81–83
    creative visualization for, 8, 13
    Grateful List for, 83–91
    sensitivity and self-appreciation from, 84, 86, 91–96
attitude of ingratitude, 82

boastful resumes, 82–83, 86–87, 91–92
Briggs, Katharine, 202
brochure design,
    popularity of, 100, 111, 112, 114
    samples, 75–78, 102–104

Canfield, Jack,
    Chicken Soup for the Soul, 8
career change,
    realistic goals for, 36–40, 41–42
career counselors,
    evaluation instruments used by, 19–20, 25, 26, 201
    goal discovery help from, 13–14
career development centers, 13–14, 19–20, 26
Career Link Worldwide (electronic job postings), 57, 61
Career Maps,
    for goal setting, 30, 32–36
career plans. *See* proactive career plans
careers vs. jobs, 4
Chicken Soup for the Soul (Canfield and Hanson), 8
computers, 62
    for electronic job searches, 56, 61, 114–115
contemplation, 12–13, 28
    See also creative visualization
counselors. *See* career counselors
cover letters,
    design guidelines for, 100, 113
    high-impact openings in, 24, 52–54, 79
    See also individual samples
creative visualization,
    affirmations in, 8, 13
    creating the position in, 7–12, 13–14, 17
    in pre-writing exercises, 33, 35, 65
    setting realistic goals with, 9, 12, 28, 30

designs. *See* formats
details. *See* writing details

doodling (pre-writing exercise), 65–66, 67, 71
    resume written from, 74–80
education, 31–32, 47, 65
e-mailing resumes, 115
emotional appeal,
    formats for, 97–116
employment, part-time or temporary, 26, 31
employment history. *See* writing details
envelope size, 101
evaluation instruments, 13–14
    See also *Myers-Briggs Type Indicator; Strong Interest Inventory*
executive summary page, 100, 110, 112, 115, 116
expectations,
    objectivity in, 28, 29–30
    eye appeal. *See* formats

family as influence, 29, 44, 114
faxing resumes, 112, 114, 115
feelings. *See* attitude of gratitude
follow-up letters, 100–101, 108
fonts and point size. *See* formats, design guidelines
formats,
    brochures, 75–79, 100, 102–104, 111, 112, 114
    design guidelines, 54, 95, 113–114, 115, 116
    executive summary page, 100, 110, 112, 115, 116
    length (size) of resume, 111, 113
    resume as sales tool, 97–111
    See also writing details
friends as influence, 29, 44, 114
functions, 202

goals, realistic,
    and career changes, 36–40, 41–42
    creative visualization for, 9, 12, 28, 30
    discovery of, 13–14
    education for, 31–32
    influences on, 29–30, 44
    long-term, 12, 15–26, 30
    objectivity and honesty in setting, 28, 29–30, 32–36, 37–38
    and patience, 40, 43–44
    proactive search strategies based on, 15–26
    short-term, 12, 32, 34, 39
Goldberg, Natalie,
    Writing Down the Bones, 66
GOTs (General Occupational Themes). See under *Strong Interest Inventory (Strong)*
gratitude. *See* attitude of gratitude

Hanson, Mark Victor,
    Chicken Soup for the Soul, 8

217

We Want to Hear from You!

Please take a moment to let us know who you are! Tell us how you were successful in your career using the Heart & Soul approach. Let us know what other career topics and issues interest you. Complete this form and send it to our office in the most convenient way available to you:

Visit our Web site: www.mindspring.com/heartsoul
Send this information via e-mail: heartsoul@mindspring.com
Fax this form to our office: (615) 329-3569
Mail this form to our office: Heart & Soul Career Center
dba ResumePLUS, Inc.
1808 West End, Suite 1012
Nashville, TN 37203
Phone: (615) 329-0300

Name_____

Address _____

City, State, Zip_____

Phone (   ) _____ Fax (   ) _____

E-mail _____

Please send me more information on the following:

❏ **Heart & Soul Resume Tool Kit**—Save time writing your resume by utilizing our resume styles and formats already on disk. Choose from hundreds of sample Heart & Soul resumes and cover letters (different from what is in the book) to help you generate ideas. Listen to our audiocassette and hear the authors explain in detail the important steps in successful Heart & Soul resume preparation. The audiotape works in conjunction with the *Heart & Soul Resume Manual.* Tool kit includes manual, computer disk, and audiocassette.

❏ **Heart & Soul Proactive Job Search Tool Kit**—Build and track a comprehensive proactive job search plan with our in-depth *Heart & Soul Job Search Manual.* Find the fastest-growing, most future-oriented, and highest-ranking Heart & Soul companies to work for. Track your networking calls, job opportunities, and contacts with our practical and insightful *Heart & Soul Job Search Calendar.* Listen to our audiocassette and hear the authors illustrate the important tools necessary for a quick, easy, and meaningful job search. Tool kit includes manual, *Heart & Soul Job Search Calendar,* computer disk, and audiocassette.

❏ **Heart & Soul Interviewing Tool Kit**—This kit provides you with today's hottest interviewing questions, ideas, and common problems job candidates face, and serves as a Heart & Soul resource to use with the audiotape. Listen to real-life interviews that illustrate the do's and don'ts in an interview. Use the many encouraging Heart & Soul tips and motivating thoughts to help you succeed in your most challenging interviews. Tool kit includes manual and audiocassette.

❏ **Heart & Soul Creative Visualization Tool Kit**—A collection of effective creative visualization techniques and exercises to open your heart and help you uncover your hidden talents, goals, and missions in life. Use the audiocassette in conjunction with the manual to develop your own creative visualization exercises, as you listen to real-life techniques for discovering your inner guidance and true self. Tool kit includes manual and audiocassette.

❏ **Heart & Soul of Starting a Home-Based Business Tool Kit**—Use this step-by-step manual to guide you through the process of starting and growing your own home-based business. Learn which of the most profitable home-based businesses would be best for you. Hear how the founder of the Heart & Soul Career Center got started in his own home, and how he has helped others do the same! Tool kit includes manual and audiocassette.

❏ **Heart & Soul seminars, workshops, and appearances**

❏ **Heart & Soul professional resume writing, career consulting, and job search assistance**

❏ **Career professionals in your area who believe in the "Heart & Soul way"**